D0041142

THE BRONTË CABINET

ALSO BY DEBORAH LUTZ

*The Dangerous Lover: Gothic Villains, Byronism, and
the Nineteenth-Century Seduction Narrative*

*Pleasure Bound:
Victorian Sex Rebels and the New Eroticism*

THE BRONTË CABINET

Three Lives in Nine Objects

DEBORAH LUTZ

W. W. Norton & Company

NEW YORK — LONDON

For information about permission to reproduce selections from this book, write to
Permissions, W. W. Norton & Company, Inc., 500 Fifth Avenue, New York, NY 10110

For information about special discounts for bulk purchases, please contact
W. W. Norton Special Sales at specialsales@wwnorton.com or 800-233-4830

Manufacturing by Quad Graphics
Book design by Brooke Koven
Production managers: Louise Mattarelliano

Library of Congress Cataloging-in-Publication Data

Lutz, Deborah.
The Brontë cabinet : three lives in nine objects / Deborah Lutz. — First edition.
pages cm
Includes bibliographical references.
ISBN 978-0-393-24008-5 (hardcover)
1. Brontë, Charlotte, 1816-1855. 2. Brontë, Emily, 1818-1848. 3. Brontë, Anne, 1820-1849.
4. Women authors, English—19th century—Biography. 5. Sisters—England—
Yorkshire—Biography. I. Title.
PR4168.L88 2015
823'.809—dc23
[B]
2014046935

W. W. Norton & Company, Inc.
500 Fifth Avenue, New York, N.Y. 10110
www.wwnorton.com

W. W. Norton & Company Ltd., Castle House,
75/76 Wells Street, London W1T 3QT

1 2 3 4 5 6 7 8 9 0

For Tony and Pamela

Contents

Illustrations

Color Insert

Acknowledgments

THIS BOOK WOULDN'T have been written without Amy Cherry, my editor at W. W. Norton, who backed it in many ways with her alert intelligence, her ideas, and her belief in it from start to finish. A conversation with Amy, her assistant Laura Romain, and Renee Zuckerbrot, my agent, about found objects, archives, collecting, and a dog called Pilot (named for Rochester's Newfoundland in *Jane Eyre*) helped shape the project from its conception.

Many friends read parts of this book. Polly Schulman tirelessly and enthusiastically commented on drafts of chapters as I wrote them, providing astute guidance as an editor and thinker. Kristofer Widholm enriched these pages with his sensitive, deft feedback and his skills as a writer, reader, and confidant. I am grateful to Talia Schaffer for her constant and long-standing support of my work, which has involved not only reading pretty much all of it (bless her!) and providing brilliant advice from her knowledge of all things Victorian, but also penning letters of praise, too numerous to count. I am lucky to be a member of a smart, hardworking writing group of Victorianists, many of whom read parts of this book: my gratitude to Carolyn Berman, Caroline Reitz, Tanya Agathocleous, Tim Alborn, and, as always, Talia. Dennis Denisoff I thank for his guidance on my dog chapter, for sharing his knowledge of dog nature, and for many (but not enough) fine dinner discussions about donkeys and meeting the eyes of animals. Tim Moreton of the National Portrait Gallery, London, provided thoughtful feedback on my walking chapter, showed me many death masks, and gave of his wide-ranging knowledge of portraiture, literary history, and museum artifacts over many delightful meals. Benjamin Friedman fixes and polishes my prose expertly and provides loyal friendship. Maggie Nelson contributes encouragement at all turns.

This book stands as a testament to the kindness I have received from curators, librarians, and staff at libraries, archives, and museums in America, Great Britain, and Western Europe, many of whom went out of their way to be helpful. Sarah Laycock and Ann Dinsdale at the Brontë Parsonage Museum, Haworth, West Yorkshire, were endlessly patient in showing me hundreds (literally) of objects, books, manuscripts, and little slips of paper. They let me sit in their quiet library on numerous trips, handling, studying, sniffing, turning about, and brooding over these many things to my heart's content. Heather Millard at the Manor House Museum and Art Gallery, Castle Yard, Ilkley, shared her enthusiasm about the manuscripts we looked at together, and she went far beyond the requirements of her job to help me investigate the weather in Haworth during the Brontës' lifetimes. Her willingness to open the Bradford archives to me, to send me pictures of Charlotte Brontë's purse and other Brontë artifacts, and to lend me her time and energy was without compare. The charming Elizabeth Denlinger and her staff at the Pforzheimer Collection brought out all sorts of relics for me, and she assisted me with her knowledge of artifacts around New York and the United Kingdom. John Vincler and Maria Isabel Molestina at the Morgan Library gave of their time, setting out envelopes, letters, manuscripts, and association copies, as did Isaac Gewirtz, Joshua McKeon, and Lyndsi Barnes at the Berg Collection, who put up with many, many visits and retrieved piles of manuscripts and relics for me. Susan Halpert and Leslie Morris and other staff welcomed me to the Houghton Library at Harvard University. I am grateful to Kathryn Jones at the Royal Collection and Alexandra Barbour at Windsor Castle, who dug around Frogmore to unearth for me some of Queen Victoria's more obscure jewels and objects. Thanks to Bruce Barker-Benfield of the Bodleian Library for his help with Shelley relics and books bound in human skin, and for giving me a kind welcome to Oxford and its research collections. Suzanne Canally, librarian at the Senate House Library at the University of London, told me about many death-inflected things in London. Thanks also to Lisa Darms and Charlotte Priddle at the Fales Collection, New York University.

Many thanks to the staff and curators at the following collections for hosting me and generously fulfilling requests. In the United Kingdom: the British Library, the Victoria and Albert Museum, the British Museum, the Wellcome Collection, the National Maritime Museum, the Keats House, the Hunterian Museum, the Foundling Museum, the Freud Museum, the Charles Dickens Museum, Sir John Soane's Museum, the Museum of London, the Florence Nightingale Museum, the Apsley House, the Highgate Cemetery, and the Pitt Rivers Museum. In the United States: the New York Public Library's Rose Main Reading Room, the General Research Division, the Art and Architecture Collection, and the Photography Collection; the Butler Library, Columbia University; the Bobst Library, New York University; the Thomas J. Watson Library, the Metropolitan Museum of Art; and the Mütter Museum, Philadelphia. Other places: the Keats-Shelley House, Rome; the Sigmund Freud Museum, Vienna; the Kunstgewerbemuseum, Berlin; and the Treasury in St. Mark's Basilica, Venice.

I owe a special debt to Robert Douglas-Fairhurst, of Magdalen College, for his kindness in welcoming me in numerous ways to Oxford and arranging for me to speak at Magdalen about Victorian relics.

Thanks for the glamorous meals and the words of encouragement and support. Many in the English faculty at Oxford were generous with their time and ideas, especially Stefano Evangelista and Sally Shuttleworth. Thanks to the attendees of the Victorian Research Seminar for letting me try out some of these thoughts on Brontë artifacts on them, and for their feedback and criticism.

The company, conversation, and work of still others—colleagues, friends, writers, curators—supplied thought, fuel, inspiration, and vision. I am grateful to Elaine Freedgood, whose friendship has meant so much to me; Will Murphy, for his help with making the leap from academic publishing to trade; Sharon Marcus; Marcia Pointon; Claire Harman, for our talks about all things Brontë; Wayne Koestenbaum, for teaching me to use appealing verbs; Eve Kosofsky Sedgwick; Avital Ronell; David McAllister, for chats about death and for his invitation to speak about death masks at Birkbeck; Deborah Rubin, for teaching me all sorts of things; Steve Kirschner and Janice Gitterman, for discussing chapter titles; Melissa Dunn; Domenick Ammirati; Jean Mills; Rachel Szekely; Will Fisher; Tom Fahy; Cara Murray; James Bednarz; John Lutz; Duc Dau; Joanne Mariner, for lending me her apartment in London and her house in the woods, and for her nighttime birdsong; John Kucich; Richard Kaye; Pam Thurschwell; Anne Humpherys; Gerhard Joseph; Jeff Dolven; Sina Najafi at *Cabinet*, who also felt heartbroken about the dolphin who died in the Gowanus; Dr. Gabriel Heaton, at Sotheby's, London, for sending me pages of auction catalogs; and Roland Albrecht and Marianne Karbe, of the Museum der Unerhörten Dinge.

Many people pondered Emily Brontë's "puzzle" wafer seals with me. Members of the National Puzzlers' League, especially Ronnie Kon and Treesong, decoded a number of them for me. Deb Amlen cracked the codes of some too. Bill Lunsford of the American Cryptogram

Association was also a big help, as was Betsy Rohaly Smoot and Rene Stein at the Center for Cryptologic History, National Security Agency.

There has been so much extraordinary work done on the Brontës, I could write a whole book of thanks, and I have tried to include as much as possible in my endnotes and the list of further reading. Juliet Barker's work has been especially foundational for me and for anyone working on the Brontës. Margaret Smith's edition of Charlotte Brontë's letters has been seminal and is an astounding piece of scholarship. I have been inspired by the writing of Steven Vine, Stevie Davies, and Elisabeth Bronfen.

At Long Island University, I am grateful to my students for discussions about Victorian women and collaboration, especially ABC (Amanda Beth Campbell), Nikki Cosentino, and Nicole McGovern. At the library, I thank the interlibrary loan staff, especially Claudette Allegrezza, for all their help. A sabbatical gave me time to complete this project, and a grant from the LIU Post Faculty Research Committee provided funds for the illustrations.

Thanks to the staff and fellow patrons at various cafes and bars where I felt my way through these chapters, especially at Ashbox, Troost, Propeller, Turl Street Kitchen, Kings Arms of Haworth, and Black Bull.

I am grateful for the affection of my family: Pamela, Sandy, Doug, Veronica, and Leroy.

Finally, I am beholden to Tony Sebok for a whole host of generosities: for his ceaseless interest as I talked for hours about Victorian dog licensing, fern fever, and much else; for the main title of the book; for his comments and ideas at all stages; for always being a loving fan of my writing.

The Private Lives of Objects

*Every spirit passing through the world fingers the tangible
and mars the mutable, and finally has come to look and not
to buy. As shoes are worn and hassocks are sat upon . . . finally
everything is left where it was and the spirit passes on.*
　　　　　　—MARILYNNE ROBINSON, *Housekeeping*

*The world is so full of a number of things
I'm sure we should all be as happy as kings.*
　　　　　　—ROBERT LOUIS STEVENSON, "HAPPY THOUGHT"

THE STRANGE BED in Emily Brontë's *Wuthering Heights* has always haunted me. We read about Catherine Earnshaw's "large oak case" before we know anything about her. A wooden box entered via sliding panels, it has cutout squares near the top that resemble "coach windows," as if one might crawl in to travel somewhere. The cabinet, its own little private room within a room, encloses a window and its ledge, where Catherine long ago stacked her small library and scratched her name into the paint. She once read there, scribbling her diary in the margins of her books.

As one who favors reading in bed, I find this oak box charged with meaning, especially when encountered while settled in my own, the lamp a circle of warmth carved out of the late-night darkness. Just as the wardrobe in C. S. Lewis's *The Lion, the Witch and the Wardrobe* is moved through by the children until the layers of fur coats become flakes of snow and tree branches, the bed opens into other worlds, the plenitude of the imagination. Heathcliff believes in this capability too; he gets into the dead Catherine's box believing he can find her. He perishes there himself, and the novel hints that the bed provides a portal to another sphere, the one of ghosts.

There are few books I'd rather carry me late into the night than *Jane Eyre*, *Wuthering Heights*, and *Villette*, few books whose worlds I'd rather crawl into and inhabit. I have even felt, somehow, *known* by their heroines, as if they might recognize me when I enter their spheres. I move around in those rooms with Jane or Lucy, sit in the antechamber of Bertha Mason's prison, and also peer with wonder as the candlelight plays over "the doors of a great cabinet opposite—whose front, divided into twelve panels, bore in grim design, the heads of the twelve apostles, each inclosed in its separate panel as in a frame." My intimacy with these books has led me, like so many others, to want to come closer to their authors. So alive are these novels that I wish I could resurrect the Brontës themselves, their daily living and breathing, their material presence.

Catherine's box bed and the cabinet with the apostles' heads glimmer with animation, seeming to lift off the page. I remember the uncanny sensation when I saw the real apostles cabinet, a seventeenth-century Dutch cupboard that Charlotte encountered when visiting a grand house with her friends, which she then transported to the top floor of

Thornfield Hall in *Jane Eyre*. Did Emily, as well, base her oak sleeping closet on one she actually saw? If so, does it still exist somewhere?[1]

Even ordinary objects can carry us to other times and places. Old things gain an extra patina of significance for this reason. Take, say, a striped dress from the 1940s, hemmed by hand, that I found in a thrift store. Holding it makes me wonder, What did it witness? What did the wearer feel and see with this very fabric against her skin? That body may well now be dead. Still, I feel the deep mystery of the lives of others in this palpable emissary of past moments, now impossible to recover. The texture of those lost days settles into possessions that outlive their owners, it seems to linger in a mended tear, a stretched elbow, a corner's roundedness. Resurrecting this old matter by wearing or using it feels almost as if we respect the absent, whomever they might be, call them back for a brief moment before the door shuts for good. We, too, will leave behind things we have nicked with incident, warmed with wearing. Will they carry our history, abide in our place without us? Will our clothing still bear our gestures?

The Victorians were more likely than we are to find remnants of selfhood in possessions that belonged to their dead. Their culture had less squeamishness about the dead body than ours usually does; sentimental thoughts about corpses were cultivated in many circles. Dying happened mostly at home, and then the living swept into the rooms and beds of the dead and kept on using them. The fashioning of death masks was still common, and the photographing of corpses had its day. A lock of hair taken from a corpse connected the living, many believed, to an afterlife where the dead resided. A nightshirt, a ring, a book, infused with the past, might reanimate it, when approached with all the senses.

I was struck by a sense of bodies long gone when I held the artifacts I describe in the following chapters. Books especially bear the leavings of inky, soiled, or oily fingertips and palms. The Brontës scribbled, doodled, and inscribed in their books—stuck plants, drawings, visiting cards in them—making their presence manifest. Some of these well-used volumes transmitted even more than evidence of reading; they had a certain scent to them, which seemed, to my nose, a fleshy smell. I was lucky to be able to touch (often without gloves), turn over, bring close, and even sniff the things I handled in libraries and museums. My great fortune reminded me of the attenuation of all the senses but sight in most museums today. We look—and only look—at things behind glass. It is hard to imagine how this could be different, since we want these works to be preserved, to last; yet it once was. In the seventeenth and eighteenth centuries, museums still retained some aspects of the private collections from which they grew, and visitors were invited to touch artifacts on display. A woman in 1786 described a trip to the British Museum where she reached into an ancient Greek urn to caress the ashes. "I felt it gently; with great feeling . . . I pressed the grain of dust between my fingers tenderly, just as her best friend might once have grasped her hands." When one Zacharias Conrad von Uffenbach visited the Ashmolean Museum in Oxford in 1710, he complained that "even the women" were allowed in: "they run around here and there, grabbing at everything." When the Victorian collector Captain Henry Lane Fox, who later took the name Pitt-Rivers, began gathering tools, art, and ceremonial items from all over the world so that the "lineaments of past ordinary lives" would be revealed, he wanted people to come to his collection (now the Pitt Rivers Museum in Oxford) and "hold in their hand an idea expressed by the hands."[2]

Making use of objects to recover history has been a popular method for at least the last couple of decades. Borrowing from archaeology and anthropology, the field of "material culture" (also called "thing theory") in literary studies flourishes: taking an object depicted in fiction and using it to explore the story and the culture in which the tale is embedded. Elaine Freedgood, for instance, uses the mahogany furniture in *Jane Eyre* to discuss the violent histories of deforestation and slavery in Britain and its colonies, forms of mastery that appear also in Jane's need to suppress herself and others. Even more radical approaches to the object realm have emerged lately. Metaphysicians of objects see them as autonomous from our perception, withdrawing from our direct access. As a philosophical or poetic meditation, as a way for us to loosen our human-centered hubris, the theory that the object has a secret existence seems worthy of exploration.[3]

Yet, as much as I favor the idea of inanimate things having lives concealed from us, I still feel that an object's meaning—its slumbering life—comes from our own desires and passions, the shadows we let play over it. All such theories have their roots, I believe, in ancient faiths. The body parts of saints, their clothing, and the objects they had touched exuded oils, perfumes, miracles, and healing. They could suddenly bleed, cry, levitate, or gain weight in a desire to not be moved. Matter, for Catholic believers in the Middle Ages, was fertile, "maternal, labile, percolating, forever tossing up grass, wood, horses, bees, sand, or metal," as the historian Caroline Walker Bynum explains. Spontaneous generation and spontaneous combustion—ancient notions that animate bodies could emerge from nonliving substances or could suddenly disappear altogether—still had currency in the nineteenth century. So did "animal magnetism," the belief in a fluid that permeated everything and that allowed objects (and people) to influence each other, even from afar. Certain gems could ward off the "evil eye," and "touchpieces," often of slate and worn around the neck as jewelry, carried the healing qualities thought to reside in the touch of the monarch. Objects had agency in British law. Belongings that had caused an individual's death were accursed or had to be given up to

God, which meant forfeiting them to the church or the Crown to be converted for pious uses, a practice called "deodand." The custom in Scotland when a fisherman had fallen out of a boat and drowned, of beaching it, cursing it, and leaving it to decay apart from its "innocent" mates, continued up until at least the early twentieth century.[4]

Since things are mute, their interpretation leaves much latitude for conjecture. Writing about the belongings of authors one greatly admires, as I do in this book, can be fraught with the dangers of "over-reading." Too much of oneself can be projected into the silence, making history personally nostalgic. All biography takes these risks, especially when little is known about a subject, as is the case with Emily Brontë. Lucasta Miller, in *The Brontë Myth*, explores how the Brontë sisters have been construed according to different agendas and the concerns of varied ages. With these myths born of Brontë love in mind, I sometimes had to laugh at my own zealousness. Poring over an artifact, I found myself wondering if some scratch in the wood of, say, Emily's desk box, formed words or initials. Was this a message from the dead, or just the results of a bump into a table? I felt like a detective looking for clues, traces of evidence, even bodily fluids. But here no crime had been committed.

Can we let objects speak on their own? Probably not even the metaphysicians of objects would think this possible. What I set out to do here is place each object in its cultural setting and in the moments of the everyday lives of the Brontës. I coax out what the thing might have "witnessed," how it colored its human settings. This has meant covering some well-worn biographical ground—a whole library could be filled with books published on the Brontës, many of them so excellent that one feels there need be no more. I speculate at times, but I also take care not to overlay these objects with too much intensity of my own. Through the "eyes" of thread, paper, wood, jet, hair, bone, brass, fur, frond, leather, velvet, and ash, new corners and even rooms of these Victorian women's lives light up for us. There has been little writing on most of these artifacts, on some not a jot. I find these things and their Victorian mates wholly beguiling. I wish with all my heart that they would step forth and speak, maybe even rise from the page. If they unlock themselves only a little—are brought to voice—then my task has been accomplished.

CHAPTER ONE

Tiny Books

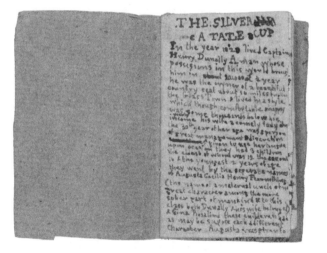

*I took my dingy volume by the scroop, and hurled it into
the dog-kennel, vowing I hated a good book. Heathcliff
kicked his to the same place.*

—EMILY BRONTË, *Wuthering Heights*

*Reading is my favorite occupation, when I have leisure for it
and books to read.*

—ANNE BRONTË, *Agnes Grey*

It was October 1829, Charlotte Brontë was thirteen, and she was concocting a tiny text with whatever was at hand. She probably sat at the kitchen table, as she often did when writing as a child, the family's beloved servant Tabby knocking about, cleaning and baking cakes. The Elland stone–flagged kitchen, just behind their father's study, was regularly occupied by the Brontë girls, who might be writing there, but could just as well be kneading dough, cutting up hash, or feeding the dogs some of their oatmeal porridge. The weather for October had been steadily drenching, the raindrops tapping the windowpanes of their house in Haworth, West Yorkshire. A peat fire under the stove kept out the damp.[1]

Charlotte's early years bristled with dark incident. The family had moved into the gray, ashlar-stone parsonage, perched on an eminence overlooking an expanse of moorland hills, in April 1820. Her father, the Reverend Patrick Brontë, had been appointed the perpetual curate of Haworth. The two-storied eighteenth-century house teemed with people. In four bedrooms and a two-seated outdoor privy, ten bodies had to find space for dreaming and moving about: Charlotte, her parents, her five siblings, and two live-in servants. Her mother was Maria Branwell, a southerner from the mild-weathered port town of Penzance, with bluestocking tendencies. Maria had been attracted to Patrick, an Irish clergyman, not only for his dignified beauty and his rough warmth—she called him "saucy Pat" in their love letters— but because he used his Cambridge education to write thoughtful sermons accessible to the unlearned. He had literary ambitions too, publishing the occasional poem or story before his job and his family filled almost all of his time. Not many months after their arrival in Haworth, Maria took to bed. She passed seven-and-a-half agonizing months in her upstairs bedroom, dying of cancer. At times she slipped into a delirium. The certainty of leaving behind her children preyed most on her mind. The nurse heard her cry out often, "Oh God my poor children—oh God my poor children!" She died on Saturday, September 15, 1821, with the children, Patrick, and her sister, Elizabeth Branwell, gathered around her bed. She was interred just next door, under a vault in the church. The mural tablet marking her burial chamber admonished the passerby to "be ye also ready."[2]

Charlotte's father was left with a throng of children, the eldest— a second Maria—seven years old and Anne, the baby, not yet two. Aunt Elizabeth Branwell soon moved in to help. Further relief came when Patrick discovered a school set up for children of clergymen who were missing one or both parents. Subsidized by donations from the wealthy, the Clergy Daughters' School at Cowan Bridge wasn't expensive, an essential consideration for Patrick, whose curate's salary was barely enough to support his large family. He tutored his son, Branwell, at home, and Anne was too young to go, so he sent the other four daughters there. Maria and Elizabeth, who as the eldest had become maternal figures for the younger children after their mother's death, left for school in July 1824. Charlotte followed in August, Emily in November. The institution would become notorious for its grim, cruel conditions when Charlotte fictionalized it as Lowood school in her second novel, *Jane Eyre*, published in 1847. Both Maria and Elizabeth became ill of consumption. Eleven-year-old Maria was sent home sick in February 1825. When she died in May, her sisters were still at school. A few weeks after Maria died, ten-year-old Elizabeth was sent home, wasting away with the same illness. Charlotte and Emily were brought home in June and watched their sister die.

In October 1829, when Charlotte was assembling her small manuscript, the house, still packed with inhabitants, had pockets of felt absence. In a short diary of the year, written a few months earlier, she mapped out the location of the remaining family members, as if to reassure herself they were still above ground. She first placed herself: "I am sitting by the table writing this in the kitchen." Then she gave accounts of those in her immediate vicinity and included one of the dead in parentheses. "Tabby the servant is washing up after breakfast and Anne, my youngest sister (Maria was the eldest), is kneeling on a chair looking at some cakes which Tabby has been baking for us." In the parlor down the hall Emily is "brushing it" (the room, presumably). Aunt Branwell is upstairs in her room, and her brother, Branwell, has gone with "Papa" to Keighley, a town a few miles away, to get a copy of the *Leeds Intelligencer*.[3]

Despite one grim incident after another befalling her, Charlotte crammed these early years with inventing hilarious tales. She then created booklets to hold them, as she was doing this October. She began by snipping out eight sheets into squares of about two by one and a half inches, then folding each down the middle. The jagged edges of the white rag paper show some clumsy scissor wielding. Charlotte had small hands—her friend and first biographer Elizabeth Gaskell described the shake of one as "like the soft touch of a bird in the middle of my palm." In later years her fingers could work expertly on delicate paintings and embroidery, but at thirteen their childishness made her cuts dip and sway as if she were on a boat while at her craft. Taking a used piece of parcel wrapping paper, brownish gray and fibrous, she cut out a square slightly larger than the white ones. This too she folded once down the middle. Stacking the leaves together, with the brown sheet on the outside forming a front and a back cover, Charlotte sewed them along the seam with needle and white thread. Now she had—empty and waiting—a rudimentary booklet of sixteen pages, about the size of a matchbook.[4]

Dipping her quill pen into an inkpot, Charlotte copied into the volume from a text she had already drafted in the weeks before she arrived at this stage of "publication." She used a print, modeled after the type of real books, so minuscule it is difficult to make out without a magnifying glass. The illustration at the beginning of this chapter is more than twice the actual size, but the following is what she wrote on the first page, close to its real tininess:

In the year 1829, lived Captain Henry Dunally, a man whose possessions in this world bring him £200,000 a year.

He was the owner of a beautiful country seat, about 10 miles from Glass Town and lived in a style which,

though comfortable and happy, was some thousands below his yearly income. His wife, a comely lady in the

30th year of her age, was a person of great management and discretion, and given to use her tongue upon

occasion. They had 3 children, the eldest of whom was 12, the second 10 and the youngest 2 years of age.

They went by the separate names of Augusta Cecilia, Henry Fearnothing (the name of a maternal uncle of

no great character among the more sober part of mankind and to this class both Dunally and his wife belonged)

and Cina Rosalind. These children had, as may be supposed, each a different character. Augusta was given to

What Charlotte was after was an imitation, in miniature, of her favorite journal of the day: *Blackwood's Edinburgh Magazine.* "The most able publication there is," Charlotte enthused. All four siblings—Charlotte, Branwell (twelve years old), Emily (eleven), and Anne (just nine)— read and adored the monthly Scottish periodical, lent to them by their friend Mr. Driver. Published by William Blackwood from 1817, the magazine was a "miscellany" of a common type in England at the time. Short stories or poems, mostly gothic-tinged and busy with ghosts and murders, were mixed with Tory-leaning political articles about current affairs, sheet music, reviews of paintings and books, imaginary conversations in a tavern among tipsy characters, and other odds and ends. Articles were signed with pseudonyms, such as the Ettrick Shepherd, James Hogg's sometimes alias. It was Charlotte's brother, Branwell, who first had the idea to make imitations of the magazine. He started his dwarf-sized "Branwell's Blackwood's Magazine" in January 1829, with himself as editor and primary author, writing under various names, such as PBB, Sergeant or Captain Bud, and Young Soult. Charlotte occasionally "contributed," under her own name or as one Captain Tree. After about six issues in as many months, Charlotte took over the "serial," now calling it "Blackwood's Young Men's Magazine," with Branwell sometimes appearing in her pages. Her first issue of August 1829 was "edited by the genius CB." To Elizabeth Gaskell, who read these little magazines many years later, they seemed "the wildest and most incoherent things." They gave her the "idea of creative power carried to the verge of insanity."[5]

The volume pictured at the opening of this chapter is the October issue of Charlotte's "Blackwood's." As with other miscellanies, she included fiction, poetry, a section called "Military Conversations" modeled on the tavern talk of *Blackwood's*, and a table of contents at the end. Advertisements appear on the last page, for objects and books such as *How to Curl One's Hair*, by Monsieur Whats-the-reason. The most pungent piece in the magazine is the first story, "The Silver Cup: A Tale," which opens on a scene pulled from her own experience: a family listening as one member reads a novel aloud. The story is interrupted by a peddler at the door, who sells the father an embossed silver cup. The cup carries with it a curse, as the father eventually realizes in a dream, and misfortunes begin to befall the family. Many of these involve children wildly misbehaving, such as the youngest girl, Cina, smashing into bits a miniature ship composed of glass, kept in a rosewood box. These little ruffians are threatened with having their brains knocked out against the wall or are given "hearty beatings," a kind of dark slapstick that the Brontës reveled in as children and which continued in the adult writings of Emily and Branwell. All is made right when the cup is drained of its evil magic by an anti-genie potion. The influence of the *Arabian Nights*—the children were reading and copying obsessively from it—is obvious here in the trouble-making genie. A more subtle idea Charlotte poached is that seemingly innocent objects might radiate with animation and meaning. "Open sesame" moved the stone door that locked up mounds of treasure; a rub of an ancient lantern thrown up by the sea fulfilled mad desires. The delicate crystal ship in Charlotte's tale was "mended by invisible hands" as if a vital spark burned low at its center, ready to be stoked. The inverse could also happen: people might transform into objects. Charlotte's Captain Bud gets so depressed sometimes that he supposes himself turned into a stone, an oyster, or a heather-bell shrub "apt to be blown away at every blast of the wind."[6]

Children especially can hold in their minds two contradictory ideas: that a toy is made of just wood and paint and that it is a quivering thing, breathing and rushing into adventures. The many stories and books the young Brontës created in tandem emerged from fantasylands and people cooked up in their own heads, like the Glasstown Confederacy where their early characters roamed and played out their dramas. Yet most of their tales were also tethered to the real and tactile.

The "Young Men" plays that Charlotte drew on for her "Blackwood's Young Men's Magazine" began life as a set of twelve wooden soldiers (the "Twelves") given to Branwell by Patrick. Charlotte recounts how, on the night of June 4, 1826, their father came home from Leeds carrying presents for them. Branwell's present of a box of soldiers became the most evocative when he burst in on his sisters the next morning. Emily and Charlotte "jumped out of Bed," and Charlotte, snatching up "the prettiest of the whole," named it after one of her heroes, the Duke of Wellington, and proclaimed, "It shall be mine!" Emily's wooden man was grave and thus took the name Gravey. Anne's was "a queer little thing like herself" and took the odd name of Waiting Boy; Branwell's was Bonaparte, after Napoleon.[7]

In Branwell's account of that morning, he imagines himself as an immense and terrible monster seizing the twelve brave soldiers as they are exploring the interior of Africa (and waging a war against the Ashantees, represented by Charlotte's set of ninepins, brought by their father on the same night as the soldiers). He takes them to "a hall of inconceivable extent and splendor," that is, the girls' bedroom, which was in reality small and shabby. Here, three other giants become involved. All of them become the genies—Brannii, Tallii (Charlotte), Emmii, and Annii—that sometimes protect the soldiers and sometimes do evil things in the towns the soldiers establish.[8]

These weren't the first toys to be pressed into service. In "The History of the Young Men," thirteen-year-old Branwell lists his key acquisitions. In the summer of 1824, "papa" bought him his first box of soldiers from Bradford. A second set came from Keighley but didn't last the year because they were "either maimed lost burnt or destroyed by various casualties they 'departed and left not a wreck behind!' " Then came two bands of Turkish soldiers and the "Twelves," mentioned already. In 1828 he purchased a "band of Indians."[9]

The mythologizing of these figures included a made-up language the little "men" spoke in, called "the old young men tongue," which seems to have been a Yorkshire dialect spoken while pinching the nose. The siblings also appeared in the stories in their own persons, such as in Charlotte's first volume of the "Tales of the Islanders," where school-children were punished in a secret dungeon by Colonel Naughty and his gang. "Unjust torturing" would go on "if it was not that I keep the key of the dungeon and Emily keeps the key of the cells." The children in this way stepped into the stories they created, inhabiting different identities, speaking in multiple voices. They also imbued their toys with narrative and with their own selves, in the way most children do, as if their bodies could meld with the tiny wooden frames, their skin becoming paint.[10]

While some of the tales had their origins in toys, others unfurled on specific furniture or in particular rooms. The raw cellar where beer was kept, reached by descending stone steps into the dark, served as a model for countless dungeons and prisons. The bed that Charlotte and Emily shared as girls—a common practice at the time and a necessity in the overcrowded parsonage—worked as a nighttime space of free invention. Charlotte called the tales spun here "bed plays," the reper-tory of which began to form on the night of December 1, 1827. "Bed plays mean secret plays," Charlotte explained two years later. "They are very nice ones. All our plays are very strange ones."[11]

Fancies arose when sitting around the kitchen fire. Charlotte describes how their play of the Islanders evolved one evening, also in December 1827. "One night, about the time when the cold sleet and dreary fogs of November are succeeded by the snow storms and high, piercing night winds of confirmed winter, we were all sitting round the warm, blazing kitchen fire, having just concluded a quarrel with Tabby concerning the propriety of lighting a candle, from which she came off victorious, no candle having been produced." After a long pause,

Branwell remarks in a lazy manner, "I don't know what to do." Emily and Anne echo his boredom.

"Wha ya may go t'bed," Tabby points out, in her broad Yorkshire.

"I'd rather do anything than that," says Branwell.

"You're so glum tonight, Tabby. Well suppose we had each had an island," Charlotte chimes in.

"If we had, I would choose the Island of Man," says Branwell.

Everyone picks an island and their "chief man," but their inspiration is interrupted by the "dismal sound of the clock striking seven," and they are called to bed.[12]

The cherry tree growing beside the house was another object brought into their games, transmuting inevitably into fiction. Acting out scenes from the Restoration, Emily, around eleven years old, played King Charles II. She escaped from her siblings, in character as Roundheads, by stepping out of a second-floor bedroom into the branches of the tree, which had become the Royal Oak, where Charles is said to have hid from his enemies. In the one novel she completed in her lifetime—*Wuthering Heights*—Emily places a fir tree just outside Catherine Earnshaw's second-floor bedroom window at the Heights. Years after Catherine's death, her daughter— also called Catherine—uses the fir as an escape ladder when she is imprisoned in the house by her father-in-law Heathcliff, on a rampage against all of Catherine's relatives. She climbs out the lattice onto the limbs, then slides to the ground.[13]

A few months later, in a dream, the fir becomes infused with the first Catherine's spirit. When the stranger Lockwood comes to visit the Heights, a sudden snowstorm blows in, and he is forced to spend the night in the long-dead Catherine's bed. The driving snow and wailing wind knock the fir branch against the casement. Annoyed by the sound, he attempts to unhasp the window. Finding the hook soldered shut, he pushes his knuckles through the glass and grasps the branch. Instead of the slim bough, his fingers close on "a little, ice-cold hand!" Clinging to him, the sobbing girl calls herself Catherine. She begs to be let in, crying that she has been a waif for twenty years. Lockwood starts awake and tells Heathcliff about his dream. Believing Catherine really is out there, Heathcliff wrenches open the lattice and bursts into "an uncontrollable passion of tears. 'Come in! Come in!' he sobbed. 'Cathy, do come! Oh, do—*once* more! Oh! my heart's darling, hear me *this* time—Catherine, at last!' " An exit strategy and then a ghost girl, the tree is like the laurel into which the mythological Daphne is transformed, as her only means to escape Apollo's pursuit. Catherine speaks, like Daphne, when the wind rustles through her leaves.

As with *Wuthering Heights*, the Brontë children's tales unfolded from real-life matter—toy, bed, kitchen fire, tree—and came full circle as concrete things when recorded in their little books. Starting in 1826, the Brontë siblings probably produced around a hundred of their micro tomes (so many have gone missing, an exact count is impossible). The earliest surviving one is Charlotte's 1826 book about and for Anne, which opens, "There was once a little girl and her name was Ane," and contains six watercolor illustrations. They probably first began making their books small because paper was dear and scarce (more about this later). Yet their penmanship became so minute the adults couldn't read it. These books were tangible secrets, private domains made more private by their miniaturization. Dispatches from their hidden fantasy world, their works were curated for an audience of four only. Tiny books generated others, in a long chain that appeared for a time never ending, stretching through their teenage years and into their twenties. They found miniaturization to be funny, suggestive. Their minuscule books initially fit well with their child bodies, as if the books were emanations of those undersized fingertips and palms. Or little worlds for small bodies to climb into, open sesame. Another way to think about the size of the books in relation to their bodies: the tiny pages and print made their fingers and frames seem gigantic. They liked to imagine themselves as giants, carrying around contrastingly diminutive objects. Charlotte writes about an island inhabited by their "Chief Men" who are ten miles high. Branwell relishes the notion of himself as a huge monster, carting around elfin soldiers. Yet they also appear in their stories as pigmy queens and a king. In the guise of a "famous Little Queen," Charlotte appears in her "Tales of the Islanders" as a "little shrunk old woman." Extreme sizes of bodies and books on both ends of the scale sparked endless invention. They could fit seemingly infinite spheres into cramped, contracted spaces. Yet they also packed these expansive stories with action and movement, filling out any gaps.[14]

While all of the books we have left were made by Charlotte and Branwell, some were surely crafted by Emily and Anne and are now missing, probably destroyed. Other lost artifacts that can be sensed by their lack are those made by or belonging to Maria and Elizabeth. Did they also create miniature books? Maria was apparently a precocious intellectual—fictionalized by Charlotte as the girl Helen at Lowood school in *Jane Eyre*—and it is hard to imagine that she didn't also throw herself into writing and handicraft, perhaps even teaching it to her younger siblings.

By 1829, all the surviving Brontë children were seized by what Branwell, using his newly learned Latin, called *furor scribendi*. They named their ability to come up with imaginary people and lands "making out." To egg each other on, they would urge, "But go on! *Make it out!* I know you can." This mania for scribbling wasn't an unusual activity for literary middle- or upper-class children in nineteenth-century England (many poorer kids were working at a young age, including

Charles Dickens, who pasted labels onto jars at Warren's Shoeblacking factory and warehouse when he was twelve years old and his father was in debtor's prison). In the late eighteenth century, young Jane Austen filled the beautiful notebooks her father had bought her with sparkling imitations and parodies of fashionable society novels, calling them "Volume the First," "Second," and "Third." John Ruskin made a forty-five-page book with red covers, ruled with blue lines, when he was just seven. Using a "book print" like the Brontës, he included illustrations and called it "Harry and Lucy." Mary Ann Evans (who later took the pen name George Eliot) wrote a fragment of a historical novel in a school notebook when she was fourteen. Charles Dodgson scribbled family magazines, sewn into cardboard covers, with his ten siblings, such as one called "Mischmasch." His adult writing continued in this same vein of delightful ramblings, published under the name Lewis Carroll. The young Stephens had their family magazine, produced weekly, in the 1890s, with Thoby and Virginia (later Woolf) as the main authors and editors and Vanessa and Adrian as contributors. It was an early practice run for the Bloomsbury Group.[15]

Not just writers inking up paper, these children wanted to be *bookmakers*. Books, in those days, were precious and rare, things to be treasured and copied (which didn't necessarily exempt them from being used as missiles, as Heathcliff and Catherine do with their prayer books in the quotation at the beginning of this chapter). Published books were expensive possessions, much less disposable than they would become in the twentieth century. Their high cost was partially due to the book trade being technologically behind other industries during the first half of the nineteenth century. Steam didn't widely replace hand labor until the 1840s. Premade cases into which sheets were glued were invented around the same time, quickly replacing the time-consuming and hence costly operation of sewing the binding around the leaves. The

Brontës knew, even as children, all about rare and gorgeous books. Sumptuous works like "the French classics, bound in watered silk, gilt and lettered" are pictured as family heirlooms in their early writing.[16]

Like most middle-class families, the Brontës belonged to circulating libraries, joined by a subscription fee, and kept book buying to a minimum. Of the volumes in the Brontë household, many were gifts by patrons or appreciative friends or were won by Patrick as prizes for academic work during his college days at Cambridge. Others they bought secondhand (or third-, fourth-, or fifth-hand). Books that had belonged to their mother had salty stains on them and smelled briny. They had been salvaged from a ship carrying her belongings after it became stranded on the coast of Devonshire, her box "dashed to pieces," and most of her things "swallowed up in the mighty sea."[17]

Branwell dramatized, in his ill-spelled and punctuated childish scrawl, the arrival in their home of a new book of Ossian's poems in his "Blackwood's" of June 1829. In a pretend letter from "Sergt Bud Jen TSC" to the "Chief Genius Bany," he explains, "I write this to accwaint you of a circumstanc which has happend to me & which is of great importance. to the world at large On May 22 1829 the Cheif Genius Taly [Charlotte] came to me with a small yellow book in her hand." Later, when Charlotte became something of a celebrity after the publication of *Jane Eyre*, her letters to her publishers conveyed the thrill of receiving the boxes of books by their authors that the publishers had sent her. She thanks them, noting that she will "take care, and keep them clean, and send them back uninjured" after the family has read them.[18]

Some volumes the Brontës owned had so many lives, they became gritty palimpsests of heavy use. One book pressed into extreme service by the siblings works as an example of many. An edition of *Russell's General Atlas of Modern Geography* that Charlotte had at school no longer carries any white pages. Doodles, rows of numbers, and random inscriptions crowd out empty spaces, as do inky fingerprints. The leather binding is ragged and frayed, the edges of the pages blackened from being turned by many fingers, leaving small amounts of soil and grease. Most of the leaves are so winnowed down, their jagged edges so chipped away, they are missing a quarter of their original mass. The volume exudes a fragrance: quite possibly the smell of sweaty flesh that pressed and held it has imbued the pages and binding. The Brontës' relish for tattered and grubby books appears in their childhood writings. Branwell, in his endless ribbing of Charlotte and her authorship, pictures her fictional alter ego scribbling away and then rising up, "brimfull of himself" and taking the "Manuscript in his greasy hand." Another oily lad draws "a bundle of dirty-looking blurred manuscripts from his pocket" in Charlotte's evocatively titled "Leaf from an Unopened Volume." Books that have absorbed the smell of the cigar smoke of the man Lucy Snowe loves, in Charlotte's later novel *Villette*, become aromatic reminders of his presence.[19]

Depending on their state of dilapidation, books lived in different rooms of the parsonage. Those still well bound were ranged along the shelves in Patrick Brontë's study. Those that had been greedily consumed by all the family and had become shabby were kept on the shelves in the upstairs bedrooms, hidden from visitors. "Up and down the house" were lodged books of all sorts. In fact, the state and location of the books in a house of the period said something about the inhabitants. Working-class people, for instance, rarely owned books, except Bibles, generally given to them by clergymen like Patrick Brontë and paid for through donations from wealthy patrons. In many nineteenth-century novels, an introduction to a character's books is an introduction to the character. The Brontës often utilized this device in their fiction. If books appeared well used and spread around the house, this implied a genteel erudition. Anne, the least known of the three sisters who would become published novelists, presents the heroine of her second novel, *The Tenant of Wildfell Hall*, in a parlor with "an old bookcase on one side of the fireplace, stocked with a motley assemblage of books." An apparently widowed woman who supports herself and her young son as a painter, Helen Graham can't afford richly bound volumes. Yet the description of her "limited but choice collection of books" tells us that she is meant to be taken seriously, as a reader and a thinker. Likewise, we are not meant to lend much credence to characters who have books merely for show, with expensive spines, shiny because never opened. These volumes are just furniture, expressions of wealth. In a story written when the two were still kids, Branwell makes fun of Charlotte's pretensions as a writer by picturing her work printed in a book with "Blue morocco back with gilt edges." If it needs such fancy gilding, it can't be intrinsically worth much.[20]

Whether sea-stained, scruffy, handmade, or too new, the book was savored, by the Brontës and other bookish people of their time, as a material object, as a papery thing that might be fusty, fragrant, even tasty. Rather than just a holder of "content" or text to be read, like today's electronic books, books were *things* to be manipulated, made personal, appreciated in a tactile way. Books purchased with paper covers were usually rebound in leather, or sometimes the owner herself would make a unique binding by hand. When they became threadbare, volumes often received a re-covering in handsome boards. The poet Robert Southey, an ardent book collector, had two daughters, Bertha and Kate, who rebound around fourteen hundred of his volumes in fabric from their cast-off dresses, stocking an entire room, which he called his "Cottonian Library." Inscribing books was such a common practice that it is hard to find a volume from a personal library before the mid-nineteenth century that does not have some sort of handwriting in it, or at the very least a bookplate glued onto its boards. A friend gave

Patrick *Sermons or homilies appointed to be read in churches in the time of Queen Elizabeth* and penned on the flyleaf, "The Reverend P. Bronte's Book—Presented to him by his Friend W. Morgan as a Memorial of the pleasant & agreeable friendship, which subsisted between them at Wellington, —& as a Token of the same Friendship, which, as is hoped, will continue for ever."[21]

The Brontës were incessant inscribers, a practice copied from their father. Patrick came from a poor Irish family, and he carefully kept his early books and marked them as his. Scenes of giving were commonly recorded in volumes. Charlotte wrote in her little diary of 1829 that "once papa lent my sister Maria a book. It was an old geography book and she wrote on its blank leaf, 'Papa lent me this book.' " Charlotte felt a sense of awe for this textbook that had belonged to her sister, dead already for a few years. She considered it a sort of relic of the saintly Maria, containing her handwriting—a remnant of her personality. "The book is an hundred and twenty years old," she continues. "It is at this moment lying before me while I write this."[22]

The ownership, recorded through inscription, of such precious books as Bibles could become quite a tangled web. Charlotte had her own Bible—as did all of her siblings—that had its record of possessors written in it. The New Testament was first given to Jane Branwell Morgan, Maria Branwell's cousin, by her husband, William Morgan, on June 30, 1825. The first inscription marks this romantic gift: "J.B. Morgan's Book from W. Morgan." The Bible was passed on to Elizabeth Branwell when Jane died. William Morgan recorded this transfer of the book: "A memorial of J. Morgan presented to Miss Branwell by W. Morgan, Sept. 29, 1827." When Aunt Branwell died, she bequeathed it to Charlotte, who also put her name in it. What is crucial about this Bible, why it still exists today, is not the printed text but the chain of relationships it represents, made tangible by handwriting on the page.[23]

Charlotte pondered the nature of books as memory devices. When she began making her micro tomes in 1826, she savored this possibility, but she continued to use the idea throughout her writing life. In her fourth and final novel, *Villette*, her character Paulina, by taking down his books from his bookcase, rediscovers a man she knew when she was just a child. As she looks them over, she studies his inscribed name. She recollects their time together by turning the leaves, palpable greetings from the past. Not only does she pore over the books, but "she gently passes over the characters the tips of her fingers, accompanying the action with an unconscious but tender smile, which converted the touch into a caress." His personality and their experience together have been embedded in the paper, ink, and leather, to be rediscovered by physical encounter.

Emily also cared about books as containers for personal memory. In the opening scenes of *Wuthering Heights*, the first introduction we have to her main character, Catherine Earnshaw, is through her handwriting and her books, found by Lockwood in her bed. When he first arrives in her personal space, before he had the nightmare already discussed, he finds a small collection of "antique volumes," bound in calfskin. Mildewed things piled in a corner, they evoke paper damp to the touch, darkened with organic matter. Accidentally burning one with a candle, he finds the air perfumed with the smell of roasted leather, as if the book might be something to cook and eat, conjuring up the senses of taste and smell. Cracking open the singed, "dreadfully musty" Bible, his eyes fall directly on the handwritten inscription on the flyleaf, which reads, "Catherine Earnshaw, her book." As he looks through the other books, he reads only Catherine's marginalia. Accounts of her days, doodles, and caricatures fill "every morsel of blank that the printer had left." Rather than using these books for reading, Catherine asserts herself in and on them, claiming her experience as more essential than the text. Crowding out the black letters with her own handwriting, her character, Catherine puts herself into these books. After her death, they still evoke her, especially her hands and her body.

What Catherine was up to in *Wuthering Heights* was based on the Brontës' own practice. All the siblings repurposed their books as notebooks or diaries. Branwell penciled a poem about Greece on the endpaper of his father's Greek prayer book, given to Patrick by William Morgan as a memento of his wife Jane when she died (all of which is naturally recorded in inscription). When Charlotte was in her twenties and studying in Belgium, she recorded her immediate feelings in the grimy *Russell's General Atlas of Modern Geography*. Written upside down in neat print in the corner of the last page is this little bit of diary:

Brussels – Saturday morning Oct. 12th 1843 – First Class – I am
very cold – there is no fire – I wish I were at home With Papa –
Branwell Emily – Anne and Tabby – I am tired of being amongst
foreigners it is a dreary life – especially as there is only one person
in this house worthy of being liked – also another who seems a
rosy sugar-plum but I know her to be coloured chalk.[24]

Not just written on, volumes had sentimental souvenirs stuck in them, making them safekeepers of relationships. Books weren't always distinguished from albums or keepsake, souvenir, scrap, or commonplace books. In Anne's first novel, the title character Agnes Grey is given a clutch of primroses by the man she loves, Mr. Weston. She preserves the petals in her Bible: "I have them still, and mean to keep them always." Used to store things, printed books had boxlike qualities. An 1827 book of botany in the Brontë library has real herbs pressed between its leaves. Their brown leather copy of *Songs in the Night* holds plants, tipped into many pages. Newspaper clippings, reviews, or arti-

cles were tucked into novels or into volumes of verse. Letters, signatures, and notes crept in. Books could be hiding places for secrets. In
Wuthering Heights, Catherine Earnshaw's daughter, at the time living
at Thrushcross Grange, has been forbidden to communicate with her
cousin Linton Heathcliff, living at the Heights. But she receives letters
from him, which she hides by stuffing them into a book. Pretending to
read the book, she can enjoy the letters, even with disapproving adults
in the room.[25]

Books fossilized a moment, a memory, an identity. The Brontës
sometimes wrote incantations in their volumes meant to keep time
from slipping away, as if books could somehow fix the ephemeral or
even predict the future. Patrick often wrote some version of "to be
retained forever" in his books, usually after an inscription recording
the experience of receiving the book. In his copy of Homer's *Iliad*, for
instance, he penned, "My prize Book, for having always kept in the
<u>first class</u>, at St. John's College—Cambridge—P. Bronte, A.B. To
be retained—semper." Anne's godmother Elizabeth Firth gave her
a Bible in October 1823. Written in what is probably Patrick's hand
is this sentiment: "Remember, my dear Child, frequently to read this
book, with much prayer to God—and to keep it all your lifetime,
for the sake of the donor." Anne has penciled lightly on the verso,
"Began about December 1841 What when & how shall I be when I
have got through?" Charlotte sensed that paper and books had talismanic qualities. They marked time for her, in magical ways. On
September 25, 1829, she placed a scrap in a copy of *Life of the Duke
of Wellington*, a biography of her hero. As part of an obscure vow,
she burned it at one end, after writing on it the names Charles and
Arthur, her alter egos in her fiction and the real-life sons of the Duke.
She recorded the act on another piece of paper, which she then folded
and kept. We don't know what these steps signified, but somehow

their enactment required slips stored in the leaves of books, as if components for a spell.[26]

Yet the Brontë children knew well that books and manuscripts couldn't last forever. As physical things, they were mortal. With an impressive amount of sophistication for a thirteen-year-old, Branwell used complicated literary devices to tell the "ancient history" of the "young men." Relying on old manuscripts "translated" from the "old young men's tongue" by a scholar named Leaf, he often has to break off his tale because parts of the manuscript he is using are mutilated or missing and can't even be found in any of the "great libraries."[27]

The book as an entirety wasn't always needed to retain these many layers of meaning. The simple paper itself, bound in the volume or loose-leaf, could do the trick in certain cases. The Haworth stationer remembered the importance of paper to the Brontë girls. They came to him to buy their supplies, in amounts that made them seem voracious. He wondered what they were doing with it, speculating at first that they might be contributing to magazines. When he ran out of stock, he worried about their reaction if they came to buy more, his being the only establishment in town for paper. Their possible distress at being turned away empty-handed led him to sometimes walk ten miles to Halifax to have a ream on hand. While their need bewildered him, he had a desire to please these girls who seemed so different from anyone else in the town: quieter, more intensely feeling.[28]

Paper had a habit of lingering around an early-nineteenth-century household, appearing in different domestic guises. Its high cost, another reason for the expense of books, was a result in part of its makeup from recycled materials such as old rags, before the rise of cheaper wood-pulp paper in the late nineteenth century. Paper shortages, such as the acute one during the Napoleonic Wars, pushed the price up farther. A paper tax, not repealed until 1860 by William E. Gladstone, the Chancellor of the Exchequer, added to the expense. Because it was so precious, paper, especially from newspapers and journals, but even from discarded books, was often recycled in turn. The Brontë children, knowing all about the dearness of paper, wrote with envy of people, real or imagined, who could afford luxury paper, such as Charlotte's fictional version of Sir Henry Hardinge, who scrawls army estimates on a "gilt-edged sheet of Bath-post," shiny letter paper used by wealthy vacationers at Bath. The rich keep vellum manuscripts in caskets of wrought gold. Another character wraps a book to be given to the woman he loves, first in silk paper, then in "blue embossed, hot pressed satin paper, sealed in green sealing wax, with the motto 'L'amour jamais.'"[29]

Scattered throughout their fiction, clippings, twists, reams of paper, and even whole books get reused in all sorts of ways. Poetry is so bad it is rolled up and ignited to light a pipe (this was young Charlotte making fun of Branwell's poetic pomposity). Shirley, a character in Charlotte's novel of the same name, believes that her old school copybooks have been recycled as curlpapers by the servant girls. But the man in love with her has actually saved and treasured them, as a means to possess her when she's gone. Books used as notebooks or journals were sometimes simply the only writing materials in the household. The second Catherine in *Wuthering Heights* is so starved of paper at the Heights, she doesn't even have "a book from which to tear a leaf" so that she can write a note. Bibles became records of births, marriages, and deaths often merely because, in humble houses, they were the only place to write anything down.

The Brontë children repurposed whatever paper came their way. They used, for their mini booklets, scraps of anything available that suited their fancy. In crafting the 1826 book for Anne, Charlotte took for the cover a sample of spotted flower wallpaper, as if, rather than a book to fill with ink scratches, it were a room to decorate and inhabit. Paper that came through the post wrapped around packages or newspapers—in brown, gray, or yellow and sometimes with the address and conveyance still legible—were ripe sources for book backings, such as for Charlotte's "Blackwood's" serials. The first issue of Branwell's January 1829 "Blackwood's" is encased in an advertisement for *The Life of John Wesley* and Thomas à Kempis's *Imitation of Christ*, sewn together with heavy brown yarn (see color photograph). Branwell scrawled his story from the "Our Fellows" series of 1828, called "History of the Rebellion in My Fellows," on a sheet of music, fastened together by green thread in a parcel paper cover. Sturdy blue sheets wrapped numerous manuscripts. The jacket for Charlotte's story "Albion and Marina" still has the label "Purified Epsom salts, SOLD BY WEST, CHEMIST & DRUGGIST, Keighley" on its verso. Other blue covers were salvaged sugar wrappers. These particular volumes still smell sweet.[30]

The Brontës felt an intimacy with these closely handled books, made by their own limbs and clothed with materials familiar from the kitchen or the parlor. This closeness of the body and the book was an ordinary feature of daily life in the nineteenth century, a relationship no longer obvious today. One reason for this different relationship was paper's multiple lives. The literary historian Leah Price explains that through a long chain of recycling, clothes that had kept limbs covered became reading matter. Printed paper was then reused to line cupboards and pie plates; it became food wrappers, holding cheese, meat, and fish-and-chips (the paper bag didn't come into wide use until the 1860s)—and toilet paper. Because of its linkage to food and the privy, Leah Price points out, paper had a recognizable connectedness to bodies and their functions. Ingestion and defecation were stages of the lives of most books, intertwining them with fleshly parts other than eyes (to read) and hands (to open and hold the book). The covers for the Brontës' miniature books began their lives as clothing, then they became spice holders, then wrappers for literary compositions. After Charlotte's novel *The Professor* had been rejected nine times, she worried that if she sent the manuscript to the publishers of her other novels it might, prematurely, be used to line butter barrels (and leather traveling trunks).[31]

Most volumes of the time were still bound in leather, making books printed matter fastened together with the hides of animals. The terms "calf" and "sheep" appeared in catalogs as shorthand to refer to books, a clear reminder that their covers came from the skins of livestock. Some books even contained animal paper: parchment and vellum derived from animal carcasses. Each type of skin had a distinct smell, and book collectors learned to recognize different bindings using their noses. Puns related books to meat or other types of food. One such joke concerned a pigskin edition of Sir Francis Bacon's *Essays*, made juicier when set beside his aphorism "Some books are to be tasted, others to be swallowed and some few to be chewed and digested." A geography text that had belonged to Hugh Bronte (he didn't put a mark over his "e"), Patrick's Irish father, was sloppily rebound by hand. The rough leather that is stretched over the cover of the book still has a patch of hair protruding out of it. Books in such cases held the marks of once being living flesh.[32]

Sentimentalists tucked human mementos into books. Curls of hair were especially suitable for stashing in volumes. Lucy Snowe, the main character in Charlotte's *Villette*, has a memorandum book in which she keeps, nestled between its leaves, the plaited lock of hair from a now dead friend. The Romantic poet Percy Bysshe Shelley's red leather diary still has a circle of perfectly preserved hair (anonymous) slipping out from between its pages, sealed with black wax and a kind of crest with an esoteric code. According to legend, Mary Shelley kept the heart of Percy Bysshe, her husband, in a large-format, paperbound copy of his elegy for Keats, titled *Adonais*. Percy drowned in 1822 when his schooner went down in a storm in the Gulf of Spezia, in Italy. The Italian health authorities insisted that his badly decomposed corpse, washed up days later, could be moved only if it was cremated. His friends Leigh Hunt, Lord Byron, and Edward Trelawny arranged for its incineration on the beach at Viareggio, and Trelawny melodramatically claimed that Percy's heart "remained entire." Trelawny snatched it from the flames. Mary carried the heart (or a tiny pile of ashes, according to some versions of this tangled legend) back to England, wrapped in a leaf torn from the book (or in silk) and stashed between its covers. Later the remains were buried with their son, and the book went to the Bodleian Library, Oxford.[33]

Trelawny also claimed to have gathered ash and bone fragments before the burial of Percy's remains in Rome's Protestant cemetery. Some of this material made it into libraries. Fragments of his skull, looking like pieces of dried leaves, can be seen in a plastic case, with authentication letters, at the Pforzheimer Collection in the New York Public Library. At the British Library, a red levant morocco–bound book has two glass-covered cavities set inside the front cover, visible when the volume is opened, containing a lock of Percy's hair and one of Mary's. Inside the back cover, an urn-shaped cavity holds some of his ash and bone. The book, titled *Percy Bysshe Shelley: His Last Days Told by his Wife, With Locks of Hair and Some of the Poet's Ashes*, incorporates manuscript records of his death, such as a letter from Mary detailing his drowning and cremation. A kind of cross between a volume and a crypt, the tome has a fragrance of what seems to be smoke lingering about it.[34]

The Brontë children had a deep interest, along with a ghoulish fascination, in the reuse of body parts, as recorded in many of their Glass-town Confederacy stories, having read of the controversy about the dissection and the recycling of corpses that raged in the 1820s in the newspapers and in *Blackwood's*. The busy traffic in corpses and their parts came about because the only cadavers that could legally be dissected before the Anatomy Act of 1832 were those of executed felons. A constant shortage of corpses for students and doctors to use for research and teaching led to "resurrectionists" robbing recent graves for bodies to sell. William Burke and his colleague William Hare, notorious resurrectionists of the time, were hanged in 1829 for murdering people in order to have even more bodies to sell. In a gruesomely fitting gesture, a pocket book was made from the skin of Burke.[35]

Loads of body snatching happens in Branwell's early writing. He also invented a class of Parisian criminals who flayed their victims alive, tied them to trees, and used their skin as umbrellas to shield them from the elements. They also made tools of their victims' bones. Charlotte penned a story on June 17, 1830, about Young Man Naughty and his crew being caught exhuming a corpse to illegally recycle. A curious thing happens when they open the coffin. "If I don't declare it's full of books instead of bones, and here's ever so many chests crammed with the same kind of traffic." Some locals have been plundering the public library, using the coffins for safekeeping. Both corpses and books are worth stealing and reselling. Charlotte ponders the possibility of one transforming into the other: book into body, or body into book.[36]

Charlotte, Branwell, and the other siblings knew all about mortality from their own personal experience, and somehow the body's survivability became linked in their minds with the book's. Concrete evidence of death infusing life at all turns surrounded them. The church graveyard, "terribly full of uptight tombstones," ran right up to the parsonage wall. Forty-four thousand burials were said to have taken

place there by 1856, when there were complaints about overcrowding.
Charlotte told Elizabeth Gaskell that she believed the parsonage house
was built on top of old graves. Funeral bells frequently tolled, and the
"chip, chip" of the mason, as he carved the gravestones in his shed near
the churchyard, gave the air around the parsonage a mournful heaviness. Boisterous, drunken funeral feasts, called "arvills," were thrown
at the nearby tavern, the Black Bull. Years later Branwell quoted from
a *Blackwood's* article that he read around the time his sisters died, probably remembering his own feelings at their funerals: "That hour so
far more dreadful than any hour that now can darken us on this earth,
when she, her coffin and that velvet pall descended,—and descended—
slowly—slowly—into the horrid clay, and we were borne death-like,
and wishing to die, out of the churchyard that from that moment we
thought we could never enter more."[37]

Not long after their sisters' deaths, the remaining children began
obsessively crafting their books. Fashioning the tiny volumes probably
functioned as a form of consolation, as Brontë biographers surmise. The
multiplying booklets and the yarns unfolded in them packed the spaces
of absence with inked pages, with worlds replete with people. Death led
them to tap a deep well of invention. While it must have become obvious
at the start that books cannot replace bodies, the children never stopped
trying to find in the act of writing a means to overcome death. One
poignant piece of magic appears again and again in their childhood stories. When characters are killed off during the innumerable battles that
play out in the tales (especially Branwell's), they can be "made alive"
again. There were various ways of achieving this end. The genies could
resurrect characters with their incantations, a plot device used so often
it became referred to as "in the usual manner." Since the genies were
the Brontës themselves, there is a neat simplicity to this feat. But other
means were also invented, as if death needed numerous sly methods to

be got around. The character Doctor Hume Badey, a notorious body snatcher and dissector, has a "macerating tub" that revives dead people if they spend two days and two nights in it. While authorship and miniature publications didn't hold the magic of the macerating tub, they did bring a certain spirit to the workaday life at the parsonage.[38]

Books offered other consolations. Held, opened, assembled, disbound, doodled on, sewn, repurposed, books were also *read*. Because of the high rate of illiteracy and the expense of paper during the early nineteenth century, books and newspapers were often shared by reading aloud. An ordinary family entertainment, reading to each other could be a means of collaborative education or of wiling away time together. Their sister Maria used to read the newspapers to the other children in a room upstairs that the servants called "the children's study." On Sunday evenings, the household gathered in Patrick's study for his catechism and declaiming of passages from the Bible. As a young girl, Emily was known to be excellent at reciting and reading aloud, skills she apparently cultivated. In the summer, Aunt Branwell read in the afternoons to Patrick.[39]

Anne and Charlotte later brought these experiences into their novels. Anne shows the goodness of her character Agnes Grey by describing her reading to poor cottagers. Caroline Helstone, in Charlotte's *Shirley*, asks her cousin Robert Moore to read Shakespeare's *Coriolanus* one evening to her and Robert's sister. Caroline, in love with Robert, hopes that he will see parts of his own character in Shakespeare's hero and reform himself. He excels at reading the haughty speeches and tragic parts, but he gives the book to Caroline to act out the comic bits. This shared reading melds into a love scene: in the "deep, fast flow" of the lines of verse, "the heart and mind of reader and listener" interknit. The activity of reading aloud also holds an erotic charge in *Jane Eyre*. Rochester often asks Jane to read to him, beginning when they have just met and she works for him, and continuing to the end of the book, when he is partially blind and can no longer read for himself.

Reading alone also unloosed rich pleasures. Poring over a book silently, caught up in one's own mindscape, became a deeply important practice for the children. Privacy was difficult to carve out in the parsonage. The girls especially had no room of their own, nor even a bed to themselves. But reading might be done in any room, and could dip the reader instantly into a private world. Window seats, all through the house, provided nooks where sitting absorbed in a book could be mingled with looking out over the expanse of the moors. Emily would often settle on the rug with her nose in a book, her hand resting on her dog Keeper stretched out beside her. If she found herself in need of a title in the parlor and there were guests in the house, Emily had the knack of darting in without looking at anyone, retrieving the volume, and leaving again without a word or glance. Since the girls were often required to do housework, they figured out how to read (and write) while at other tasks. Books were not out of place in the kitchen. They read while watching over the cakes rising, and Emily, who made the bread for the house, could be found "studying her German out of an open book, propped up before her, as she kneaded the dough." Charlotte had an odd way of focusing intensely on texts because of her shortsightedness. "When a book was given her," a schoolfellow related, "she dropped her head over it till her nose nearly touched it, and when she was told to hold her head up, up went the book after it, still close to her nose, so that it was not possible to help laughing."[40]

Books were taken along for roaming on the moors. Local weavers remembered the Brontë "lasses" passing on their return from a walk. Out reading, books in hand, they were so lost in their own worlds they didn't look up. Anne has the heroine of *The Tenant of Wildfell Hall* start off on leisurely rambles with a book. In *Shirley*, Caroline Helstone often wanders about outdoors, reading or making sketches. When sad and alone, she sits in the garden, whiling away the time reading "old books, taken from her uncle's library." A green hollow is made into a study in *Wuthering Heights*. Books were used as an excuse for a nap, for daydreaming, for reverie. Characters yawn over newspapers, and Agnes Grey walks about with a book for several hours, "more thinking than reading." Jane Eyre sometimes *endeavors* to read, but her thoughts swim between her and the page. Like Jane, Caroline Helstone in *Shirley* often means to be reading. In one passage, she has lent the servants books "fit for Sunday reading," and they are silently engaged with them in the kitchen. She has a similar type of book open on the table, "but she could not read it." Her mind is too busy, "teeming, wandering, to listen to the language of another mind."[41]

Whether they are read or not, books can further romance. Having a book open in front of one can be a covert means of observing and courting others. Louis Moore, in love with Shirley, the eponymous heroine of Charlotte's novel, wants to be in her presence even when she is in a sour mood. He manages this by taking his book and sitting quietly in the window seat. As he reads, he steals a look at her now and then, watching for her countenance to soften and open. As a way to woo Helen, Gilbert Markham, in Anne's *Tenant*, lends her books. It starts when he purchases an elegant, portable edition of Walter Scott's *Marmion* for her. It continues: "So we talked about painting, poetry, and music, theology, geology, and philosophy: once or twice I lent her a book, and once she lent me one in return." He becomes so desperate to see her at a certain juncture that he takes from his bookcase an old volume, barely presentable in its dilapidated condition, but just good enough as an excuse for a visit. Gilbert doesn't even learn her first name until he sees it inscribed in her books. Their romance reaches a critical juncture and begins to unravel when he cracks open a copy of Sir Humphry Davy's *Last Days of a Philosopher* sitting on her desk and finds written on the first leaf, "Frederick Lawrence," a man he believes is a rival suitor.

Jane Eyre opens with a famous scene of reading. Glad that a walk outdoors is impossible because of a penetrating rain, Jane withdraws from the hostile Reeds—relatives who reluctantly raise her after the death of her parents. The Reeds are gathered in the drawing room, but she escapes into the adjoining breakfast room. She soon possesses herself of a volume from the bookshelves and crawls into the window seat. She sits cross-legged, "like a Turk," and draws the red moreen curtain closed around her, shutting herself into a hidden nook. She further withdraws by slipping into the world of her book. With Thomas Bewick's *History of British Birds* (a volume the Brontës had in their own library) open before her, she finds herself, for once, happy. Reading draws around her a charmed circle. The self-sufficiency she develops in her practice of hiding out with a book, the fund of pleasure found in inwardness, is what later makes her so desirable and mysterious to men like Rochester and St. John.

The ten-year-old Jane doesn't have this free space for long. Her cousin John Reed, an expert bully, breaks into her protected space. Calling her out of the window seat, he hits her for "your sneaking way of getting behind curtains, and for the look you had in your eyes two minutes since, you rat!" Knowing that this would sting above all else, he forbids her to use his books. Even though just fourteen, he knows that as the only son, his father deceased, the property of Gateshead really belongs to him rather than his mother. Jane, as a female relative and orphan with no money, is completely dependent on him. John continues his abuse by flinging the heavy book at her, and its sharp corner cuts open her head. Her retaliation comes when she accuses him of being a slave driver, like a Roman emperor, an idea learned from a recent reading of Oliver Goldsmith's *History of Rome*. When John doesn't understand the classical reference, he looks like an idiot. This knowledge gleaned from books becomes a rare source of power for a plain, penniless girl.

In many of their novels, Charlotte, Emily, and Anne depict reading, or pretending to read, as a way to escape difficult situations or impossible households. Helen Burns in *Jane Eyre* attempts to alleviate the oppressions of Lowood school by retreating to the fireplace. She is "abstracted from all round her by the companionship of a book, which she read by the dim glare of the embers." Lucy Snowe, in *Villette*, also finds consolation in her books and papers when at a foreign school. Comfort might be discovered under the lid of her desk, "nestled between the leaves of some book, gilding a pencil-point, the nib of a pen, or tinging the black fluid in that ink-glass." Women often cry over or behind books, their tears absorbed by the pages. When the marriage of the Huntingdons in *The Tenant of Wildfell Hall* begins to unravel, the husband hides behind his newspaper, the wife behind a novel. Emily gives her character Cathy, the daughter of Catherine Earnshaw, reading as the only means to elude the brutal, male world of the Heights. She kneels on the hearth and pores over a book by the aid of the blaze while the men around her argue and give orders. When Heathcliff robs her of reading material, she exclaims, "But I've most of them written on my brain and printed in my heart, and you cannot deprive me of those!"

The Brontës' writing was, in the final analysis, about books. They handcrafted them, read them, and wrote in, on, and about them. Charlotte and Emily (and Anne, to a lesser extent) were to become famous for authoring them. After all of her siblings had died, Charlotte looked back to this earlier time when "there was no inducement to seek social intercourse beyond our domestic circle, [and] we were wholly dependent on ourselves and each other, on books and study, for the enjoyments and occupations of life." In 1829, their homemade publications, the miniature books that began this chapter, were stuffed with all of living. Despite this, they were also fragile objects. Vulnerable to dissolution and decay, these artifacts could have been destroyed in countless ways, as some of them undoubtedly were. Today, handling and turning the leaves of these testaments to early talent is to open the book of the past, to touch what hands now quiet once touched.[42]

CHAPTER TWO

Pillopatate

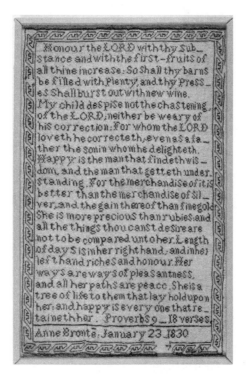

She by no means thought it waste of time to devote unnumbered hours to fine embroidery, sight-destroying lace-work, marvelous netting and knitting, and, above all, to most elaborate stocking-mending. She would give a day to the mending of two holes in a stocking any time, and think her "mission" nobly fulfilled when she had accomplished it.

—CHARLOTTE BRONTË, *Shirley*

NOVEMBER 24, 1834, was a clear day. It was just past noon, and the kitchen was in an untidy state. Anne and Emily paused in the middle of their chores to write a short account of what they, and the rest of the household, were up to. It was close to five years after Charlotte crafted her miniature book, and the three girls were helping out with preparations for dinner, which would be boiled beef, turnips, potatoes, and apple pudding.[1]

Emily had just fed their pheasants, named Rainbow, Diamond, Snowflake, and Jasper. Anne and Emily "want to go out to play," but they have together made a muddle of their duties. "Anne and I have not tid[i]ed ourselves, done our bed work or our lessons," Emily reports, nor have they finished their piano exercise, which "consists of b major." Branwell came in earlier from a walk to Mr. Driver's with news that, as Emily writes, "Sir Robert peel was going to be invited to stand for Leeds." While the lack of capitalization of "peel" could merely be the result of Emily's indifference to such rules, it might be a deliberate poetic play, turning an illustrious name into a common verb: from "Peel" to "to peel." Without a period ending the sentence about Sir Robert, she launches into the next one: "Anne and I have been peeling Apples [for] Charlotte to make an apple pudding." Emily connects the country's politics to what average English girls do to prepare dinner. Needless to say, the wealthy Sir Robert Peel, who was to become prime minister in a few weeks, never did any peeling in the kitchen.[2]

Different versions of "peel" run throughout the diary, at times reflecting Tabby's broad Yorkshire accent. Emily goes on: "Charlotte said she made puddings perfectly and she was of a quick but limted intellect Taby said just now come Anne pillopatate (ie pill a potato Aunt has come into the Kitchen just now and said where are you feet Anne Anne answered on the floor Aunt." While it is not exactly clear if Charlotte is making a joke at her own expense or if Emily is teasing her, nor what their Aunt Branwell means with her question to Anne (perhaps she is checking to see that Anne doesn't have her feet on the fire fender, an unladylike habit of hers), Emily's report has a comic, even slapstick, quality. It is also the work of a budding poet who is reveling in the sounds of words as they come from different mouths: from "peel" to "pillopatate" to "pill."

Emily exchanges her quill pen for a peeling knife, both implements for work done in the home. When Tabby insists that Emily stop writing the diary to peel, Emily saucily puts her pen in Tabby's face. Tabby grumbles, "Ya pitter pottering there instead of pilling a potate." Emily answers, "O Dear, O Dear, O Dear I will derictly." Just before she puts down the pen, though, she dips into the girls' shared imaginary world. Not even a period separates the realistic domestic scene with their made-up adventures set in the land of Gondal: "Papa opened the parlour Door and gave Branwell a Letter saying here Branwell read this and show it to your Aunt and Charlotte—The Gondals are discovering

the interior of Gaaldine Sally mosley is washing in the back Kichin."
On the page, Anne has drawn a long tress of a Gondal character's
hair—one Lady Julet—as if she is sitting next to them at the kitchen
table, her locks sweeping the paper. Layering high and low activities,
Emily accentuates with her lack of punctuation and experimental style
(a kind of stream-of-consciousness, a term not yet invented) a certain
equality: the country's political activities, the workaday life at the parsonage on a Monday washday, and their writing, both of the actual and
of the fantastical, are all crucial and "happening" just then. To the two
sisters, these events all carry weight; being Sir Robert Peel and being a
peeler of potatoes and apples, with a rich fantasy life, are equally worthy objects of slapdash lyricism.

This was the first in a series of "diary papers," as Anne and Emily
called them, that give rare glimpses of the daily running of the house,
especially Anne's and Emily's roles, and the intertwining of this labor
with that of writing. Every three to four years over the next eleven
years, they filled a scrap of paper (usually they each wrote their own),
front and back, with the minutiae of a parsonage day in micro script.
Then they folded the papers to make them even smaller and put them
into a two-inch-long tin box. The rules for the diary papers multiplied
by the 1840s. They were to be written on Emily's birthday—July 30—
and on the same day they would open and read the previous ones, written four years earlier. Lord Byron's diary, which Emily and Anne were
reading just then, via the pages of Thomas Moore's *Life of Byron*, provided a model for this kind of writing. Byron's chronicle, with its gambling, tippling, ennui, violent passions, and visits to mistresses, made
for racy reading for the sixteen- and thirteen-year-old girls. Rather
than the sex and drugs (laudanum, in particular) of Byron, in the diary
papers we have the relative quality of pudding making among the girls
of the house.[3]

These diaries were Anne and Emily's private scheme. Charlotte and Branwell probably knew nothing about them. By 1834, allegiances among the siblings had shifted. Emily and Charlotte's "bed plays" of 1827 had speedily dissolved, and Charlotte and Branwell continued to build their intertwined tales of the Glasstown Confederacy, which they moved into the newly made-up land of Angria in 1834. While the lost manuscripts of Emily and Anne's collaboration remain forever a mystery, their stories at the time apparently ran along different lines from those of the older siblings. Charlotte and Branwell wrote of wars and sweeping dramas, but Emily's and Anne's work was more domestic and "female" in character. Charlotte complained about the dullness of Emily's "Parry's Land" in her August 1830 "Blackwood's." Writing from the point of view of her hero Charles Wellesley, Charlotte has him wander into the strange place. He is immediately struck with "the changed aspect of everything. Instead of tall, strong muscular men going about seeking whom they may devour, with guns on their shoulders or in their hands, I saw none but little shiftless milk-and-water-beings, in clean, blue linen jackets and white aprons." They wear bibs when dining, and "Lady Emily" has a child named Eater "habited in a most dirty and greasy pinafore."[4]

While Anne and Emily had been collaborating for at least a year, their writing partnership was cemented in 1831, when Charlotte left home to attend school at Roe Head, on the outskirts of Mirfield. Emily and Anne became "like twins, inseparable companions, and in the closest sympathy which never had any interruption," a friend observed. This is probably when the two began inventing their world of Gondal, out of which so many of Emily's great poems would flower. While these two grew closer, Charlotte began to form alliances outside the family. Nothing like the Cowan Bridge school, Roe Head would be a great benefit for her, not least because she would meet girls who would become lifelong friends, especially Ellen Nussey and Mary Taylor. Charlotte returned to Haworth during the summer of 1832, lording her new education over her sisters. She took on the task of teaching them, and she never really gave up this drive to guide, critique, and even control their actions and sometimes their writing. Emily bridled at Charlotte's domineering nature, sometimes treating Charlotte with a touch of devilishness. Out on the moors, Emily liked to lead shortsighted Charlotte into situations that seemed dangerous to the more timid sister—the edges of drop-offs, high spots, and the like. Emily amused herself by bringing the unwitting Charlotte, afraid of unknown animals, in close proximity to bulls and unfriendly dogs, and then laughing at her horror. Yet Anne was passive with her stronger-willed sisters, willing to be led and taught, to be considered the baby well into adulthood. It was Anne's custom "to bear whatever was unpleasant, with mild, steady patience," Charlotte recalled. Unlike her sisters, who were complainers and noisy rebels, Anne was "milder and more subdued" and "long-suffering, self-denying," with a quietude that covered her mind and feelings with a "nun-like veil." This was probably due to the influence of her conventionally feminine Aunt Branwell, who, since Anne was the youngest, shaped her mind more than the other children. In some ways, Anne followed the gender rules laid down by the society of her time. In the 1840s, while Emily created the strange and stormy *Wuthering Heights*, Anne penned a comparatively straightforward, realistic narrative of the trials of the life of a governess, based closely on her own teaching jobs. As she made clear in *Agnes Grey*, she wanted the novel to be instructive to others. In writing a novel of moral guidance, Anne moved smoothly along the grooves set down for women, as self-effacing teachers of others.[5]

All three girls took up the usual women's household labors on a regular basis. Domestic work and the writing life went hand in hand for them, a twinning somewhat unusual for the time. "It was not thought proper for young ladies to study very conspicuously," Harriet Martineau, a writer and leading intellectual who grew up around the same time as the Brontës, explained in her autobiography, "especially with pen in hand." When visitors called, women needed to be careful not to show "any signs of bluestockingism," Martineau recalled, by taking care to "sit down in the parlour to sew." Martineau did her writing and intellectual work early in the morning and late at night, since the daytime had to be spent "making my own clothes, or the shirts of the household." When she published her first essay in a magazine, her beloved elder brother said gravely, "Now, dear, leave it to other women to make shirts and darn stockings; and do you devote yourself to this." Yet, after all, Martineau prided herself in *not* embodying the dreaded stereotype of the time: "a literary lady who could not sew." Glad to be a contradiction, she could not only write but also "make shirts and puddings, and iron and mend, and get my bread by my needle, if necessary."[6]

Emily, who was to do more and more of the chores as Charlotte and Anne went to work as governesses, became especially adept at developing lines of verse or passages of *Wuthering Heights* while doing housework. One of their servants described Emily's practice of carrying out creative work while ironing clothes: Setting down the "tally iron," she would scribble something on a piece of paper. "Whatever she was doing ironing or baking, she had her pencil by her." At the end of Emily's 1845 diary paper, she announces that she must hurry off to her "turning"—a thrifty practice of picking out the seams of collars, cuffs, and even entire dresses, turning them inside out and resewing them in order to conceal the worn or dirtied side. She also has "plenty of work on hands," the "work" a shortened version of "needlework." In this list of things she must rush off to get done, she includes writing, probably an early drafting of *Wuthering Heights*, finished about a year later.

Putting down the pen and picking up needle and thread, or the knife to "pillopatate," became a part of the rhythm of her writing process.[7]

It is no accident that the character who "tells" most of the story of *Wuthering Heights* is the servant Nelly Dean, who sews as she spins out the tale. The structure of Emily's novel is famously convoluted, and some of this confusion comes from the fact that the story is told by Nelly, the observant housekeeper of Wuthering Heights, to Lockwood, a stranger to the family and the area. When the novel begins, most of the story has already happened—Catherine Earnshaw has been dead many years, Heathcliff has worked his revenge on the two families he feels slighted him. Lockwood gives the reader his impression of these strange creatures when he decides to rent Heathcliff's house, Thrushcross Grange, and then goes up to Wuthering Heights and meets the family that is left. The story of their past is recounted to Lockwood and to us, the readers, when he falls ill and asks Nelly to give him an account of his landlord's life. She settles next to him with her "basket of [needle]work," commencing stitching and narrating. Emily has storytelling and needlework develop in tandem, the rhythms of one informing the cadence of the other. The female servant at her domestic work is given the agency to frame, reshape, and knit together the life plots of those around her, something like the novelist herself.

The type of needlework that had the most potential to be storylike was the sampler. Creating a sampler, like Anne's pictured at this chapter's start, meant, in most cases, "writing" a text, where thread stitched into cloth replaced ink on paper. The Brontë girls learned at a young age how to do all sorts of needlework, from the "fancy" to the most tiresome mending of stockings. They sat with their Aunt Branwell in her room upstairs as she taught them, and some of their earliest works—to perfect and prove their skills—were samplers. Anne completed this one just after she turned ten, in January 1830. Its text is in brown thread, which may have faded from black, in a cross-stitch, on a background of light brown, roughly woven cloth. Moths have opened numerous holes in it, including one that has caused about an inch of the border to disappear. The sampler stands as a testament to the hours Anne spent in close toil, an emblem of her work ethic and sense of duty, on the one hand, and her pleasure in aesthetic creation, on the other.[8]

All the girls of the family made samplers, often more than one. Anne had already worked one in 1828, its simpler pattern—with bands of abstract designs, the alphabet, numbers, and two short biblical quotations—a standard boilerplate for nineteenth-century girls. It ends with the line "Anne Bronte: Finished this Sampler Nov: 28: 1828." The two elder sisters, Maria and Elizabeth, each made one in 1822, rare testimonials to the activities of their brief lives. The years, and perhaps sunlight, have drained the color of the lettering to the same drab beige as the back cloth, giving the samplers the quality of epitaphs on old tombstones, requiring pencil rubbed on paper to be deciphered. Their mother, Maria Branwell, stitched one in 1791, and her sister, Elizabeth, worked hers one year earlier. Charlotte and Emily completed two each, their first primarily composed of alphabets, like Anne's first. Charlotte's second sampler, finished April 1, 1828, has a series of verses also from Proverbs, but full of fear and trouble, such as "A house divided against itself cannot stand," and "Better is a dry morsel and quietness therewith than a house full of sacrifices, and strife." As befits the sister who would eventually handle the domestic duties, Emily clearly had more skill, her second sampler of March 1, 1829, being the longest and neatest of all. Both Charlotte and Anne found themselves often having to split words between lines—as can be seen here with Anne's—or to squeeze in a letter or word wherever it might awkwardly be stuck. Emily spaces out the letters of her quotation from Proverbs neatly, only having to split one word. Hers soothes, with the lyricism of God's creations expressed in nature's beauty: "Who hath gathered the wind in his fists?" And, "Who hath bound the waters in a garment?" Branwell never made a sampler, of course, nor was he ever required to help with the housework or cooking. Not for him was the reminder to "despise not the chastening of the LORD," and to "not be wearied of his correction," as Anne laboriously worked into her sampler, a text that fits with her dutiful and self-disciplined nature, although it's possible that all of these biblical quotations were chosen by their Methodist aunt rather than by the girls themselves. Whatever the texts, the samplers were early attempts to think through how words and letters interact on a "page," to understand the material nature of composition.[9]

Samplers were used to teach young girls embroidery and elementary literacy. Originally examples ("samples") of patterns and techniques that a professional needleworker created in order to have a kind of notebook of work that could be referred to later or shown to potential clients, samplers increasingly came, by the late seventeenth century, to be stitched by children. Girls of all classes churned out these alphabets and religious quotations or moral sayings throughout the eighteenth and nineteenth centuries. Unlike the earlier tools of a trade, girls' samplers were usually framed and saved as mementos. These squares of cloth and thread provide the historian with a chronicle of what a particular youth was up to during a specific set of days. For many girls, especially those who grew up in poverty or in orphanages and workhouses, very few, if any, records of their lives remain. Samplers are often the only documentary evidence of their existence and activities, and signatures and dates give them an added immediacy. Since most samplers followed a standard pattern, they didn't provide much opportunity for individual expression, but more unusual ones still exist that give us a better window into these now obscure lives. Map and solar system samplers helped the producer learn geography and the night skies. Mourning samplers remembered the dead; family trees traced in thread on cotton kept alive the names of distant ancestors. Some girls depicted their homes, or towns (one Ann Woler made a sampler of the Haworth church), with family members and pets standing stiffly in front of buildings. Occasionally human hair was used instead of thread, like one sampler stitched entirely with black hair, ending, "Eliza Yates aged 9 / years, done at / Sileby School 1809." Many samplers celebrating the Great Exhibition of 1851, a sort of world's fair set up in London's Hyde Park in a temporary glass structure called the Crystal Palace, were stitched by girls. Probably the must unusual and poignant sampler made in nineteenth-century Britain came from the needle of Elizabeth Parker, a nursery maid living in Ashburnham. Her 1830s sampler is a biography, "written" in red cross-stitch on a white background, of loneliness and despair. She admits to thoughts of suicide, breaking off mid-sentence with, "what will become of my soul . . ."[10]

Victorian women often represented their experience through needlework. Sewing was a type of women's labor that had visibility, unlike peeling, kneading, and most everything else, which disappeared soon after completion. Some hand-sewn articles, as we have seen with samplers, not only lasted longer than the lifetime of their makers but also are still around today to make legible their workaday industry. The act of sewing itself had something of a public character, since women were expected to keep their hands busy, even among company. Advice manuals taught how best to show off skills and elegant hands while at needlecraft, even as a way to potentially attract a mate. Charlotte has a character always "trifling over some elegant piece of needle-work" when a man she loves comes to visit, so she can "set off her white hands." As a social activity, needlework happened along with all sorts of other things, in the parlor or any part of the home. The rhythms of sewing punctuated events such as confessions of passion and secrets, a confluence nineteenth-century novelists were fond of utilizing as plot devices.[11]

The Brontës gave sewing an integral place in their fiction. So much so that when *Jane Eyre* became a sensation in London, with speculation rife about the gender of "Currer Bell" (Charlotte's pseudonym), Harriet Martineau knew the author was a woman because a passage "about sewing on brass rings, could have been written only by a woman or an upholsterer." Charlotte was especially adept at realizing needlework's dramatic potential. In an early passage of *Jane Eyre*, young Jane finally gathers the courage to tell her Aunt Reed how cruelly abusive she has been. Her aunt feigns disinterest by focusing on her needlework. As her fingers pause in their nimble movement, a moment opens up for Jane to give voice to her feelings of injustice. Jane knows she has won this small battle when her aunt's "work had slipped from her knee." Dropping one's sewing shows agitation in many a Victorian novel, as does stabbing one's finger with a needle, which Caroline does when Robert Moore, in *Shirley*, confesses his romantic past in order to clear the way to propose to her. Lucy Snowe of *Villette* is prickly with other women, which is handily expressed when she puts pins in her girdle to ward off the physically affectionate Ginevra Fanshawe, who would otherwise be "gummed" to her.[12]

The motions of plying the needle, or pins and other implements, often expressed a female character's hidden emotional life. Romance blossomed through needlework, just as it did through reading and book giving. Shirley and her lover, Louis Moore, sit so close he is "near enough to count the stitches of her work, and to discern the eye of her needle," an elegant figure for bodily intimacy. When M. Paul Emanuel, in *Villette*, sees Lucy Snowe knitting a silk and bead watchguard (another term for a watch chain or fob, used to secure a man's pocket watch to his clothing), he is jealous, thinking this intimate gift is being made for another man. But Lucy keeps secret the fact that it is a birth-day present for him, making the final moment of giving all the more poignant for him.

Shy women hide out with their needlework. Jane, forced by Rochester to join the brilliant company in the parlor at Thornfield, sneaks in early and slips into an unobtrusive window seat. She tries to avoid being noticed by the likes of the Ingrams, and especially to avoid showing her longing for Rochester, by concentrating her "attention on these netting-needles, on the meshes of the purse I am forming." She tries to train her desire and vision to narrow to the "silver beads and silk threads that lie in my lap." Agnes Grey, in Anne's novel, often avoids situations that make her uncomfortable by stepping over to the window with her nee-dlework, with the excuse that she needs more light, but secretly meaning that she needs fewer people.

Even the tools of needlework had the power to speak out of a wom-an's inner self. Handled on such a daily basis, often around others, sew-ing implements had a close association with the body of the woman who used them, the archaeologist Mary Beaudry explains, and with their personal gestures and motions. Especially ubiquitous during the Victorian era was the workbox. Needles, pins, and other instruments, still expensive in the early nineteenth century, especially to relatively poor girls like the Brontës, were carefully stored and guarded in work-boxes (or work-cases, -bags, -baskets, or -tables). It is hard to imagine a Victorian home without at least one; even the spartan Moor House, where Jane Eyre meets her long-lost cousins, has a "brace of work-boxes." When M. Paul, the man who falls for Lucy Snowe in *Villette*, sets up a small house and school for her out of his diminutive savings, it is only complete when he provides a workbox "on a gueridon with a marble top." Sold in shops specializing in fancy goods, such as the renowned "Temple of Fancy" in London, workboxes were usually made of wood with metal fittings, although cheaper ones could be had in such materials as papier-mâché. They almost always came fitted with sets of matching tools.[13]

Much like clothing, workboxes reflected a woman's disposition and status. Caroline Helstone carries her "gay little work-bag" to the Moores' house, in *Shirley*. As a child, Paulina, in *Villette*, has a little "toy white workbox of white varnished wood." When she becomes a young woman and a wealthy countess, "the white-wood workbox of old days was now replaced by one inlaid with precious mosaic, and furnished with implements of gold." Workboxes or workbags could be signs of poverty and forced humility. Part of the Lowood uniform for the orphans, in *Jane Eyre*, are "little pockets of Holland (shaped something like a Highlander's purse) tied in front of their frocks, and designed to serve the purpose of a work-bag." The Brontë girls were expected to bring workbags with them to Cowan Bridge, the prototype for Lowood.[14]

Some of the most elaborate workboxes took pride of place in the Great Exhibition, many made as souvenirs to commemorate the event itself, picturing the Crystal Palace on their lids. The dearest workboxes were the French Palais Royal. One model called a "secret book," popular in the court circle of Charles X, took the shape of a small volume, made of burr amboyna wood. An early-nineteenth-century French Empire workbox has what looks like books fitted into the case, with their spines visible when the box is opened. When one slides out the "books," their function becomes clear: two are pincushions, one a needlebook, another a silk tape measure. Workboxes also had the booklike quality of carrying inscriptions, to commemorate friendships, scenes of giving, or community service. One box, made by Fisher, of 188 Strand Street, has an inscribed lid: "Presented to Miss Boundy / In grateful acknowledgement of her gratuitous services for several years as organist at Bethany and afterwards at Argyll Chapel Swansea, 15th July, 1875."[15]

The Brontë women naturally had their workboxes. Aunt Branwell owned at least two: one had a "Chinese" design on the top and the other an "Indian" one. Like many a middle-class woman of some privilege, she bought finely crafted boxes made by artisans in the East, seen by the British as a form of exoticism with a suggestion of luxury. The girls each had a workbox. Charlotte seems to have had a couple and also a morocco leather work-case. Her rosewood workbox, an average type for the time and much simpler (and cheaper) than her aunt's, was saved with most of its contents intact. With mother-of-pearl inlay on the top and sides and lined with blue paper, the box has a tray with ten compartments and a pincushion in the middle (see color photograph). Removing the tray exposes a larger space for swatches of material and other whatnots. The usual tools that came with workboxes are found in Charlotte's: pins, needles, spools, ivory bobbins, scraps of lace, ribbon, braiding, buttons, fasteners, an ivory measuring tape, another one made out of a cowrie shell, purple silk thread wrapped around a flat piece of bone, and an acorn-shaped thimble holder.[16]

Despite their semi-public nature, workboxes were treated like private spaces, and it is in this respect that they give voice so eloquently to the nature of the woman who carried them around. Like Charlotte's, most of them were subdivided in multiple neat ways, with pouches let into the lids, cubbies, and nooks. A fad for secret compartments in workboxes had its day, usually a drawer held in place by a long bolt that would release a spring in the bottom of the box, pushing the drawer out. The inscribed workbox given to one Miss Boundy for her service as an organist, for instance, has a hidden spring that opens a secret drawer and another that releases a mirror. Most had locks, like Charlotte's and like Lucy Snowe's in *Villette*, but a lock doesn't prevent Lucy's employer, the crafty Madame Beck, from searching through the box in order to keep tabs on her. Obnoxious children ransacked their governesses' workboxes and turned them inside out, depicted as a serious invasion of privacy. Agnes Grey's workbag is rifled by an especially evil child, who then spits in it. Intimacy with another's workbox and its contents could be welcome when a desirable hand is involved, as when M. Paul slips a romance into Lucy Snowe's, a clandestine offering of affection. When Shirley first meets Caroline, she reaches into her own workbox for a section of silk, then uses it to tie a bouquet that she gives to Caroline. This marks the beginning of a devoted friendship, full of shared confidences.[17]

Victorian women stuffed all sorts of things in their workboxes, making them catchalls for the everyday detritus of living. In Charlotte's we find stray items that were more personal: paper patterns for cutting out clothes to be sewn, the snipped-off finger ends of kid gloves (possibly used as finger protectors), a piece of a whalebone stay, a pair of black silk cuffs, and some round, pink pillboxes with pills still intact. Martin Yorke, in *Shirley*, "extracted from his mother's work-basket a bunch of keys" to a medicine cabinet. In Anne's workbox she stored a hoard of rocks collected on the beaches of Scarborough, where she traveled as a governess with a family on vacation, some of the rocks later polished to intensify their colors. Charlotte's box also had some pebbles, gathered on walks, and writing paper with doodles. Locks of hair ended up here; Charlotte stored two tresses (now anonymous) in hers, lending it a somatic character. Caroline, in *Shirley*, discovers a black curl belonging to Robert Moore in his sister's workbox. The discovery provides her with an excuse to ask Robert for one for her workbox, giving the box an erotic charge—part of the body of her lover now mingling with her sewing things.[18]

The Victorians had a penchant for depicting inanimate objects as thinking, feeling, and speaking things, with the workbox and its contents especially expressive of vitality. Lewis Carroll has his Alice spend "a minute or so vainly pursuing a large bright thing that looked sometimes like a doll and sometimes like a workbox." In an 1858 tale called *The Story of a Needle*, by Charlotte Maria Tucker, in which said needle is a sentient being who speaks to the reader of his experiences, there is a chapter called "Conversation in a Workbox." The scissors complains to the needle about how they are always blamed for human inadequacies, but then the thimble, who is a superior being, waxes eloquent about human ingenuity and the blessings of working for them. Other sewing implements stretch, chat, and explain how they were manufactured, like Mrs. Pin in *The History of a Pin*. Many a narrative of an object telling its life story appeared in the nineteenth century, a time when household goods were increasingly mass-produced: *The Adventures of a Pincushion*, *The Silver Thimble*, *The Memoirs of an Umbrella*, *Adventures of a Black Coat*. The popularity of these odd tales probably stemmed in part from discomfort with the way that the people who made these things, or even bought and used them, came to seem like objects and machines themselves. If needles and pins stirred to life, speaking of how nice it was to be employed, then maybe people, too, could maintain animation and agency. If the workbox, a dead, factory-made thing, was an extension of a woman's body, might the woman herself become more mechanical and wooden, just an appliance completing domestic duties, a kind of sewing robot?[19]

Needle-cases also walked this line between being mass-produced—and near ubiquitous—and sometimes being distinctive and imbued with original character. They could be purchased in an astonishing array of shapes and sizes; one popular version took the form of a tiny, closed umbrella made of bone, with a miniature spyhole (called a Stanhope viewer, after the inventor, Lord Charles Stanhope) in the "handle," showing tourist sights such as the Crystal Palace, which housed the Great Exhibition. Handmade or hand-adorned needle-cases were gifts for close female friends, and patterns for cutting and stitching them appeared in women's magazines. Little Maria Brontë, just before she died, gave an embossed cardboard and ribbon needle-card to a friend, inscribing it like a book: "To my dear Margaret from her affectionate schoolfellow, Maria Bronte." Charlotte stitched together a needle booklet, using white paper covers with ribbon edging, and, inside, pink tissue paper and two sheets of a flannel material for the needles to be stuck into, and gave it to one Eliza Brown. On the front and back covers are flowers and vines made out of pinpricks in the paper, which perhaps once held embroidery thread. Charlotte may have bought the parts premade and ready for her to piece together and embellish, as such sets of perforated cards, meant to be decorated with colored silks worked through the holes, could be bought in shops. She also personalized a needle-case for herself with pencil drawings—a sketch of a bird's nest with eggs on one side and a running spaniel on the other. Charlotte's best friend Ellen Nussey sent her a "housewife," also called a "hussif"—a fancy needle-book that often included scissors and a pincushion. Ellen's gift had the formal title of a "Housewife's Traveling Companion," and Charlotte thought it "a most commodious thing; just the sort of article which suits me to a t—and which yet I should never have the courage or industry to sit down and make for myself—I shall keep it for occasions of going from home—it will save me a world of trouble in collecting together little necessaries: it must have required some thought to arrange the various compartments and their contents so aptly." Housewives, like workboxes, came in the form of books, bearing legends like "Essays" or "A Stitch in Time." Charlotte had a leather, book-shaped housewife with "Souvenirs" printed on the spine, creating a neat symmetry between sewing, novel writing, and collecting.[20]

Needlework cemented intimacies between women. Pincushions, often homemade, also marked friendship or devotion by becoming gifts from one needleworker to another. The Brontës had many: one in the shape of a basket and another like a closed book, with the place for the pages being stuffed with cloth into which pins could be stuck. One of Charlotte's was inscribed, "C. Brontë, from a sincere friend and well-wisher, A. M., October, 1835." There were mourning pincushions—black with black pins—and "sticking pincushions," with pins inserted so that the heads spelled a phrase, like "ever true to you" or "ever love the giver." One had a memorial to the poet William Wordsworth painted on its glass top, picturing his tombstone along with his daughter's in a graveyard; others commemorated the Great Exhibition. A pincushion made by Lucy Snowe and given to her godmother Mrs. Bretton, in *Villette*, plays a crucial role as a memory device. After being ill and collapsing in the street, Lucy wakes up in a strange room that has ghostly reminders of the past. Especially startling is a pincushion "made of crimson satin . . . and frilled with thread-lace" with the letters "L.L.B." formed in gold beads, Mrs. Bretton's initials. When she recognizes she made it, Lucy begins to form ties with a past of friendship and love that has been lost to her until now.[21]

The relationship between Charlotte and Ellen Nussey can be followed as it flowered and deepened by tracing the handmade needlework gifts they exchanged through the mail. Charlotte spent many months in 1839 and 1840 working a bag for Ellen and lamenting in letters that she hadn't time to finish it. Ellen sent Charlotte some "pretty little cuffs" to keep her wrists warm, and then, later, "wrist frills," and a collar for Emily. Materials to be "made up" into something went back and forth between the two. In 1840, Ellen posted to Charlotte "very pretty Turkish looking things," but since she "can get no cord and tassels at Keighley," it must "lie by a time longer." In 1845, Charlotte scolded Ellen (a common means of showing gratitude between the two) for sending her some pretty slippers, which she will have "made up" to bring along when she goes to see her. Such gifts were used as occasions to compliment the friend's skills and denigrate one's own. "Will you condescend," Charlotte writes to Ellen in 1847, "to accept a scrubby yard of lace . . . I thought I would not offer to spoil it by stitching it into any shape. Your creative fingers will turn it to better account than my destructive ones."[22]

Sewing was a way for women to be together, to mark time in each other's company, not so different from reading aloud. In fact, the two often went together, with women sewing while another read to them or told stories. Charlotte developed the habit of reciting poetry when busy with her needle, especially Thomas Moore, such as "O Thou Who Driest the Mourner's Tear" and "The Bird, Let Loose in Eastern Skies." In *Agnes Grey*, the sisters Agnes and Mary pass many happy hours "sitting at our [needle]work by the fire," probably based on Anne's experience sewing with her own sisters. The three girls also occasionally worked on the same article, such as a colorful patchwork quilt they all stitched but never finished. Like the micro books they handmade as children after creating shared imaginary worlds, the plan for the quilt was cooked up among the three, reusing household scraps to give their ideas a physical, lasting shape. As we shall see, their first novels were also crafted with the help of each other, as domestic work among women that would become highly visible.[23]

The term "craft" links much of the Brontës' aesthetic work, whether it refers to piecing together a poem, making a bead bag, or sketching a portrait of a family dog. The more mundane sorts of crafts, including "fancy" needlework, were strewn about the average middle-class woman's parlor, signs to visitors of her investment in the housewifely sphere. Time for crafts meant excess leisure, so handcrafts were also tangible expressions of class status, proudly displayed in the most public rooms of the house, as badges of privilege. The parlor of Ellen Nussey, Charlotte's friend, gives us a sense of the layers of craftwork filling a typical Victorian living space. There we would find a pair of embroidered pictures; an octagonal bamboo table with embroidered cover; an oak occasional chair, with embroidered back and seat; two sofa cushions in needlework; a walnut sideboard, with panels on the doors embroidered with Shakespearean subjects; a needlework footstool and circular wool cushion; an embroidered table cover; a needlework tray cloth; and ten crocheted mats. Ellen even had an embroidered toilet cover. There were, of course, other crafts that kept women's hands busy, such as fashioning flowers from shells, wax, feathers, paper, or sand which were then placed behind or under glass. Homemade taxidermy was assiduously and skillfully developed by many a lady, learned through instructions in women's magazines and craft books. Leaves were skeletonized by dissolving the fleshy parts and leaving only the delicate filaments; seaweed was made into collages; and fish scales left over from a meal were sewn upon silk or satin to form flowers, leaves, or ornamental borders. Leftover cherry pits decorated picture frames, tables, and workboxes. The early Victorians were inveterate recyclers, as we have seen with paper goods, so even flimsy luxury items made to show off one's free time revealed a cleverness in reusing common household waste. One of these handicrafts that combined both thriftiness and hours of careful labor was paper filigree work, sometimes called "quilling." This involved rolling tiny strips of paper into circles or other shapes and pasting them onto the outside of workboxes and other sorts of containers as a form of delicate ornamentation. Charlotte made a quilled tea caddy, probably as a gift for Ellen. Like the Brontës' reuse of household wastepaper for their tiny books, quilling gave paper yet another life.[24]

But crafts and fancywork were for the privileged few. Most working women practiced "plain" needlework as a necessity. The pay for such work was scandalously low, and women who attempted to eke out a living by sewing were forced to do it all day and well into the night, often ruining their health in the process. By the 1860s they had to compete with machine-made needlework, making their tasks even more arduous. The exploitation of the seamstress was a perennial topic in the Victorian press, and an inspector in 1842 found that there was "no class of persons in this country, living by their labour whose happiness, health, and lives are so unscrupulously sacrificed as those of young dress makers." The seamstress's labor was not usually "visible" as it was for more privileged women. The pieces she made were rarely treasured and kept, and if they were, the woman who did the stitching slipped into anonymity. It is unlikely that someone sat with her admiring her hands at work, as we have seen with middle-class women, and she probably couldn't afford a workbox, unless of the most basic kind. The divide between fancy and plain work was a gap in quality of life most profound.[25]

The Brontës did both types of needlework (although as adults, Charlotte seems to have done more fancy work than her sisters, perhaps simply because she lived longer and had more friends for whom to make fancy things). Sewing drudgery filled many hours for the girls. There were the mountains of work for the parsonage household. In 1839 we find them "busy as possible in preparing" for Branwell's departure for a private tutoring job, "shirt-making and collar-making" for him, which occupied all their time. A few years later, on the eve of her trip to Brussels, Charlotte writes Ellen that she has "lots of chemises—nightgowns—pocket-handkerchiefs & pockets to make—beside clothes to repair." On some of their clothing that still exists can be found small mended or darned patches, such as Charlotte's black silk stockings with a hole that has been carefully closed. In addition to the regular mending and turning, they also made many of their dresses. Anne writes in her diary paper of July 31, 1845, that "this afternoon I began to set about making my grey figured silk frock that was dyed at Keigthley [*sic*]—What sort of hand shall I make of it?" A common refrain in the diary papers follows, about the seemingly endless pile of needlework to do: "E. and I have a great deal of work to do—when shall we sensibly diminish it?" Worse than sewing for oneself and one's family was being required to do it for others, which had a degrading tinge of the lower orders about it for middle-class women struggling to maintain their gentility. Charlotte complained when she was asked to do needlework at governess jobs. When she took a temporary post in the family of John Benson Sidgwick in Lothersdale, near Skipton, she found that Mrs. Sidgwick overwhelmed her "with oceans of needlework, yards of cambric to hem, muslin nightcaps to make, and, above all things, dolls to dress." Being forced to make dresses for some charge's dolls was a particularly galling waste of time.[26]

In their novels, the Brontës made plain sewing carry varied shades of significance. Sometimes it is used as a way of contrasting a serious, dutiful girl with a frivolous, empty-headed one, as Anne does in *The Tenant of Wildfell Hall* with the sisters Mary and Eliza Millward.[27] The reader is clearly meant to approve of Mary, who sits "mending a heap of stockings" for the family or hemming a "large, coarse sheet," while Eliza, who we discover is a crafty liar, works on "some piece of soft embroidery" or adds a deep lace border to a cambric handkerchief. Charlotte also makes sewing carry this moral message, such as when the shallow Ginevra Fanshawe gets Lucy Snowe, in *Villette*, to do her "needle-drudgery" like hose mending, and sticks to such vanity work as embroidering fine cambric handkerchiefs, apparently a practice that should make the reader suspicious of the character of the woman at it.

Yet Charlotte gives needlework a more sweeping social weightiness in *Shirley*, her most feminist novel. Caroline Helstone is a middle-class woman who has nothing to do, which strikes her as infinitely burden-some. She lives with her uncle, a misogynist who ignores her, and she has been banned from seeing the man she loves. She tries to stay occupied with the tasks genteel women were expected to do—needlework, read-ing, drawing, and charity work. The latter involves a great deal of sewing for poor women or making fancy-work to sell at bazaars, with the money going to those in need. The endless hours of stagnation at home become grim. Trying to dutifully fill up the hours, she plies her needle "continu-ously, ceaselessly," but breaks down, crying on her "busy hands." She comes to realize she must find an occupation outside the home, and she asks her uncle to let her look for a governess job. He forbids it because it might lower their worth in the eyes of their neighbors. This leads her to question the justice of a society where men can go out for professions, while "their sisters have no earthly employment, but household work and sewing." Stuck at home in tedium, their "minds and views shrink to wondrous narrowness." The independent and strong-willed Shirley sews, but "by some fatality, she is doomed never to sit steadily at it for above five minutes at a time: her thimble is scarcely fitted on, her needle scarcely threaded, when a sudden thought calls her upstairs: perhaps she goes to seek some just-then-remembered old ivory-backed needle-book, or older china-topped workbox." We might say she is too good for the work of sewing, or at least Charlotte thinks so.

A well-known scene in *Jane Eyre* begins with Jane pacing the roof of Thornfield, wishing she could throw herself out into the stirring world, rather than be shut up in a gloomy mansion in the countryside working as a governess. She thinks of women of all sorts, in rebellion against their lots:

> Women feel just as men feel; they need exercise for their faculties,
> and a field for their efforts as much as their brothers do; they

suffer from too rigid a restraint, too absolute a stagnation,
precisely as men would suffer; and it is narrow-minded in their
more privileged fellow-creatures to say that they ought to confine
themselves to making puddings and knitting stockings, to playing
on the piano and embroidering bags.

While Jane is thinking this, she hears a maniacal laugh, coming from,
she is led to believe, the servant Grace Poole, who sits in a third-story
room sewing. Perhaps sewing has unhinged her? Only later does Jane
discover that the laugh comes from Rochester's mad wife, locked away
permanently in the little room upstairs, another illustration of the house
as prison for women.

Refusing to do needlework became a recognized means for women
of the time to show their iconoclasm. In the early nineteenth century,
the unconventional Ellen Weeton, who attempted to escape the domestic sphere by taking long walking tours alone throughout Britain and
Ireland, became fed up with sewing. She wrote in her diary, "I have,
for some years, entirely given up all kinds of needlework which has no
real utility to recommend it. I do not say anything in condemnation
of ornamental needlework, although I could say much, and I think,
justly." A little later in the century, in the 1850s, a cousin described the
feminist Bessie Raynor Parkes (who became Madame Belloc), a leader
in the fight for the vote and university education for women: "She will
not wear corsets, she won't embroider; she reads every heretic book she
can get hold of, talks of following a profession."[28]

Considering samplers in this different light, they gain an oppres-
sive quality. In the case of schoolgirls at charity institutions, making
samplers or doing other types of arduous sewing was often an exercise,
in part, in instilling humility: lessons in the worth of hard work for its
own sake. At Lowood institution, in Charlotte's *Jane Eyre*, the orphan

girls are required to make all their own clothes, and sewing for hours every day is part of the curriculum. Jane, who is around nine at this point in the plot, has a teacher put in her "hands a border of muslin two yards long, together with needle, thimble, etc, . . . with direction to hem the same." Such menial work is made more degrading when the cruel head of Lowood, the evangelical Mr. Brocklehurst, buys bad needles and thread, to save money.[29]

To return to Anne's sampler pictured at the beginning of this chapter, its message fits well with the enforced submissiveness of many Victorian girls, with its acceptance of correction and chastisement. Thankfully, for the Brontës and posterity, these particular girls had writing to turn to when the sewing could be put down, when the pudding was made and eaten, and the pile of mending appreciably diminished. As mentioned earlier, Anne's novels can, from a certain standpoint, be read as teacherly and didactic in the approved way for Victorian women. Did Anne ever escape her samplers?

Anne was of a different cast of mind than her sisters. Behind her retiring and shy demeanor, she was more reasoning and rational, altogether more hardheaded. The only one of all the siblings to hold down a job outside the house for any length of time, Anne worked as a governess for the Robinsons at Thorp Green, near York, for five years, only leaving when the youngest child grew too old for a governess. (Charlotte's longest teaching job lasted less than three years and involved a mental breakdown; Emily's, six months.) There are no flitting ghosts in her novels, no madwomen in attics. Demonic heroes do not stalk her realistic plots; indeed, the men of her books are never grand, stirring, or mysterious. Some of them are honest, hard workers, such as Agnes Grey's Edward Weston. But most of them are petty and small-minded, even when heroes, such as Gilbert Markham in *The Tenant of Wildfell Hall*. In her character study of Arthur Huntingdon, Anne takes the tormented, self-destructive hero and seriously deflates him into a tedious, cruel alcoholic. She makes the reader question the attraction (and plausibility) of the popular sentiment, expressed by a flighty girl who makes a bad marriage in *Agnes Grey*, that "reformed rakes make the best husbands, *everybody* knows." In Anne's hands, the rake and the Romantic hero are exposed as no more than selfish cads who force women to run their houses and keep them in clothes, while they are out hunting, gambling, and sleeping with other women.[30]

An argument can be made that Anne's novels speak out against the unjust elements of a Victorian woman's lot. *Agnes Grey* chronicles the dull, dreary life the governess was forced to lead, like *Jane Eyre* does, but in a much more detailed, unremitting manner. *The Tenant of Wildfell Hall* works as a sustained critique of the laws that made it difficult for a woman to leave an abusive husband and impossible if she wanted to keep her children by her side. There is something steadily subversive about Anne's books, as if a hidden spring of resistance runs just underneath the conventional ground of the plot. They represent a Victorian woman's working life, free of much of the fantasy and passion of her sisters' plots. Indeed, this is how life was for Anne, for most of her adulthood, except perhaps when she was writing.

The Brontës sewed, peeled, made puddings, did some writing, then went back to household duties. Domestic arts made them women of their time, lending a dash of the real to their novels. They undoubtedly found some of their labor wearisome, although it provided meat for novel plots (and the table). One suspects that novel crafting could itself be monotonous toil at times, hard work with only flashes of inspiration and romance. We readers are given windows into the lives of Victorian women not only through their plots but also through the swatches and cloth fragments they stitched, turned, and hemmed: the physical monuments to the business of their days.

CHAPTER THREE

Out Walking

Come, the wind may never again
Blow as now it blows for us.

—EMILY BRONTË, "D.G.C. TO J.A."

Woods you need not frown on me
Spectral trees that so dolefully
Shake your heads in the dreary sky

—EMILY BRONTË, UNTITLED POEM

WALKING OUT ON the moors was, by all accounts, a necessity for Emily as a teenager. Gentler landscapes wouldn't do. In July 1835, less than a year after penning the diary paper with Anne, sixteen-year-old Emily was sent to school at Roe Head—all green pastures and soft curves—with Charlotte, who returned as a teacher. Anne stayed home for the time being, and Branwell, who wanted to train as a professional artist, went to London to enroll at the Royal Academy. Emily lasted at school for only three months. Charlotte wrote (years later) that Emily's pining for liberty, for the vision of the moors that rushed on her every morning when she woke, caused her to sicken. Charlotte saw her "white face, attenuated form" as evidence of a rapid slide to the grave and insisted she be sent home. Emily's poems attest to the unfettering of mind and body that came from setting out into wide-open spaces of moorland. After her return home, she wrote of escape from a "drear dungeon" by following, in spirit, the resounding flux of the "high waving heather 'neath stormy blasts bending." Midnight, moonlight, and bright shining star blend with the "mighty voice." of the "life giving wind" into a glory that leads to rejoicing and swift change. Cleared of clutter by keen gales, the heights swept open the mind.[1]

Rambles on the moors were a near-daily ritual. Ellen Nussey claimed—surely exaggerating—that the Brontës didn't really live in their house except for eating, drinking, and resting: "*They lived* in the free expanse of hill moorland, its purple heather, its dells and glens and brooks." Sometimes all the siblings set off together, but more often walks were done singly or in twos. Anne and Emily regularly hiked to favorite spots, like the confluence of South Dean Beck with an unnamed stream, about three miles into the Pennine mountains, which they dubbed the "Meeting of the Waters." Here they would sit "hidden from the world" with only "miles and miles of heather" and the broad sky in view. It was seclusion they were after, and a certain rugged play, nothing like the delicacy associated with the conventional idea of womanhood at the time. They forded streams instead of picking their way around them, and delighted in cliff, crag, and bog. They knew their mosses, skylarks, grouse, and bluebells, and studied the seasonal changes of the tundra-like flora and fauna. References to the landscape of high-altitude heath-land are found everywhere in the poetry and fiction of all the Brontë siblings. Emily begins a poem with a list of experiences to be had on an everyday tramp, as if the walk itself produced the poem: "The linnet in the rocky dells, / The moor-lark in the air, / The bee among the heather bells." When Jane Eyre walks out on Rochester—bereft, homeless, and in penury—she finds herself on great moors, where the heather "grows deep and wild." She has no friend but the "universal mother, nature." Striking out straight into the heath, she finds a "moss-blackened granite crag," where she spends the night, with a turfy swell for a pillow. Nature, for this moment, is to her a benign home.[2]

When Emily couldn't endure the airlessness of school, Anne was sent to replace her. Not long after Charlotte and Anne left for Roe Head in the middle of October of 1835, Emily began composing poems for herself alone, surely not coincidentally. With both her sisters gone, Emily started on a career of slow study, a specialty of the walker and poet. Her first poem, an early 1836 fragment that begins, "Cold clear and blue the morning heaven / Expands its arch on high," is probably grounded in solitary moor roaming. Many of her poems that can be accurately dated reflect the weather in Haworth at the time: they spring directly from lived experience, from the precise moods of a day. She tells in a poem of exchanging fantasies of wealth and learning for something actual, tangible: a walk. This is no grand sojourn or communion with the heroic past, but a simple act compelled by her own nature and her "first feelings." "I'll walk," she says, "Where the grey flocks in ferny glens are feeding; / Where the wild wind blows on the mountain side." These lonely mountains reveal to her "more glory and more grief" than she can encounter anywhere else.[3]

Branwell was another serious walker in the family. As with Emily's short stay at school, he also returned quickly, failing to thrive away from home. Were the features of the home landscape also a requirement for him? His experience in London is shrouded in mystery: no one knows why he didn't enter art school, and some biographers argue he didn't go to London at all. Whatever happened to Branwell in London or wherever he went, he was at home with Emily and their father by January 1836. Anne and Charlotte, at school, were homesick, not so different from Emily when there, but they focused more forcefully on their duty to learn and to teach. Both also fell ill, Anne with some sort of fever that brought her near death and Charlotte with what she called "hypochondria," her name for a nervous depression, referencing the term's Greek etymology, which related it to melancholy rather than paranoia about illness. This would become a serious mental illness that would plague her periodically throughout her life. Meanwhile, at Haworth, Branwell continued to scribble the tales of Angria, to work on becoming an established portrait painter, and to try to get the editors at *Blackwood's* to publish his works, with little success. He went out on walks, with Emily or alone, savoring a "little lonely spot" retired among trees, which, according to a fragment of a poem written during this spell at home, is happily "by all unknown and noticed not / Save sunshine and the breeze."[4]

On his wanderings, Branwell probably took along a walking stick. The fells around the parsonage could make for rough travel, and a stout staff was of great use. In some spots they were steep, with slippery rock, cliffs, defiles, and, in wintertime, frozen pathways. Perhaps he took along the stick pictured here, said to have belonged to him, although it is possible his sisters used it. Family tradition had him giving this stick, toward the end of his life, to a local acquaintance, J. Briggs, while at his favorite drinking spot, the Black Bull. Made of one piece of blackthorn or hawthorn, both trees indigenous to Yorkshire, the stick has a knob handle, possibly from a burl (a knot in a tree), and distinctive bumps, with the bark intact, where side branches once grew. Blackthorn sticks were coveted for their straightness and toughness, and when cut and cured properly with the bark maintained, they lasted so long they often became family heirlooms. The making of thorn sticks, originally a traditional Irish craft, was mastered by English woodworkers in the nineteenth century. Blackthorn walking sticks were already classics by the 1830s; a gentleman walker in the country was bound to have at least one. Patrick himself carried one so faithfully that friends called him "Old Staff." Charlotte gives one to an Irish curate, Mr. Malone, in her novel *Shirley*, which he treats as a type of weapon, or "shillelagh." Branwell's knob stick may have been cut and cured by the local carpenter, who did other woodworking and joining for the Brontës. His name was, aptly enough, William Wood.[5]

Branwell and Patrick carried sticks on most outings, but did the girls carry them? Most nineteenth-century men used walking implements of some sort, whether they were city men strolling with silver-tipped Malacca canes or farmers with oak staffs that kept sheep in line, knocked apples off trees, and supported them on long treks. Women rarely carried canes, unless they were elderly; instead parasols or umbrellas served a similar purpose. Some daring women carried flexible switches—as Anthony Reál reported in his 1876 history of the walking stick—"in the street, at the promenade, and at the races." An active woman on a serious hike in the country might take along a staff, especially if she didn't care much about fashion and was willing to be viewed as eccentric. Emily fit this profile. While Anne, with her violet eyes, was thought the prettiest by most who met them and was never sartorially criticized, Charlotte and Emily were described throughout their lives as awkward dressers. Charlotte experienced anxiety about her "plain—high-made, country garments," especially when she visited London as an adult, and she made adjustments to try to appear unremarkable. Yet when Emily was teased about her relish for puffy leg-of-mutton sleeves and skirts that clung to her thin legs—styles that had fallen out of fashion decades before—she didn't seem to care. Haworth townsfolk also noted heavy boots upon the three, a tomboyish eccentricity. Such mannish footwear would have gone well with walking sticks, and Emily did not shy from using accessories considered to be solely for men: Patrick taught her to fire his pistols, according to some sources, and she was a good shot. If a walking staff helped her to scale the heights up to the dear and remote Top Withins farmhouse, then Emily probably had one often in her hand.[6]

Straying outside when the spirit moved them, the Brontës also walked more deliberately. They didn't have a choice but to walk to go places. They couldn't afford to own horses, nor did they have a carriage, although they did occasionally hire conveyances of various sorts, like gigs and covered carts, including a double-phaeton that the wealthier and more conventional Ellen Nussey found "shabby-looking," "a rickety dogcart, unmistakably betraying its neighbourship to the carts and ploughs of some rural farmyard." While the railway through Leeds (twenty miles away) opened in September 1834, it wasn't until 1846 that a train could be caught at nearer Bradford. An extension to Keighley wasn't opened until March 1847 and didn't reach Haworth until after the entire family had died, in 1867. So they trudged eight miles round trip to Keighley over steep hills to pick up and return library books and to attend lectures and other events, sometimes returning in the dark. They also took these moorland tracks and field paths to catch the regular coach (like a bus with set routes but pulled by horses that were changed at coaching inns along the way) from Keighley to Bradford or Leeds, major connecting points for other destinations. When Branwell moved in 1839 to Bradford to set up a studio as a professional portrait painter (an endeavor that also didn't work out for him), he would often walk back to Haworth over the moors, which was about twelve miles each way. This is nothing compared to a legendary walk he took when he was thirteen or fourteen to visit Charlotte at Roe Head School: twenty miles each way. Charlotte's letters to Ellen Nussey are full of details about the complications of their visits to each other. On one visit, Charlotte walked four miles to Keighley, took the coach to Bradford, arranged to have her box carried, then walked five and a half miles to Ellen's house in Gomersal in the evening. Patrick walked all over the parish to do his work, often covering, by his own account, forty miles a day, stick in hand. Emily depicts a "long spell" of a walk in *Wuthering Heights* with a mysterious, overdetermined significance: Mr. Earnshaw treks sixty miles each way to Liverpool, in three days. On the way back he carries, "bundled up" in his greatcoat, a dark child picked up freezing on the streets of Liverpool, whom he names Heathcliff after his boy who died. Half dead with fatigue, Earnshaw declares he "would not have such another walk for the three kingdoms."[7]

Under these conditions, a walking stick quickly gained miles of use. The relationship between walker and stick was intimate. A good stick was made with the height and weight of the walker in mind, and with much use the wood became molded to reflect the gait and lean of the walker's body. The handle took the shape of the hand. As the poet and ardent walker Edward Thomas saw it, "In slow course of years we acquire a way of expression . . . gradually fitted to the mind as an old walking-stick to the hand that has worn and been worn by it, full of our weakness as of our strength, of our blindness as of our vision." Canes were expressive of the person, like Thomas Hobbes's, which had an inkhorn and pen in its handle so he could record ideas that came to him while meandering. Staffs or canes that had steadied the way of saints were treated like precious relics when the saints died, as if the smoothing of the grasp infused them with blessings. The faithful believed that to touch the walking stick of Saint Catherine of Siena, for instance, who traveled around the Italian city in the fourteenth century attending to the poor, was to touch her flesh, a tangible contact with the eternal. A splinter of the walking stick of Saint John of God is said to be encased in his statue. The legend of the staff of Saint Christopher, the patron saint of travelers, encapsulates the mythic vitality of such objects as living symbols. He planted his staff in the ground upon the instructions of Christ, and, the story goes, the next day it flowered, like Aaron's rod in the Bible, which sometimes turned into a serpent and at other times grew blossoms and edible almonds.[8]

Authors who loved walking had sticks that became characters in their writing lives, something like saints' staffs and their legends, but tools aiding composition rather than connection to God. The heroic walking tours of the Romantic poet Samuel Taylor Coleridge were part of his poetic process and a way to live his philosophy of the divinity of nature. Well before mountaineering became widely adopted, conventionalized through standardized clothing and equipment, Coleridge developed special gear for his travels afoot. For an early tramp through Wales, while he was a student at Cambridge, Coleridge bought a five-foot walking stick that, he claimed in a letter, was carved on one side with the head of an eagle, eyes representing the rising sun and ears meant to evoke Turkish crescents. On the other side was carved a portrait of himself. He lost this stick at Abergele but got it back when he discovered that it had been "borrowed" by a lame elderly man staying at the same inn. Rambling about in rugged workmen's jackets and trousers, Coleridge and the college friend who accompanied him, Joseph Hucks, looked like "two pilgrims performing a journey to the tomb of some wonder-working saint." They covered over five hundred miles by foot on this particular trip alone. Later Coleridge went on epic hikes in the fells of the Lake District, carrying a portable inkhorn, notebook, and stick. One of these sticks was a broom handle fashioned into a climber's staff.[9]

A writer's cane could sometimes gain a quasi-relic status. Dickens would go off on tramps around London, or whatever his locale was at the time, to burn off the hours he had sat writing. Few could keep up with his frenetic pace, and he would often cover twenty miles in a single sojourn. He would "swing his blackthorn stick" as he went along, and sometimes act out his characters, as a way to write while walking. Naturally, his pocket compass and his ivory-handled walking stick, with a timid dog's face carved into the top of the shaft, entered collections. Charles Darwin, whose travels across the seas would be so important for evolutionary theory, was known to stride with his whalebone and ivory walking stick, its pommel in the form of a skull.

Virginia Woolf, who reported that the whole of *To the Lighthouse* came to her in an involuntary rush while ambling around Tavistock Square, left behind her crook-handled cane when she drowned herself in the river Ouse. One can almost imagine the stick, now a prized object in the New York Public Library's Berg Collection, as a material witness to the terrible event.[10]

Walking sticks pick up meaning as they roam. Pilgrims' staffs are the best examples of this accretion of value with miles and handling. Before the Protestant Reformation, pilgrims journeyed to sacred sites such as Canterbury and Walsingham to pray at the saints' shrines, to ask for pardon for sins and for divine intervention in illness and bad luck. For some the traveling itself, often lengthy, arduous, and even danger-ous, as thieves lurked along the much-used pilgrims' routes, worked as a form of penance, the staff serving as a prop and a companion. Even for those who saw the trek as an excuse for a holiday, ale at the inns along the way, and convivial storytelling as Chaucer depicts it in *The Canterbury Tales*, a walking stick had an integral place in the ritual. Pil-grims' staffs were often painted with images of the saint being visited, and at the pilgrimage site badges or tiles were purchased and nailed to the walking stick, a form of proof of arrival. Pilgrims of extensive expe-rience had staffs paved with badges, handy semaphores of virtue. Some staffs had compartments to hold relics gathered at shrines, becoming traveling reliquaries, themselves imbued with the sacred. Pilgrims' sticks were early versions of tourist souvenirs, and the practice became secularized in some parts of Europe, especially Germany, where long-distance trekkers bought little shields at key sites along their routes, to attach to their walking sticks, or had the names of towns they passed through carved into their sticks. The well-traveled stick then spoke for itself, like stamps in a passport but visible to all who passed.[11]

Loving their souvenirs and their walking sticks, nineteenth-century

Britons often merged the two, one example being a sycamore stick with a band of copper inscribed, "Commemorating the Death of Lord Nelson, Oct. 21, 1805. Made from Copper from H.M.S. Victory, given by the Lords of the Admiralty." A material trace of the death of Lord Nelson during the Battle of Trafalgar—the fatal musket ball entered his shoulder on his ship the HMS *Victory*—this keepsake is deeply nostalgic, as are all souvenirs. It is an attempt, doomed to fail, to keep present and stable an event that can be remembered but never recovered. Turning the memento into a walking stick makes it, rather strangely, a portable memory device and reliquary. Branwell's walking stick under discussion here was kept for the same nostalgic reasons at play with these other souvenirs, as an attempt to reconstitute the Brontë story. Yet using physical remains to retrieve history functions imperfectly, if at all. The attempt to treat such keepsakes as witnesses founders, turning them instead into poignant testimonials to the irretrievability of the past. All biographies and histories—including the one held right now by the reader—endeavor to cheat time, just as souvenirs do.[12]

Those who cared about unique places, times, and events treasured these souvenirs as a means to save that specificity. Pilgrimages and other kinds of meaningful foot travel fulfilled similar needs; they were insistently local. They pulled inspiration out of place. One must travel to the exact location where the saints' relics were kept, the precise site of the miracle. The routes to shrines were overlaid with rich history, and walking them was a means to have communion with that history through the body. For those who considered nature itself as having a sacred quality, which was the case for Emily and, to a lesser extent, for the rest of her family, an amble along well-loved pathways was like a small-scale pilgrimage. Daily meandering revived a personal history: the memory of past walks along the same ground, of thoughts, events, and life epochs. This sort of ruminating foot travel served the writing process, especially for Emily. She would go out walking to "get into a humor" for scribbling. Details of birdsong, cloudscape, or fern frond garnered while roaming were the sourcebook for much of her writing. "Every leaf speaks bliss to me," she said in an 1838 poetic fragment. The female speaker of a later poem finds visions and hope come to her with the "pensive" night winds and the "tender fire" of the stars, calling up a manifold desire. Emily even carried out onto the moors the small wooden footstool that she sat on while writing. If her daily walks can be considered as pilgrimages, then the blessings received were those of artistic inspiration. Her stick, if she carried one, was then a type of writing instrument, not so literal as Thomas Hobbes's pen-and-ink stick, but still part of the array of tools that assisted composition. It was also a pilgrim's staff, brought on solo searches for an inner sanctum, discoverable by moving over moorland.[13]

Walking as an aesthetic pursuit, as a taking in of nature to spur creativity, may have come naturally to Emily and her siblings, but it was also a practice they learned from the English Romantic poets, especially William Wordsworth and his close friend and walking companion Coleridge. The Brontë children were all born during the last decades of the Romantic period, which ended in 1830. Queen Victoria was crowned in July 1837 (an event mentioned in Emily's diary paper of the same month and coupled with the ascension of one of her Gondal queens), when the siblings were all past adolescence. The Brontës were bred by the Romantics rather than the Victorians, a literary influence transparent in Emily's writing. They all read Byron, as has already been mentioned—his satanic but appealing heroes are a source of the brooding Heathcliff and Rochester—but they also absorbed ideas about the natural world as the highest inspiration, a hallmark of Romanticism. Both Branwell and Charlotte wrote letters to major Romantic figures, asking for advice and help. Branwell sent some of his poetry to Wordsworth in 1837, and later to Thomas De Quincey. Charlotte's letter to Robert Southey brought the now notorious March 12, 1837, reply that warned her off writing because the minds of female writers became "distempered": "Literature cannot be the business of a woman's life," he counseled.[14]

Wordsworth was the Romantic who, even more than Coleridge, made walking in remote and rustic landscapes a recognized part of the aesthetic education of writers of the next generation. For Wordsworth, the rhythm of his steps brought out the cadence of his verse. But excursions out into the natural landscape also had more abstract meanings for him. When he was a student at Cambridge in 1790, preceding Coleridge there by a few years, he "took his staff" and set off with his friend Robert Jones to cover France and cross the Alps into Italy, all on foot. They caught a boat to Calais and then set a pace of about thirty miles a day. Wordsworth later wrote in a poem that when crossing the Alps he saw in the "winds thwarting winds," the "unfettered clouds" and other unfathomable beauties, the "types and symbols of Eternity / Of first and last, and midst, and without end." This feeling of stepping into the universe was found on many walks throughout his life. On a tour to Bristol with his sister, Dorothy, when they walked over fifty miles in three days, he had the experience described in his "Lines Composed a Few Miles above Tintern Abbey, on Revisiting the Banks of the Wye during a [Walking] Tour, July 13, 1798," to give the full title of this legendary poem. The steep and lofty cliffs and the wild secluded scene of the area around the ruined abbey brought on a "blessed mood" that pushed him, he believed, to "see into the life of things." During this simple act of a trip by foot, he found a reflection of his own mind in the "light of setting suns, / And the round ocean and the living air." The walk and the poem that grew out of it led him to deeper self-knowledge and a sense that his spiritual home could be found anywhere on earth. Anywhere, but also in this one spe-cific place: his emotional intimacy with the natural sphere arose from unique objects in singular localities, on particular walks. This specific-ity is what resonated for Emily. She would be what Thomas Coryate, celebrated in early-seventeenth-century England for his epic walking tours, called a "traveller in little things," or someone who roamed in order to note minutiae. While she never wrote to any of the Romantics, Emily internalized their belief that the true home was found in the land known well.[15]

Like Emily and many of their contemporaries, Branwell was inspired by the pedestrianism of Coleridge and Wordsworth. Finally realizing he couldn't make a living as an artist, he took a job in 1840 as a private tutor to the two sons of Robert Postlethwaite, in Broughton-in-Furness, a small town in the Lake District. The area most associ-ated with Wordsworth and Coleridge because of their residence there, it was the ideal place to walk in their footsteps (quite literally) and to inhabit the character they invented: the writer-pilgrim. Branwell, with a copy of Wordsworth's sonnets in his pocket, went on lengthy rambles along the River Duddon, a favorite haunt of Coleridge, Wordsworth, and Dorothy. He penned a sonnet himself, in Wordsworth's style, addressed to Black Combe, a mountain that filled the sky on his excur-sions. Branwell's sonnet lacks Wordsworth's rapture and is altogether darker. It contrasts the "invincible" mountaintop, "huge and heath clad," which rejoices in stormy skies, to man, who, losing "vigour in unstable joys," is ultimately lost.

Yet more than a creative act, walking was—Wordsworth and other Romantic thinkers believed—a statement of egalitarianism, an active means to pledge allegiance to vagabonds, the homeless, and gypsies of all stripes. Southey's sexism notwithstanding, the political radicalism of walking could also be adapted by renegade women to make a statement about their own marginalization. Stepping out onto the moors was exchanging the rule-bound home with a freer space, what Leslie Stephen, a great rover afoot who formed a walking club named the Sunday Tramps in 1879, called "escaping on ticket-of-leave from the prison house of respectability." The possibility of this sort of physical liberation from society's boxes was especially poignant for women. While women walked out on the roads for all sorts of reasons—to go to church, to get to work in a mill, factory, or farm—a woman walking long distances alone, especially if she were a stranger to the area and of the middle or upper class, was viewed with suspicion. Charlotte depicts this situation when Jane Eyre finds herself penniless after fleeing Thornfield. The townsfolk she encounters view her with mistrust; they think she might be a prostitute or even a thief. One servant says to her, "You should not be roving about now; it looks very ill." The association of the female walker and sexual looseness is made clear by the term "streetwalker."[16]

Anne Lister, a near contemporary of the Brontës and fellow resident of West Yorkshire, wrote in her diary about shocking and alarming her friends and neighbors by walking alone on a regular basis. She even went on her own Romantic Lake District tour in 1824, one day covering more than twenty miles over the mountains, with only a hired male guide as companion. On another occasion, she set out on the high road from her house in Halifax to meet a carriage bringing her lover. After walking over ten miles through a "dreary mountain moor-scene," she flagged down the carriage, got in, and explained that she had traveled there by foot. The passengers were astonished, even "petrified" of her because of her strange act, and her lover was so "horror-struck" that it marred their relationship irreparably. Another great woman walker was Ellen Weeton, mentioned earlier as despising needlework, whose life could have been written by Anne Brontë. She worked as a governess and companion for various disagreeable people, then married a blackguard who took her small fortune and drove her away (although years later they reconciled). Her one real pleasure was walking, and she loped along mile after mile on her long legs, once covering thirty-six miles in a day. She delighted in "places unfrequented by those of my own species, that my thoughts, as well as my feet, may ramble without restraint." She especially savored climbing mountains, an unusual practice for a woman alone in the early nineteenth century. "Running wild among" grand scenery thrilled her, made her feel "free and unrestrained as the air I breathed." Some of her pleasure was marred, and some of her walking tours curtailed, by the fear of insult and assault by men. They sneered and laughed at her and sometimes tried to stop her from ascending mountains because it wasn't "done." Anne Lister also had these troubles when out on walks, but her situation was made worse by her masculine appearance (she preferred women over men and much of her walking was a means of cruising for women). Once a man "suddenly attempted to put his hands up my things behind," but she escaped by wielding her umbrella to good effect.[17]

While the Haworth townsfolk became used to the eccentric Brontë girls walking about, Emily took a big dog along when alone. Still, Charlotte, when attempting particularly long walks to see Ellen, faced opposition from her father and aunt. Once, not able to reserve the only gig available at the time in Haworth and wanting to meet Ellen for a seaside foray, she planned to walk to Keighley, catch a coach to Bradford, then walk the last six miles, but the elders in the household blocked her from such unladylike travel, in part because she would be traveling in unknown places, where she herself was a stranger. She was invited to tour the Lake District in 1850 when her fame brought her offers from the wealthy and titled. In contrast to Branwell's solitary wanderings, however, Charlotte had to see everything from a carriage.

She "longed to slip out unseen, and to run away by myself in amongst the hills and dales," she wrote in a letter to a female friend. But she was forced to control her "erratic and vagrant instincts," because such behavior would draw too much attention to herself, a "she-artist." [18]

Because of the widespread belief that there was something not quite correct with wayfaring women, the act of walking became a recognized form of defiance. Dorothy Wordsworth was on the vanguard of women who asserted their agency by walking. As her biographer Frances Wilson puts it, "Exchanging the nursery, the parlour and the cultivated garden path for the liberty of the highways and the byways, Dorothy walked out of the life that she and others expected of her." She did some mountain climbing with her friend Miss Barker, an unmarried older woman who lived alone. Because of her long walks, Dorothy faced censure from her relatives, especially when she joined her brother on cross-country feats, once covering thirty-three miles in one day. Her great-aunt wrote with deep disapproval of her "rambling about the country on foot." Dorothy put up a vigorous defense: "So far from considering this as a matter of condemnation, I rather thought it would have given my friends pleasure to hear that I had courage to make use of the strength with which nature had endowed me." Courage and physical strength, terms not often associated with women of the time, became rubrics for personal rebellion. [19]

Jane Austen, Dorothy Wordsworth's near contemporary, was well aware of such debates, and she shows the daring and somewhat radical views of her character Elizabeth Bennet in *Pride and Prejudice* through her vigorous walking. When her sister Jane falls ill at Netherfield while on a visit to the Bingleys, Elizabeth decides the three-mile walk from her house is just what she needs. Despite her mother's protest, she sets out, "crossing field after field at a quick pace, jumping over stiles and springing over puddles with impatient activity." When she arrives, the

Bingley sisters find it "almost incredible" that she should have walked so far by herself. "She really looked almost wild," one of them remarks, "to walk three miles, or four miles, or five miles, or whatever it is, above her ankles in dirt, and alone, quite alone! What could she mean by it? It seems to me to show an abominable sort of conceited independence." Austen presents such walking as not only controversial but also progressive, as having a flavor of the egalitarian principles behind the best aspects of the recent French Revolution and the earlier American one.

When the agitation for women's rights was becoming more visible a little later in the century, feminists found walking to be a fit way to assert their equality. Two of the most important feminists of the Victorian era, the painter Barbara Leigh Smith (later Bodichon) and the poet Bessie Raynor Parkes, the abstainer from sewing already discussed, understood from their love of Wordsworth and Shelley the ideological nature of self-reliant pedestrianism. They did the usual touring of the Lake District, but they also went on a European walking tour in 1850, just the two of them without any male chaperones or guides, something almost unheard of for English women at the time. For their trek, they left behind their corsets, shortened their skirts to give freedom to their legs, and wore black boots. (In contrast, the Brontë sisters wore their usual long skirts when out walking and probably whalebone corsets of the type saved in the Brontë archives.) Walking set Parkes and Smith on their way to their later work advocating voting rights for women.

Like Austen a few decades before her, Emily created a heroine who broke convention by using her two feet. When Catherine Earnshaw is a "wild, wick slip" of a girl, with a "bold, saucy look," she rebels against home rules by running off "to the moors in the morning and remain[ing] there all day" with the young vagabond Heathcliff. Becoming a woman, she is squeezed into silk dresses and tamed into marrying the proper Edgar Linton and keeping his house, but her longing for the wild freedoms of the past splits her apart. Her mind becomes unhinged and she feels, as the "lady of Thrushcross Grange," in exile from herself. She burns with desire to be "out of doors—I wish I were a girl again, half savage and hardy, and free!" Although it is winter and she is dying, she asks Nelly to throw open the window so she can feel the wind coming off the moors: "I'm sure I should be myself were I once among the heather on those hills," she exclaims.

In order to be free, Catherine must reverse time. What she must do is get rid of her woman's body, which has enmeshed her in gender rules.[20] She sees it as a "shattered prison," unlike her girl body in which she had an androgynous autonomy, a liberty to slip into the universe, Wordsworth-like. "I'm tired," she laments, "tired of being enclosed here. I'm wearying to escape into that glorious world, and to be always there; not seeing it dimly through tears, and yearning for it through the walls of an aching heart; but really with it and in it." The only way she can do this is to die, which she then does forthwith. Cathy isn't one to let such trifles as life and death stop her from her heart's desire.

After Catherine perishes, it is possible that she is finally able to be really *with* and *in* it. Emily hints in more than one passage that Catherine roves the moors as a ghost, and that, once Heathcliff dies, they together imbue with their spirits the desolate stretches of heathland. In the oft-quoted passage of Catherine's dream of dying and going to heaven, she seems to foretell her future afterlife. The Christian heaven would be a miserable place to her, she explains to Nelly when she is still a girl living at the Heights. In her dream, heaven is not her home, and she breaks her heart with weeping to return to earth, "and the angels were so angry that they flung me out, into the middle of the heath on the top of Wuthering Heights; where I woke sobbing for joy." For her, Mother Nature, not God our father, provides paradise.[21]

Emily took her place in the history of radical female walkers.

Haunting the moors as a teenager, she was already developing Catherine's character in her Gondal heroines—her Augusta G. Almeda calls herself a "mountaineer." Unlike Catherine, Emily didn't have a Heathcliff, but she did have the heath and the cliff, usually all to herself without any man around. While Emily's experience out roving the area around her home has become central to our understanding of her, her sensations and thoughts on actual walks remain somewhat fugitive; we don't have Emily's version of Dorothy Wordsworth's delightful Alfoxden and Grasmere journals. It is in Emily's poetry that her relationship to nature can be traced, but even here it is difficult to separate personal reverie from invented Gondal scenarios. Emily remains a shadowy figure despite the plethora of books written about her and Charlotte's need to interpret her sister, to shape her image. There is something fitting about Emily as a secret, straying subject.[22]

Yet, after all, Haworth townsfolk and her family told of her setting out and her absorption in the natural world. In a characteristic description, the church sexton reported seeing Emily from the church windows go through the stile followed by her dogs, "hundreds of times." "No matter what the weather was, she loved the moors so much that she must go out upon them and enjoy the fresh breezes." Other accounts speak of her loose-limbed boyishness while out roaming. The tallest person in the family except her father, she "slouched over the moors, whistling to her dogs, and taking long strides over the rough earth." A "solitude-loving raven," Charlotte called Emily, "no gentle dove."[23]

Emily's inwardness had, at times, a flavor of iconoclasm, a turning away from the conventional. She developed no friendships outside of the family and was described by those who knew her as deeply reserved. "My sister's disposition was not naturally gregarious," Charlotte famously remarked of Emily, "circumstances favoured and fostered her tendency to seclusion; except to go to church or take a walk on the hills, she rarely crossed the threshold of home." Ellen Nussey, who as Charlotte's friend was one of the few people outside the family circle who saw Emily with some frequency, found her to be impenetrable, with "a strength of self-containment seen in no other." Emily encompassed a "law unto herself, and a heroine in keeping to her law." Around this time Emily picked up the nickname "the major" for her assertive, masculine ways. A teacher later remarked that "she should have been a man—a great navigator," because of her powerful reason and her "strong, imperious will," never daunted by opposition or difficulty. This will and tenacity were given free play by the harsh landscape around her; she could push against it as hard as she pleased, like Catherine is given Heathcliff to push against.[24]

"Wildered," an archaic term meaning straying, lost, or wandering (kindred to the later "bewildered"), describes a state common in Emily's poems. It can be sorrowful, as for a Gondal character: "Sad he stood a wildered stranger / On his own unbounded moor." The clouds that "wilder me" are exciting, if unsettling, as is a breeze that "whirls the wildering drifts." Being wildered is to be placed in the unknown, to obtain what Frances Wilson calls the "pilgrim's liminality," or the state of straying between fixed selves. Emily often tells of an extreme form of escape, which in one poem she calls "being away." She is happiest when "most away." This involves bearing her soul from its "home of clay," which is a little like Catherine's dying into nature, but also like Wordsworth's trance at Tintern Abbey, when he "is laid asleep / In body and become[s] a living soul." For Emily, it's a windy night and a bright moon that lets her ease into being not herself "and none beside." Her sublime height is reached when she is "only spirit wandering wide / Through infinite immensity."[25]

The area around Haworth is a good place to be "wildered." While not exactly a wilderness, the stark moors feel like they go on forever. From high vantage points the empty hills roll away, giving the walker a feeling of the infinite. Their dramatic loneliness stems in part from the acidic and boggy soil's inability to support anything but hardy plants such as bracken, heather, and coarse grasses. The rare tree is twisted and contorted because of the strong, and almost constant, wind. The presence of the sky, immense and moody, makes itself felt at every moment. When Elizabeth Gaskell went on her first walk there, with Charlotte, she found that the "sinuous hills seemed to girdle the world like the great Norse serpent, and for my part I don't know if they don't stretch up to the North Pole." It is a "wuthering" place, to use another archaic word important to Emily's lexicon. "Wuther," a variant of "whither," is a violent motion, sound, or force, especially in reference to what the wind does to things and what things do in the wind. It can denote "an attack, onset; a smart blow, or stroke," as in the force of a rough wind against a tree. Yet another meaning is "to tremble, shake, quiver," the motion of a tree under the influence of a strong gust. In *Wuthering Heights*, the landscape and houses are molded to this gale, as are the people, who learn quickly to face the blast boldly and become violent forces in their own right, or be annihilated. They are like the "stunted firs" and the "gaunt thorns" described at the beginning of the novel, mute evidence of the "atmospheric tumult" and powerful north wind in their excessive slant and their limbs stretched one way, "as if craving alms of the sun."[26]

Emily was seduced by this "remote and unclaimed" quality, as Charlotte described it, both in its material self and in the personal states that it led her to. In Emily's 1840 poem "The Night-Wind," she (or a poetic alter ego) sits musing at midnight at an open window. A soft draft waves her hair and tells her of the beauties she misses by sitting indoors. It whispers lowly, "How dark the woods will be!" The leaves there speak in the "myriad voices" of the wind, making the trees "Instinct with spirit secm." But she denies the "wooing" of this "Wanderer," even as its "kiss grew warmer still." "O come," it sighs sweetly, arguing that " 'when thy heart is laid at rest / Behind the church-yard stone / I shall have time enough to mourn / And thou to be alone' –." That is, the time to drink in the enchantment of night is now, not when she lies under the earth. The poem ends here, with an ambiguous dash, never telling the reader if she ventures into the speaking woods.[27]

The presence of the grave in a poem celebrating erotic vitality is surprising at first. But perhaps, after all, what the wind hints at all along is a beautiful death, of the sort the Romantic John Keats alludes to in "Ode to a Nightingale," another song to a night so beautiful it makes the poet long "to cease upon the midnight with no pain." That poem asks, as does so much of Emily's writing: Can the sweetness of nature be fully experienced without losing one's self in it, to the point of insensibility, even annihilation? Then, this question follows: If one is dead, can these sweets still be savored? If Emily's answer to these questions can be found in her writing, then it is "yes," but always with ambiguity, boundaries, and limits in sight. Catherine steeped herself in this as a girl with Heathcliff, up on Penistone Crag, but it is reported in retrospect, only after it is over. And then again, she may find ecstatic freedom in death, but this is only suggested in the novel. A few of Emily's poems contain hymns to the joy of the countryside, like the refrain in an 1838 lyric: "For the moors, for the moors where each high pass / Rose sunny against the clear sky!" Here the birds reflect the feelings of plenitude of the human stroller:

> For the moors, where the linnet was trilling . . .
> Where the lark—the wild skylark was filling
> Every breast with delight like its own.

Yet, characteristically, this is a poem about longing for a terrain that can't be had: the speaker remembers the dear place from far away because he is forced to be, the poem explains, "in exile afar."[28]

Being in exile from the true self, whatever or wherever that may be, is a common turn in Emily's poems, which Janet Gezari (the foremost scholar of Emily's poetry) characterizes as opening "oneself to one's own absence." This is the state that both Catherine and Heathcliff experience when they can't be together. Catherine sees Heathcliff as "more myself than I am": "If all else remained, and he were annihilated, the Universe would turn to a mighty stranger." When Catherine dies, Heathcliff laments that his soul is in the grave: "I *cannot* live without my life!" Many of Emily's poems situate the beloved as dead and buried, and the lover as the one lingering over the grave. In "Remembrance," the female speaker's "only Love" is "cold in the earth . . . Far, far, removed, cold in the dreary grave!" But her thoughts of the dead still hover and rest their "wings where heath and fern-leaves cover" his noble heart. There is something seductive about this grave, like the north wind. She "dare not indulge in memory's rapturous pain" or drink deep of that "divinest anguish" because then she would never seek the land of the living again. In other words, she would die to be with him, just as Heathcliff ends his life happily because he thinks he sees Catherine beckoning him just "three feet away," on the other side of the permeable divide between life and death. His lonely life, devoured by the desire to be with her, ends in Catherine's box bed, with a "gaze of exultation" on his face. Like Catherine, he quickens to death.[29]

Longing is the emotional content of most of Emily's writing, whether for a lost self or land, the perished, or for escape into death. The plangent call in her poems, the ache arising from absence, can at times bring a complicated ecstasy along with pain. This love of longing has a philosophical dimension, expressed by Romantic thinkers with the German term *Sehnsucht*. The grandeur and the tragedy of the finite nature of humanity brings on *Sehnsucht*, a kind of obsessive thinking about the beauties of loss. Emily's poems are in thrall to time, to the fact that we must live in it and that it must end. This brings anguish, but also the kind of pure aliveness that shines out at times in her works.[30]

The stern terrain of her home, a place of *Sehnsucht*, shaped this appetite for endlessness, for always wanting more, which became Emily's great theme. It was an emotional tendency probably already in her nature, Charlotte felt, rounded off by her native land. She saw Emily as a "nursling of the moors," carrying inside her the "purple light" of blooming heather, the shadows of the "sullen hollow in a livid hillside." Her type of brooding—a pining after infinity—had its external counterpart, for Emily, in the wind. Only visible in what it moves, the wind makes apparent empty spaces. It seems to come from nowhere and go nowhere. The title of *Wuthering Heights* aside (which basically means "wind's place"), winds appear in poem after poem as fitful, chainless souls that breathe spells, swell with divine joy, bring bright rejoicing to the trees. The west wind can be the most soothing air, calming dreams, the restless dead, flowers' blooms, but it also causes the pulse to "bound anew." The south has a gentle voice, and when it breaks the "icy grave" of the earth, then "'Tis sweet to wander here at night / To watch the winter die." The "bleak, bleak" east wind sobs, and the north roars and raves or has a bitter sigh. Wandering airs in her poems speak of sadness, are texts of melancholy, such as an autumn wind that "sighs mournfully," or a faraway gust that "comes sighing o'er the heathy sea." Winds moan as they rove; they grieve, repine, lament, wail, flit forebodingly, call the darkness down again: they are figures for loss and lack. The nightwind plays a "lonely vesper hymn"; it is, like its fellow zephyrs, a physical expression of longing.[31]

The wind brings on a desire to step outside and be in it, to let it wilder and wuther the body. A glorious blast, in a poem of July 6, 1841, sweeps the world aside, dashes memory from the mind. The walker becomes the "essence of the Tempest's roaring," a spirit pouring her presence into all, a "principle of life intense / Lost to mortality." To die in the wind is to never die because it pushes her "to reach, at last, the eternal home," a kind of perishing into infinity.[32]

While nature and the wind brought Emily a kind of spiritual transcendence, being *in* and feeling *with* the body was part of the magic of the moors for her. Walking is a way of being in the body; its restlessness and movement can make it an articulation of yearning. The importance of breath in her verse, of the throb or the tremble that came with emotional reactions to nature—the burst of tears—revealed a visceral engagement with her subject matter. Somehow she needed to transcend the body in her imaginative flights, but also be with and in it, in order to truly feel the gust on her cheek or the sunshine on her skin. It is no wonder that after Emily died, Charlotte found when walking the moors that "there is not a knoll of heather, not a branch of fern, not a young bilberry leaf not a fluttering lark or linnet but reminds me of her."[33]

It is hard to think of an author more tied to place: this stands as a testament to Emily's gifts as a writer of the local. Charlotte was the first of a long string of admirers who believed that it was only by walking on the moors that Emily's presence could be felt, if it could be felt at all. Not so much in the house itself, its rooms, or even the things that Emily used, such as, perhaps, Branwell's walking stick, can intimacy with her physical life be had, but rather in setting out into the heath. The pathways around Haworth became themselves relics, and walking them was to walk in her footsteps, to see what she saw, to try to reconstruct her flux of experience. Emily remains the *genius loci* of these miles of heath.

Not surprisingly, tourists began to flock to Haworth, beginning in the 1850s, soon after it became known that the person publishing under the pen name Currer Bell was a curate's daughter named Charlotte Brontë, born and bred in this little corner of England, along with her now-dead sisters, Emily and Anne. Pilgrimages to the homes and haunts of revered writers were made around the turn of the nineteenth century to commune with genius, and the Victorians turned the practice into a widely fashionable form of pleasurable travel. Wordsworth and other Romantics popularized the walking tour, but their belief in the centrality of the individual also brought a shift away from allegiance to religious figures to national ones and then to personal ones. One might worship Shakespeare, Robert Burns, or Emily Brontë as secular saints worthy of pilgrimage, not so different from the travels to religious shrines and relics in the past. Books on such travel proliferated, such as William Howitt's 1847 *Homes and Haunts of the Most Eminent British Poets* and Theodore Wolfe's 1895 *Literary Pilgrimage among the Haunts of Famous British Authors*. T. P. Grinsted described his project in the preface to his 1867 *Last Homes of Departed Genius*: "Our plan is, first, to sketch the edifice or locality; then, to glance at the busy lives of those who there lie sleeping, and thus to present to the reader their *first and last*." [34]

John Keats understood a walking pilgrimage to a literary shrine to be part of his apprenticeship to poetry. He trekked to the house in which Robert Burns was born, during an 1818 walking tour that covered 642 miles and included the Lake District, in order to "use [me] to more hardship, [to] identify finer scenes, load me with grander Mountains, and strengthen more my reach in Poetry, than would stopping at home among Books." It inspired him to write a sonnet about his own body standing there in Burns's house, moving toward death, a death that had already taken Burns: "This mortal body of a thousand days /

Now fills, O Burns, a space in thine own room." Charlotte visited the show house of her hero Sir Walter Scott on a trip to Scotland in 1850. Abbotsford, as Scott called it, was fast becoming a major tourist attraction, only to be rivaled in the future by Haworth. She didn't record her reactions to the historical souvenirs Scott had amassed there in his nostalgic drive to hold onto history, such as remnants of the Battle of Waterloo collected from the battlefield itself by his own hands two months after its end; a walking stick given to him by a friend, made from a hazel that grew near a key position in the same battle; and a chair made of wood from the beams of the house where the Scottish nationalist William Wallace was captured in the fourteenth century. Charlotte wrote no poem on the experience, but other visitors of the time found that the pilgrimage evoked a communing with Scott in the flesh, like Keats felt with Burns. A suit of Scott's clothes, bolstered by the presence of his walking stick, was on display, along with a lock of his hair and his death mask. One pilgrim had a walking stick made from a tree that grew out of Scott's tomb.[35]

This need to travel to the very site where the beloved author was born, lived, or died became integral to Brontë fandom from the start. The luster of Haworth as a destination for literary pilgrims began even before Charlotte's death. The Brontë scholar Lucasta Miller details how the "cult" that developed around Charlotte—the only celebrity in the family at first—and the religious awe many felt for her soon came to encompass Haworth and its environs. Haworth and the Brontës are "somehow inextricably mixed," wrote a young Virginia Woolf, herself a vehement moor wanderer and daughter of the Sunday tramper Leslie Stephen, when she went on her pilgrimage there in 1904. "It expresses the Brontës; the Brontës express it; they fit like a snail its shell." So convincing was the notion that the Brontës *were* the landscape, many writers assumed that the sisters' bodies were buried in that peaty, moorland soil, as Emily puts Catherine Earnshaw not in the chapel, nor in the tomb with her relations, but "on a green slope, in a corner of the kirkyard, where the wall is so low that heath and bilberry plants have climbed over it from the moor; and peat mould almost buries it." Despite the fact that Emily and Charlotte are buried in a vault beneath the church and Anne at Scarborough, Matthew Arnold, who met Charlotte in 1850, places them all around each other in "Haworth Churchyard," so that "the grass / Blows from their graves to thy [Charlotte's] own!" He imagines them waking from their eternal sleep with the west wind and the plovers calling. Emily Dickinson, an adorer of the Brontës, compounded the confusion by picturing Charlotte's grave as a cage (and Charlotte a dead nightingale), "all overgrown by cunning moss / All interspersed with weed."[36]

One of the first Haworth pilgrims was a young Bessie Rayner Parkes, the walker and feminist. Along with admiring the Romantic poets and practicing their radical pedestrianism, she was also a lover of Emily Brontë and *Wuthering Heights*. One wonders if her walking habit was influenced by Emily's Catherine. Elizabeth Gaskell, another early pilgrim, had met Charlotte in 1850 in, of all places, the Lake District. Gaskell came to stay at the parsonage in September 1853 and accompanied Charlotte through the "sweeping moors." "Oh! those high, wild, desolate moors, up above the whole world, and the very realms of silence," she declared in a letter. After one of these walks she decided that Emily must have been a "remnant of the Titans—great granddaughter of the giants, who used to inhabit the earth." Her 1857 best-selling biography of Charlotte dwelled on place almost as much as person, with the Brontës and their works inextricably interwoven with their home terrain.[37]

Many other pilgrims followed. Some walked from Keighley to Haworth and, after visiting the church, the graveyard, and the parsonage, would saunter out behind the house and feel the wind that "blew across these moors on that January winter's day, fiercely, coldly, but right gloriously," a visitor in 1867 remarked. Longer walking tours of Yorkshire began to include a stop in Haworth. One traveler in 1871 found the moors dreary and desolate, but could see the "charm of freedom in their wild solitude." Like many after him, he wanted to imagine the sisters there, and he fell asleep in the high grass and lost "consciousness of my own identity in trying to realize the daily influences of nature and society that had shaped and disciplined those remarkable characters." A romantic girl, Emma Cullum Huidekoper of Pennsylvania, arrived in 1866 with the "one idea . . . to fly to the moorland eyrie of her dreams and there to remain forever."[38]

The trek to Haworth became an important rite of passage for women writers, an early stage in the apprenticeship of the likes of Parkes, Gaskell, and Woolf. Sylvia Plath went with Ted Hughes in 1956, just after their marriage. They hiked up to Top Withins, and Plath wrote of the two pathways there in her journal: one "a track worn, losing itself, but not lost" and the other "across the slow heave, hill on hill from any other direction across bog down to the middle of the world . . . all eternity, wildness, loneliness." The house at Top Withins, with its two trees "where the long winds come, piece the light in a stillness." In a poem called "Wuthering Heights" based in part on her moor wandering, she says that the wind "pours by like destiny" and "the sky leans on me."[39]

Later poets influenced by Emily found that walking went hand in hand with watching the natural world from within its everyday texture, what the poet Algernon Charles Swinburne called Emily's "love of earth for earth's sake." In Anne Carson's "The Glass Essay," her remarkable poem about troubled desire and Emily Brontë, she ponders the character of the watcher in Emily's poems, which Emily spelled "whacher": "Tell me, whacher, is it winter?" Carson pictures Emily as this "whacher":

> She whached God and humans and moor wind and open night.
> She whached eyes, stars, inside, outside, actual weather.
>
> She whached the bars of time, which broke.
> She whached the poor core of the world,
> wide open.[40]

When the Haworth church was pulled down and rebuilt in the 1870s because of decay (and over the vehement protests of Brontë lovers), parts of the wooden interior were saved as relics. Pew fronts with renters' names painted on them became treasured souvenirs, and oak from furniture and rafters was recycled into many items, such as urns, vases, salt boxes, candlesticks, paper knives, picture frames, tobacco boxes, spittoons, tatting shuttles, and at least one "escritoire." And, not surprisingly: a walking stick.[41]

CHAPTER FOUR

Keeper, Grasper, and Other Family Animals

The dog was throttled off; his huge, purple tongue hanging half a foot out of his mouth, and his pendent lips streaming with bloody slaver.

—EMILY BRONTË, *Wuthering Heights*

"KEEPER IS IN the kitchen," Emily announced on July 30, 1841. But Keeper, Emily's big dog, was often in other parts of the house too, ones where he wasn't allowed. Both Aunt Branwell and Tabby were afraid of the powerful beast, who had a history of lunging at the throat of anyone who tried to punish him. Soon after his arrival at the parsonage in 1838, Keeper took up the habit of slinking upstairs when no one was about, jumping up on a bed, and stretching out on the clean bedspreads for a nap. Tabby didn't want her counterpanes dirtied, and Emily, knowing that this habit would mean Keeper's banishment, declared that she would beat him into submission if he did it again. When Tabby came to her one day to tell her that Keeper was drowsing on one of the best beds, Charlotte watched Emily's face become grim and set. Emily dragged Keeper, who was lowly growling and had stiffened his legs to make it more difficult to move him, down the steps by the scruff of his neck, Charlotte and Tabby watching in the hallway. Cornering him at the bottom of the staircase, Emily clenched her fist, and before he had time to bite her, she beat him about the eyes. She punched him until he was almost blind from the swelling. Then she led him into the kitchen and tended to his wounds herself. After this, his stubborn loyalty was directed all toward her.[1]

Keeper, whose collar is pictured here, was a gift to Emily. His exact breed is hard to determine—he was once called a "conglomerate, combining every species of English caninity from the turnspit to the sheepdog, with a strain of Haworth originality superadded." Probably mostly bull terrier—a cross between a bulldog and a terrier—Keeper might have had some mastiff mixed in his blood. The classification and standardization of dog breeds was still in its infancy in the 1830s. In 1859 the British held their first formal dog show; in 1873 they founded the Kennel Club. Humans had not yet fully invented the breeds that today we often assume are "pure." The bull terriers of the 1830s usually had longer legs than they do today, for instance, and were bred for dog fighting, badger hunting and drawing, and bull baiting (tethering a bull to a stick, to be attacked by dogs). Such "sports" were popular in rural areas during this time; in Haworth they were still being practiced openly in the 1850s. They slowly fell out of favor and were outlawed with the growing power of the Society for the Prevention of Cruelty to Animals, founded in 1824, which pushed through various laws, accumulating in the 1876 Cruelty to Animals Act. Bull terriers became known as a breed favored by women in the Victorian period, for reasons now obscure. Too large to be used as "turnspits," mentioned in the quotation above to describe Keeper's breed, bull terriers and related mixes had little in common with the small, bandy-legged worker dogs put in caged treadmills connected to spits that turned meat over a fire. Even so, some of them spent their lives working, as did other breeds. Draft dogs, usually Newfoundlands, pulled carts, carriages, trucks, and barrows, and hauled boats along rivers. One could still, in Britain in the early nineteenth century, buy gloves and wallets made of dog skin.[2]

Emily probably gave Keeper his name, but we don't know why she chose it. Perhaps because the other pups weren't for keeping, like this one was? Or was it to signal his guard dog capabilities: to keep guard, to keep safe? Perhaps he kept hold of things, once his strong jaws had locked? Or was there something else he kept, like secrets? The name Keeper, along with Grasper, another Brontë dog, and many of the canines that slink around in *Wuthering Heights*, like Gnasher, Wolf, Growler, Thrasher, and Throttler, are throwbacks to an earlier time, when animals were less likely to have human names because they were less likely to be kept as pets. These names sound more like labels for what the dogs did, or were kept to do, like gnash teeth at an intruder, or skulk about the stranger's heels with suspicion. The name "Wolf" especially evokes the long history of dogs in Yorkshire. Archaeologists have discovered Mesolithic (Middle Stone Age) dog remains in an area called Star Carr, where dogs kept the packs of wolves—who had dens in the fens among the rushes, bogs, and furze—from killing sheep in the night. Bred from wolves themselves, these dogs had jaws and teeth with both lupine and canine characteristics. Much later, ancient Romans in Britain used ancestors of such wolfish dogs to bear messages, attached to their collars.[3]

Emily probably encountered some of this history and earlier attitude toward creatures in her wide reading. There she discovered a time when animals were afforded a different kind of independent life than they generally were during her lifetime. On the continent from the Middle Ages to the early twentieth century, animals (including insects) that killed humans or ruined crops were put on trial and often sentenced to death. In 1522, for instance, a famous case was tried in Autun, France, against rats that had ruined some barley crops. A distinguished lawyer was appointed to represent them, but the trial was complicated by the fact that the rats would not appear in court, despite being summoned. Their lawyer argued that they wouldn't come because of their fear of the cats belonging to the plaintiffs. This argument worked for a time, but finally the rats were convicted *in absentia*. Trials of animals were less common in England, but in 1679 at Tyburn, Middlesex, a woman was hanged for bestiality and so was her canine partner. More informally, dogs or wolves caught killing sheep or poaching were often hanged as punishment (today they are often just shot). Shakespeare alludes to such punishments in *The Merchant of Venice*, so they must have been common enough for him to believe his audience would understand his reference (as would Emily, who knew Shakespeare very well). Gratiano curses Shylock:

> Thy currish spirit
> Governed a wolf, who, hanged for human slaughter,
> Even from the gallows did his fell soul fleet,
> And whilst thou layest in thy unhallowed dam,
> Infused itself in thee; for thy desires
> Are wolfish, bloody, starved, and ravenous.

While there is something terrible about animals being hanged for crimes, from a certain point of view these trials and punishments show a moral respect toward the animal, a belief that the fellow creature had some basic rights that could be vindicated at law.[4]

The Brontës tapped into ancient beliefs about animals and their special powers that survived into the nineteenth century in rural areas like the villages of West Yorkshire. A robin pecking at the window meant someone in the house would fall ill. Songs of wild birds were sometimes interpreted as messages to human listeners. The chaffinch's song said, "Pay your rent"; the great titmouse sang, "Sit ye down"; and the quail called, "Wet my lips! Wet my lips!" Heathcliff, in *Wuthering Heights*, is like one of these: he is a "bird of ill omen." Creatures signaled a future change in the weather, like petrels on the sea, or cats, swallows, owls, cattle, and hedgehogs at home. On Christmas Eve, horses and oxen were said to kneel in their stables, and bees to change their buzz for the special occasion. Bees needed to be told immediately when there was a death in the family, or they themselves might die, or leave permanently in anger. Charlotte wrote a poem around this time about creatures whose presence presaged death in the house. It begins:

> Like wolf—black bull or goblin hound,
> Or come in guise of spirit fair
> With wings and long, wet-wavy hair
> And at the fire its locks will dry
> Which will be certain sign
> That one beneath the roof must die
> Before the year's decline.[5]

A few years later, Charlotte would give Jane Eyre's first meeting with Rochester a supernatural air by calling on these same beliefs, specifically that spirits or ghosts could take the shape of horses, mules, or large dogs and haunt solitary ways. Jane sits in the gloaming and hears a horse approach, which brings to mind tales of the gytrash, a shape-shifting goblin. When a "lion-like creature with long hair and a huge head" glides up, she imagines it will have "strange pretercanine eyes." But it is just Pilot, Rochester's Newfoundland, who bounds ahead of him. Soon Rochester himself arrives on the black horse called Mesrour, who slips on the ice, beginning the famous romance. Emily, too, infuses the animals in her novel with a strange magic, but one difficult to explain, like when the ashes in the fireplace stir to life as a brindled cat, or when hellish dogs haunt the recesses of the Heights.

There is nothing supernatural about Keeper, however; in fact, the brutal violence of Emily's punishment of him is all too real. His name evokes the types of dogs whose lives in earlier centuries ended in hanging: mixed breeds, or "mongrel curs," who belonged to the poor and were often used for poaching. These outsider dogs were even thought for a time to be their own breed, called lurchers, before breeds were codified by the upper classes in the later nineteenth century. (The lurcher breed as it existed then disappeared, like the white terrier, the Great Irish hound, and many others.) Looking at engravings of lurchers from the early nineteenth century, one thinks of the sorts of dogs that Heathcliff keeps, in *Wuthering Heights*. Dogs in Emily's novel do get hanged. The little boy Hareton Earnshaw hangs a litter of puppies from a chair back, the usual way to kill unwanted dogs on a working farm like Wuthering Heights. Heathcliff hangs Isabella's springer, called Fanny, by a handkerchief when they elope together, almost killing the little dog. Heathcliff's shocking brutality, continued in his treatment of Isabella, is part of his project of revenge against the society of wealth and privilege that he feels has debased him, cast him out, and lost for him the one thing he cares about in the world—Catherine. Even the pampered dog is worth punishing in his mind, as it is part of the fabric of power that has crushed him; he only wishes he "had the hanging of every being belonging" to the families that have taken Catherine from him. While Heathcliff's plight is in some ways sympathetic, his treatment of animals deeply complicates the simple notion that he is a romantic hero.[6]

In contrast to Keeper and his lower-class associations, Anne's black, white, and tan spaniel named Flossy had an upper-class name and was generally a breed for the rich. He was probably a gift from the children of her employers, the wealthy Robinsons of Thorp Green. Queen Victoria adored spaniels, especially the silky-haired King Charles breed, named after another royal who also kept them. She acquired one when she was still Princess Victoria and called him

Dash, dressing him in a velvet collar and sometimes "a scarlet jacket and blue trousers." The little petted dog was portrayed numerous times by Edwin Landseer, whose fame developed largely through his portraits of the animals of the wealthy, especially the many commissions from the queen and Prince Albert to portray their dogs. In one of his famous paintings, the 1842 *Windsor Castle in Modern Times*, he included not only the queen and Albert but also Albert's greyhound Eos, sitting at his knee looking up at him with adoration. The queen's three terriers—Cairnach, Dandie, and Islay, who is begging on his hind legs—are also in the picture, as is the queen's eldest daughter, Princess Victoria, at this time a toddler. She is playing with a dead game bird, and strewn about the floor and settee are other dead birds, presumably killed on a hunt from which Albert has just returned. The painting at first appears to be another sentimental portrait of the royal family and their pets, and this is how most contemporaries would have understood it, but the dead birds make the critical viewer stop and think. The stark difference in the treatment of animals—the dogs loved, the birds slaughtered—perhaps signals the steel behind the sentimentality, the human and animal misery that went into the creation of such a large and prosperous empire, upon which, not long after this painting was completed, the sun never set.[7]

Dogs like Flossy and other spaniels and terriers were prime targets for the brazen pet kidnappers who had a wide and lucrative market in Victorian London. They would entice a dog away with chunks of meat or with little dogs rubbed in fat, slip the captured creature into a bag or wrap her in an apron, and then offer to return her for a large sum. By mid-century, the list of victims included Sir Robert Peel, the Duke of Cambridge, the Duchess of Sutherland, and Earl Stanhope. The Fancy, a well-known gang of dog stealers led by a man named Taylor, stole Flush, a beloved cocker spaniel that belonged to the young poet

Elizabeth Barrett, later Browning, in 1843 (Virginia Woolf wrote a story from the point of view of Flush, based largely on her own spaniel, Pinka). Barrett paid the ransom for the dog, but then he was stolen two more times by the same gang, a common occurrence when the owner paid up promptly.[8]

These are all scenes in the drama of the Victorian cult of the pet, with the queen and her family playing central roles. While pet keeping is an ancient practice, it reached new heights in the nineteenth century. Queen Victoria so loved dogs that she collected close to a hundred in her lifetime, most of them living in kennels on the grounds of her castles. When she was dying, her Pomeranians kept her company on her deathbed. The historian Harriet Ritvo puts the count of mid-century London street traders dealing in live animals at twenty thousand, at least a dozen of whom specialized in selling brass collars for dogs. Poems about dogs with human eyes proliferated, as did paintings and illustrations attributing human emotions to dogs, with titles like "Inseparable," "The Foster Mother," "The Best of Friends," "Silent Sorrow," and "Waiting for Master." Pictures of dogs dressed up as people doing things like teaching Latin or writing doggerel were a Victorian specialty, as were stories written from the point of view of dogs. Owners had their terriers stuffed, placed in glass cases, and displayed about the home when they died. Queen Victoria passed her dog love on to her children and their children; her granddaughter Princess Victoria had the sheddings of her brown poodle knitted into a shawl. In an even stranger act of memorialization, Charles Dickens had the paw and leg of his cat removed from its body after its death and made into a letter opener, which is inscribed, "C.D. in memory of Bob 1862."[9]

Emily didn't subscribe to the usual Victorian sentimentalism and idealization of pets. Although she can be called an animal lover of sorts, her relationship to them was more complex than this conventional phrase suggests, as is hinted at in her punishment of Keeper. The Victorian lady fawning over her lapdog, or the naturalist praising the "innate" subservience of dogs with humans as their "natural" masters (Victorians called this "love of Master"): these were all, to her, dishonest views of dogs. Dogs were selfish creatures of basic needs who would fight for dominance if required; as such, they were much like people, whose veneer of culture thinly covered their own animal natures. Yet, Emily felt that dogs were more honest in their expression of their natures and that made them superior to humans. She once argued in a school essay that humans "cannot sustain a comparison with the dog, it is infinitely too good." In fact, people were most like cats, in their excessive hypocrisy, cruelty, and ingratitude. Cats hide their misanthropy in order to be fed, Emily contended, just as people use politeness to gain what they desire. In their torment of their prey, cats are like ladies who kill (literally) their lapdogs in affection or like men who nurture foxes on their land in order to hunt them down. "The ingratitude of cats is another name for penetration," she wrote, because they guess the selfish motives that prompt humans to feed them.[10]

While Charlotte's heart opened to helpless animals, Emily's was drawn to fierce creatures with wild, unyielding natures. Sometimes Emily would show off Keeper's ferocity, Ellen Nussey reported, by making him "frantic in action, and roar with the voice of a lion." Those who knew her found her attention to animals—Keeper especially—as a possible way in to her impenetrable character and deep reserve. Dogs opened up a well of emotion in her, something humans rarely did. An acquaintance put this more strongly, opining that Emily "never showed regard to any human creature; all her love was reserved for animals." While this is probably an exaggeration, it wasn't wholly untrue.[11]

What she cherished was bodily closeness, the contact with fur and tongue, the feel of dog breath on her skin. Keeper would force himself onto Emily's lap, pushing aside Charlotte sitting next to her, and settle his tawny bulk as best he could on Emily's slender frame. He would match her stride when she went for walks on the moors, and he lay next to her on the carpet when she read. Emily probably didn't have intimate contact with other people except, perhaps, her sisters. One can imagine her hunger for touch and the satisfaction of the nearness of a dog's body. For Emily, animals weren't pets so much as they were family.[12]

Emily's unbending will made her akin to the hardscrabble dogs she relished tussling with. Charlotte wrote about one of Emily's angry rampages in an early piece in the speech of the "Young Men," comparing her not to a dog, but to "a gurt bellaring bull." Such bullishness appears in a story told about Emily by Haworth townsfolk. Keeper and another powerful dog were once fighting down the lane. A servant went to the house and told Emily, who immediately grabbed the pepper box from the kitchen. She found the two dogs locked on each other's throats while sundry men stood around, afraid to intervene. Emily seized Keeper around the neck with one arm, and used the other to dredge their noses with pepper. Thus separating them, she drove Keeper before her into the house, the men "standing there thunderstruck at the deed."[13]

Another time, Emily saw a strange mutt ambling past the house, looking ill, with its tongue out and its head hanging. She called for it to stop so she could bring it water. When she approached, the dog snapped at her in a crazed way, cutting open her arm. Worried about rabies, she went directly into the kitchen, pulled one of Tabby's red-hot Italian irons out of the fire, and pressed it against the bite to burn away any infection. She told no one about the incident until later, not wanting to trouble those of weaker spirit. While this oft-told story is generally cited as proof of Emily's courageous character—which it is—it is also the advice medical men of the time gave about how to deal with the bite of a rabid dog. Another way of thinking of this is that she treated herself in the same fierce way she treated Keeper: with a refusal to back down and even a desire to fight it out.[14]

Emily's willingness to skirmish with, to be wounded by, and to master difficult dogs exposes her view of intimacy as a difficult grappling with untamed natures. If love doesn't lead to wounds, then it's not passionate enough. This is the dark philosophy she brought to her novel, which Charlotte, who found the work to be too coarse and violent, thought was "hewn in a wild workshop, with simple tools, out of homely materials." Many Victorian critics questioned where this knotty story came from, as have many critics since. How could a well-bred clergyman's daughter create this tale of raw desire and devilish cruelty? A reviewer for *The Cornhill Magazine*, the most important journal of its day, expressed a typical sentiment, after Gaskell's biography had exposed the identity of the Brontës and the novels were being reissued: "It is fearful, it is true, and perhaps one of the most unpleasant books ever written: but we stand in amaze at the almost incredible fact that it was written by a slim country girl . . . who had little or no experience of the ways of the world." We find sources in her reading, of course: the novels of Walter Scott, Byron's poetry, Greek tragedy (read in the original Greek), Shakespeare. Local Yorkshire gossip and rustic characters made their way in. But there is another source worth considering: the lessons Emily learned from sparring with dogs.[15]

"Four-footed fiends" lurk in the opening pages. In the family sitting room at Wuthering Heights, a "liver-coloured bitch" pointer sits surrounded by a swarm of squealing puppies. She "sneaks wolfishly" up to strangers, with lip curled up and "white teeth watering for a snatch." A pair of "grim, shaggy sheep-dogs" slip forth from hidden dens, adding to the "absolute tempest of worrying and yelping." Heathcliff makes it clear these dogs are his working animals, for herding sheep, hunting, and guarding the house. Each dog is "not accustomed to be spoiled—not kept for a pet." He then punches one with his foot. Later, the guard dogs at the Heights tussle with those from the nearby Grange, leaving the latter limping, heads swollen and bleeding from their ears.

Even at the supposedly more civilized, polite Grange, dogs are not treated kindly, nor are they meant to treat strangers kindly. On young Catherine and Heathcliff's first introduction to the inhabitants, they peer through a window and see the young Edgar and his sister Isabella fighting over a puppy, nearly pulling it in two between them. The house guard dog, a bulldog by the name of Skulker, hears the two children sneaking about and gets his jaws around Catherine's ankle. Heathcliff tries to thrust a stone down his throat, but the dog doesn't let go until he's "throttled" by a servant, and he later sires a pup named Throttler.

This is a savage world where brutality is visited on beasts of all sorts. The put-upon creatures include humans, who often grow up to be as vicious as they were once treated. Mr. Earnshaw picks up Heathcliff on the streets of Liverpool, as we have seen, like a lost dog: "Not a soul knew to whom it belonged." Heathcliff is an "it," also called a "thing"—labels that show him to be as unfortunate as any dog in his fellow housemates. After being pulled out of Mr. Earnshaw's coat, "it was set on its feet [and] it only stared around," Nelly explains, "and Mrs. Earnshaw was ready to fling it out of doors." At first, "it" sleeps on the floor outside the room of its "master." It finally is given a name, although it's a recycled name, having already belonged to a son who died. Even so, Heathcliff barely sounds like a human name, at least a Christian one. He never has a last name, "Heathcliff" serving for both. When he marries, his wife is called Mrs. Heathcliff, his son Linton Heathcliff, and when he dies, his tombstone reads simply, "Heathcliff." (If Keeper married, his wife would, presumably, be Mrs. Keeper.) His name a compound of the natural features around him, he seems to ema-

nate from the elements. "An arid wilderness of furze and whinstone,"
Catherine names him. Charlotte calls Heathcliff, in what is essentially
an apology to readers after Emily's death for this "fierce and inhuman"
being, "a granite block on a solitary moor" from which is chiseled "a
head, savage, swart, sinister." Eventually, "the crag took human shape;
and there it stands colossal, dark, frowning, half statue, half rock."[16]

This rock leads a dog's life. Hindley, Earnshaw's son, forces Heathcliff to labor outdoors and flogs him brutally when he resists being
treated like a slave. Hardened to ill-treatment, Heathcliff doesn't protest much when he is repeatedly cast out of the human world of houses,
parties, and fine clothes because he is a "lurcher" type of human—a
vagabond, castaway, "lascar," gypsy, an "out-and-outer." As a boy, his
dark face causes the local magistrate to comment, "Would it not be a
kindness to the county to hang him at once, before he shows his nature
in acts as well as features?" Ground down repeatedly, he becomes more
and more like the dark "devil" he is accused of being. Growing sullen
and morose, he lets his gait turn slouching and his hair like a "colt's
mane," while he develops the expression of a "vicious cur that appears
to know the kicks it gets are his deserts, and yet hates all the world as
well as the kicker."

Heathcliff reminds us of our ties to animals. His difference from the
canines that weave in and out of his life is slight, as if Emily had dogs,
and perhaps Keeper especially, in mind when she created him. He is
Catherine's faithful pet: she calls him, with fondness, "fierce, pitiless,
wolfish." Her greatest delight comes from commanding him, making
him do her bidding. A characteristic scene: Cathy sits at the hearth,
Heathcliff lying on the floor with his head in her lap. He does put on
the sheen of a gentleman when he is gone for three years, but his nature
slips out from beneath the mask. He wants, for instance, to tear out
Linton's heart and drink his blood, and Isabella pictures him eating

his enemies, with his "sharp cannibal teeth." In their final moments together, just before Catherine dies, she springs at him, and their bruising embrace ends with Catherine fainting, Heathcliff gnashing and foaming over her "like a mad dog." Nelly, watching the fury of the scene, is convinced she is not "in the company of a creature of my own species." After Catherine dies, Heathcliff "howled, not like a man, but like a savage beast being goaded to death with knives and spears." He could, it is suggested, stretch himself over her grave and "die like a faithful dog." His permanent loyalty to Catherine, his love for her shot through with a need to be mastered by her—or to master her—calls to mind a tough, unredeemed mongrel.

As Heathcliff starts on his path of revenge, he moves past the canine and becomes a different type of creature altogether. Isabella asks, "Is Mr. Heathcliff a man? If so, is he mad? And if not, is he a devil?" His particular brand of savagery turns him into a kind of monster, a supernatural being like a goblin, ghoul, afreet, imp, fiend, and vampire—all labels he gains in the novel. Gytrash—an evil spirit taking a canine or human shape—would also be appropriate, although no character calls him this. Shakespeare's hanged wolf spirit that enters into the body of a man works even more cannily. Perhaps Emily had this passage in mind when she conjured up Heathcliff.

Hareton, Hindley's son mostly raised by Heathcliff, takes up Heathcliff's canine mantel. Despite his rabbit-like name, Hareton exemplifies the best qualities of the dog. Loyal even to those who treat him with cruelty (Heathcliff and, for a time, the second Cathy), he doesn't seem to know what it means to hold a grudge or seek revenge. His father, Hindley (whose name reminds us of a deer, but who glares "like a hungry wolf"), drunkenly throws him about and talks of cropping his ears because "it makes a dog fiercer, and I love something fierce." The second Cathy says of him, in a surly criticism, but one that rings true: "he's just like a dog . . .

or a cart-horse." He shares an affinity with those dogs at the Heights who, in the opening pages, show such a tigerish ferocity toward strangers, but are for the most part just doing their job and who turn pretty friendly under different circumstances. When "two hairy monsters" appear to fly at the throat of Lockwood, they pin him down and then seem "more bent on stretching their paws, and yawning, and flourishing their tails, than devouring me alive." One Juno deigns to "move the extreme tip of her tail, in token of owning" his acquaintance. Another "snoozled its nose over-forwardly into" the younger Catherine's face. Companionable dogs include Skulker, who, after he bites Catherine's ankle, is fed cakes by her and lets her pinch his nose, and Skulker's son, who is the only creature friendly to Isabella when she arrives at the Heights after a disastrous marriage with Heathcliff. Skulker's son pushes his "nose against mine by way of salute." When Heathcliff approaches the Grange, sure of no welcome, a large dog lying on the sunny grass raises its ears as if about to bark, but then smooths them back instead, announcing by a wag of the tail his recognition of Heathcliff.

Not only do many different sorts of creatures in *Wuthering Heights* play their role—Isabella's tame pheasant, the pony Minnie, a heap of dead rabbits on a cushion, a hive of bees—but the humans fulfill various creaturely roles, too. The first Catherine is a "little monkey," while Isabella Linton has dove's eyes, strays like a sheep out of the fold, and can be repugnant like a "centipede from the Indies." Linton, the son of Heathcliff and Isabella, pules like a chicken, shares kinship with a whelp, and exits out a door "exactly as a spaniel might which suspected the person who attended on it of designing a spiteful squeeze." Hareton not only has mongrel qualities but also takes the roles of an "infernal calf," an "unfledged dunnock," and an "unnatural cub." Creatures of all sorts share in the scuffle that is life, human and nonhuman alike, Emily seems to be saying, challenging "the settled boundaries between human and animal species," in the words of the great Emily Brontë scholar Stevie Davies.[17]

Nature's central driving principle is destruction, Emily believed. "Every being must be the tireless instrument of death to others, or itself must cease to live," she wrote in 1842, well before Darwin would publish his *Origin of Species* (in 1859), which helped popularize the notion that creatures only survived by being fitter than other creatures in vying for scarce resources. Some beasts, especially dogs, could at times rise above the fray, attain a touch of grace, in Emily's philosophy. Birds also had the potential for redemption. While the starkest picture of family life in *Wuthering Heights* is a lapwing nest "full of little skeletons," Catherine also describes them with words of yearning for freedom, not long before her death: "Bonny bird; wheeling over our heads in the middle of the moor." A pair of ousels builds a nest close to Heathcliff when he stands against a tree, rooted in mourning Catherine. The second Catherine's idea of the perfect day—of paradise—includes larks singing high overhead, and throstles, blackbirds, linnets, and cuckoos "pouring out music on every side . . . the whole world awake and wild with joy." Birdsong also runs through many of Emily's poems, such as the redbreast early in the morning: "wildly tender is thy music." In an 1841 poem, she identifies with a chained bird, who is "like myself lone wholly lone." If things were different:

> Give we the hills our equal prayer
> Earth's breezy hills and heaven's blue sea
> We ask for nothing further here
> But our own hearts and liberty

Yet the bird remains chained until its death, the poem implies, and the same might be said of Heathcliff.[18]

This chained bird takes us back to the real-life Brontë pets. To our modern sensibility, Keeper's heavy-metal collar seems to speak of this time when dogs were more likely to be used for hard work and their skin for leather. The adjustable brass strip has been extended to its largest setting, in order to fit around a massive neck. Its edges turn out, to prevent chafing. A small padlock on one side locks the adjustable band into its current setting. Slaves were sometimes fitted with collars like this, and slavery, while illegal by this time in Britain, was not yet outlawed in the United States and other parts of the world. In the eighteenth century, the London silversmith Matthew Dyer specialized in "silver padlocks for blacks or dogs; collars, etc." Keeper's collar reminds us that dogs were property in the eyes of English law, like humans were elsewhere. Its engraving—"The Revd P. Bronte Haworth"—marks the wearer as the possession of the man of the house. As a teenage girl, Emily wouldn't be considered the actual owner of Keeper, even if she and Keeper saw it differently. Patrick paid a tax on his dogs (as he did on his windows and hair powder), which had been implemented in 1796 as a way to gather revenue, ostensibly to support the Poor Rates, but in reality to fund the Napoleonic Wars. One's property could be seized for nonpayment of the dog tax: a tax collector was once murdered by an irate dog owner whose possessions were being taken away. The tax also worked to limit the humbler classes from legally owning dogs and using them for "unruly" practices, such as poaching on the estates of the wealthy (who wanted to kill their own game with their expensive hunting dogs) or letting them run around loose making trouble. In other words, the tax helped control a potentially rebellious people, their dogs an extension of their—sometimes righteous—lawlessness.[19]

There was nothing extraordinary about Keeper's collar; it was an inexpensive version of what most dogs of the time wore, although leather ones were also common. For the wealthy, silver or gold dog collars signaled status. Prince Albert's favorite greyhound Eos had an intricately decorated silver collar, and the prince also owned a Malacca walking stick that had as its handle a bulldog carved of ivory sporting a lovely gold collar—both of which Edwin Landseer depicted in his 1841 painting, *Eos, A Favorite Greyhound*. The thickness and height of metal collars protected the wearer's throat from the teeth and jaws of attacking dogs or other animals. Some had spikes on the outside for this purpose, a great aid if the dog was used to hunt large game. In previous centuries, dogs hunted boars and wolves, even men, as wars in the Middle Ages saw mastiffs, alaunts, and Great Irish hounds being used as soldiers on the battlefield.[20]

Dog collars could be bought at shops that specialized in brass or metal goods, and street traders sold them around London and other major cities—the smaller ones going for sixpence and larger ones for three shillings—with matching padlocks. Some of these metal collars had soft linings on the inside, made of fabrics, paper, or leather. Mention of brass collars appeared frequently in the pet "lost and found" columns in newspapers of the time, as a way to identify the dog that had gone astray or been recovered, such as a black-and-tan English terrier lost at Cultra Station, answering to the name of Dixey. The Dog Collar Museum at Leeds Castle has metal bands of all sorts dating back to the Middle Ages. Sturdy enough to be reused, some were turned inside out so that the old inscription would be hidden against the dog's neck; others had old engravings filed away. Pilfering one resulted in a year's prison time for one thief. They lingered so long that treasure hunters retrieved them from the bottom of the sea: in October 1841, divers searching the wreck of the *Royal George* found a brass dog collar—probably originally belonging to a Newfoundland, commonly used as working dogs on ships—engraved "Thomas Little, Victory [probably the dog's name], 1781," and they returned it to a relative. Another collar, pulled in 2005 from the HMS *Swift*, which sank in 1770 off the coast of Argentina, had belonged to one "I. Child in North Street Poplar Middlesex."[21]

Many of these metal dog collars had engraved inscriptions that recorded and commemorated events and relationships. Silver ones awarded to greyhounds that won coursing stakes or to bulldogs for top prizes in pedigree competitions noted these facts in lengthy inscriptions that included the dogs' and the owners' names, as well as the place and dates of the shows. One early-nineteenth-century silver presentation collar had three separate inscriptions, plus scenes of bear baiting, bull baiting, and two cocks fighting. An inscription on the inside stated, "Bulldog Champion collar for length of pedigree founded by The Hon'ble Arthur Wellesley [Charlotte's hero, who would become the Duke of Wellington], given as first prize at the bulldog breeding show." Two later inscriptions added on the outside of the collar recorded it being given, first "From Frank Redmond to Harry Brown Esq." and then "To Captain W. H. Patten-Saunders K.C.G.," presumably a gift from Brown. Other collars were awarded to dogs who labored on behalf of charities, usually by being led around cities wearing charity boxes attached to their collars or strapped around their middles. Such a collar was presented to a dog called Wimbledon Jack, "for his work in the Cause of Charity," who, after his death, was stuffed and displayed in a glass case at Wimbledon Station.[22]

Some collars evoked the characters of certain dogs and their jolly owners, such as a small brass one that declares, "Stop me not but let me jog for i am S. Oliver's Dog, Bicknell." Alexander Pope started something of a fad when he gave a puppy, the offspring of his Great Dane Bounce, to Frederick, Prince of Wales in the 1730s, with a collar saying, "I am his Highness' Dog at Kew / Pray tell me Sir, whose Dog are you?" This "Whose dog are you?" appeared on a number of later collars, usually bragging about the noble birth of the dogs' owners, but also a poignant reminder to the reader of the collar of the obvious fact that the dogs themselves cared nothing about human notions of status and class. (Of course, the inscriptions also carried a second meaning for the readers of the collars, reminding them that they were themselves "dogs" with "masters" that they must serve.) Numerous metal collars once worn by the dogs of the famous—like Keeper's—still exist today, such as Lord Nelson's silver collar for his dog Nileus. A leather one that belonged to Dickens has a brass plaque stating, "C. Dickens Esq. / Gad's Hill Place / Higham." Robert Burns, who wrote a poem in which the dog of a wealthy man has a "Locked, letter'd, braw brass collar," had a favorite collie whose collar said, "Robert Burns, Poet." Charlotte wrote in an early story of an "enormous dog" that belonged to the "body snatcher" Doctor Hume Badey (of the magical macerating tub) with an iron collar that says, "Surgeon. A bloody rascal." Keeper's collar is relatively mute in comparison.[23]

Another Brontë dog collar (now missing) that looks like it was made of leather belonged to Grasper. Little is known about this terrier of some sort who preceded Keeper. Emily immortalized him in the expressive pencil portrait she did in January 1834 (pictured here). An inscribed plaque on his collar is drawn so as to be illegible (a form of asemic writing). A few years after Keeper's appearance came Anne's Flossy. His smaller collar has the same inscription as Keeper's. It may have been purchased by Emily in 1846 using money she inherited from Aunt Branwell, since she records in an account booklet, "collar for F," one shilling, six pence. Its brass has a high shine, while Keeper's has scuffs, dents, and tears as if from numerous scuffles and adventures. Many biographers call Flossy a Cavalier King Charles spaniel, which is unlikely given his appearance in the watercolors Anne and Emily

made of him, in which he looks exactly like an English springer spaniel, called in the early nineteenth century a springing spaniel—no toy, but rather an extended-legged gun dog with a longish, straight snout and curls on his back. Hunters cross-bred and created all sorts of spaniel breeds in early-nineteenth-century England, some of which have now disappeared, and others, like the Cavalier, were not developed until after the 1840s.[24]

Other pets filled up the Brontë household: there was Dick the canary; the cats "little, black Tom" and Tiger; and two geese called Victoria and Adelaide (after the queen and her aunt).[25] It wasn't only Grasper who had his portrait drawn. Branwell made a pencil profile of a sleeping cat, for instance, probably a house feline. Emily drew a portrait of Nero, her merlin hawk that she had found wounded on the moors and had nursed back to health, and a now-missing picture that included Keeper, Flossy, and the cat Tiger. Keeper got his own watercolor in 1838, a sleepy one where we see him, curiously, without his collar (see color photograph). As did Flossy, who gamboled along or looked peacefully out the window (usually with his collar on) in Emily's and Anne's watercolors. We find Flossy doing things that must have been forbidden, like sleeping on Emily's bed, while she sat on her stool writing, Keeper on the rug close by, his head resting on his paws.

A kinship with animals of all sorts seemed to run in the blood of the Brontë clan. Local creatures provided another favorite subject to draw and paint, sometimes copied from prints or illustrated books, other times "from life." The Brontë siblings adored especially their two volumes of Thomas Bewick's *History of British Birds*, and all four of them drew versions of the animals (and vignettes with people) depicted in them. Charlotte did a watercolor copy of "The Mountain Sparrow," Branwell of the "Gos Hawk," and Anne a pencil sketch of some magpies standing on a rock. In one volume, Emily noticed the bird species that lived on their moors, and these are the ones she duplicated, in delicate pencil strokes: "The Winchat" and the "Ring ouzel." In the scene of reading that opens *Jane Eyre*, it is Bewick's history that Jane has in her lap and that takes her off into a fantasy world. Branwell wrote an essay admiring Bewick, whose "quiet poetry" teaches one, he felt, to muse on the simple world of nature "where every changing cloud, or opening leaf, or mossy stone, or fleeting wave, may yield something of pleasure," may even have "the greatest power or pathos."[26]

Branwell doesn't seem to have had a dog, unless Grasper belonged to him. His lack of canine companionship appears odd, especially since he owned guns and probably hunted game—like rabbits and red grouse—on the moors, an activity usually done with bird dogs, such as setters, pointers, or spaniels like Flossy. He even made an oil painting of himself with a rifle in the crook of his arm, standing with his sisters in front of dead birds, books, and papers piled on a table. Perhaps Branwell's lack of a dog was a result of his knowledge that he must make a living away from home and, as the only son, eventually support his sisters. He was dismissed from the tutoring job in the Lake District in 1840 for unknown reasons, although some sort of bad behavior is speculated, drinking perhaps, or even impregnating a local woman. Within a few months, he had found a completely different type of position, working as a clerk on the new Leeds-Manchester Railway, in Sowerby Bridge, a town close to Halifax. In 1841, while on this job, Branwell composed a poem about a popular painting by Edwin Landseer, which he must have seen reproduced in a book or magazine, called *Old Shepherd's Chief Mourner*. It depicts a collie keeping watch at twilight over his master's coffin. Branwell contrasts the human mourners, who show only the "form" of grief, with the "low heart broken whine" of the collie, who spends "long hours to pine / For him if love had power thy love could save." The dog has an emotional genuineness missing in humanity. Moved by the painting of canine fidelity in the face of death, Branwell may have been remembering the deaths in his own family.[27]

The numerous creatures about the parsonage made up a part of the fabric of the home life that was missed when the siblings left during this period, attempting to hold onto jobs. Anne was with the Robinsons at Scarborough when she wrote her diary paper of 1841, which included, like all the diary papers, a survey of the animals at the parsonage, along with the people. Sighing for the parsonage life, Anne wrote that "we have got Keeper, got a sweet little cat and lost it, and also got a hawk. Got a wild goose which has flown away, and three tame ones, one of which has been killed." Even though Emily's time away at Roe Head had failed so completely, she tried leaving Haworth again, and she was either making friends with animals where she was or missing the ones at home. She took a job teaching in 1838 at Law Hill School in Halifax, not long after Keeper first arrived in Haworth. She did some moor walking here (perhaps crossing paths with the renegade Anne Lister, or at least hearing stories about her) and developed a friendship with the school's house-dog, once announcing to a classroom of undisciplined girls that the only individual she cared for in the whole place was said mutt. She lasted six months this time.[28]

Charlotte, who had been trying out various governess jobs for the last couple of years, went away again with Emily in 1842 to a school in Belgium, and while they were gone, some of their animals were given away or disappeared. After nine months at the Pensionnat Heger, they rushed home when their Aunt Branwell died, in November 1842. Emily discovered that her hawk Nero had been "given away" along with their geese. She felt sure Nero was dead, "for when I came back from Brussels I enquired on all hands and could hear nothing of him." After this trip, Emily would stay at home with the animals, save for a few short trips around northern England, for the rest of her life.[29]

Charlotte returned alone to Brussels to work as a teacher. Sunk in a "gulf of low spirits," she wrote in a letter to Emily, she wished she could be back at the parsonage, especially in the back kitchen cutting up the hash, with Emily standing by to make sure she added enough flour, not too much pepper, and, "above all, that I save the best pieces of the leg of mutton for Tiger and Keeper, the first of which personages would be jumping about the dish and carving-knife, and the latter standing like a devouring-flame on the kitchen-floor."[30]

Anne and Charlotte expressed a simpler view than Emily of the relationship of human and animal, one with which it is easier to agree. Characters are judged by the way they treat animals. In *Agnes Grey*, it is obvious what the reader should think about the little boy who traps birds in order to roast them alive. Mr. Weston's kind treatment of Agnes's wire-haired terrier Snap starts him on the road to romantic hero-dom. Arthur Huntingdon, the drunken husband in *The Tenant of Wildfell Hall*, strikes his cocker spaniel Dash a smart blow, while the hero Gilbert Markham, contrastingly, has a much-loved black-and-white setter named Sancho. In *Shirley*, the title character's closeness to her half mastiff, half bulldog Tarter, with his "tawny and lion-like bulk," is based, Charlotte claimed, on Emily's intimate relationship with Keeper. The character Caroline finds that animals are the "true oracle" to test the temperament of the man one might marry. As she explains to Shirley, she knows that Robert will be a good husband because he is the "somebody" in the following: "We have a black cat and an old dog at the rectory. I know somebody to whose knee that black cat loves to climb, against whose shoulder and cheek it likes to purr. The old dog always comes out of his kennel and wags his tail, and whines affectionately when somebody passes." We know that the tide has turned for the harsh little professor M. Paul, in *Villette*, when we find him fondling the spaniel Sylvie and calling her tender names in a tender voice; Lucy falls for him completely.

A story about Anne at the very end of her life sums up her feelings about animals. When she was in Scarborough, dying of tuberculosis, Anne was being pulled around in a donkey cart at the beach. Worried about the donkey being urged to go faster than might be comfortable by the boy driver with a whip, she took the reins herself, despite being weak from illness. As she left the donkey, she charged the boy to treat it well. When Charlotte was visiting the seaside near there, to tend Anne's grave, her thoughts turned to Anne's dog. "I saw a great dog rush into the sea yesterday—and swim and bear up against the waves like a seal—I wonder what Flossy would say to that."[31]

Keeper and Flossy didn't seem to have lives of strife, notwithstanding Keeper's harsh punishment from Emily and the dogfights he rushed into. Flossy fathered a puppy, also called Flossy, "a most forward passionate little animal," which was given to Charlotte's friend

Ellen Nussey in 1844. He behaved "discreditably and gets his mistress into scrapes," such as one "catastrophe" that involved the ruination of a book-muslin dress. Anne wrote to Ellen in 1848 that Flossy senior "is fatter than ever, but still active enough to relish a sheep hunt."[32]

Both dogs outlived their mistresses. Charlotte tells of Keeper lying at the side of Emily's "dying-bed," following her funeral to the vault, and "lying in the pew couched at our feet while the burial service was being read." He visited her little bedroom day after day, for a long time after her death. After Anne died at Scarborough, Charlotte returned home to her father and the dogs, who "seemed in strange ecstasy. I am certain they regarded me as the harbinger of others—the dumb creatures thought that as I was returned—those who had been so long absent were not far behind."[33]

It must have been their father, Patrick, who taught his children to revere canine friends. When he faced an operation for cataracts and worried he might not make it through, what bothered him most was this: "I shall never feel Keeper's paws on my knees again!" We don't know his reaction when Keeper died in 1851. Charlotte wrote about it in a letter to Ellen: "Poor old Keeper died last Monday Morning—after being ill one night—he went gently to sleep—we laid his old faithful head in the garden. Flossy is dull and misses him. There was something very sad in losing the old dog; yet I am glad he met a natural fate—people kept hinting that he ought to be put away which neither Papa nor I liked to think of." Flossy passed away three years later, and again we know about it because Charlotte informed Ellen: "Did I tell you that our poor little Flossy is dead? He drooped for a single day—and died quietly in the night without pain. The loss even of a dog was very saddening—yet perhaps no dog ever had a happier life or an easier death."[34]

A few months after Charlotte, Patrick's last surviving child, died, he purchased two dogs from Mr. Summerscale, the Haworth teacher, for three pounds each. They were descendants of dogs belonging to Bingley acquaintances, the Busfield Ferrands. One he called Cato, a year-and-a-half-old Newfoundland-retriever mix that he believed Charlotte had admired. The other he named Plato, a mix of water spaniel with Newfoundland. A third brass collar at the Brontë Parsonage Museum may have belonged to one of these dogs, although tradition has it that Keeper wore it and then grew out of it. The two larger collars might have been reused—on Keeper first, then on Plato and Cato—especially since the engravings didn't include dog names. It's even possible future owners of the collars used them on their dogs. This third collar has a hank of soft, black dog hair still caught in the lip of the curled-over edge. From which dog body did it come?[35]

CHAPTER FIVE

Fugitive Letters

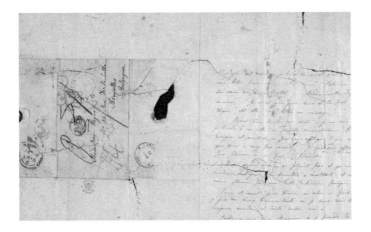

I began to study the outside of my treasure: it was some minutes before I could get over the direction and penetrate the seal; one does not take a strong place of this kind by instant storm—one sits down awhile before it, as beleaguers say . . . The seal was too beautiful to be broken, so I cut it round with my scissors.

—CHARLOTTE BRONTË, *Villette*

Sailing back from Brussels in January 1844, Charlotte joined Emily and the animals at home. For a while now she had been pondering ways to send her writing out into the world, rather than keeping it within the circle of family. One step toward this came through letters. With much practice, Charlotte had learned to make a letter, even one sent to someone hundreds of miles away, an act of intimacy. She had long developed a vivid sense of the page's talismanic qualities, sewing together those miniature books as a child. Handwriting and the autograph transmitted personality, perhaps a bit of the soul. The touch and warmth of the writer's skin could be carried in a letter, Charlotte thought, a belief worked out in much of her correspondence.

It was in letters to Ellen Nussey that Charlotte shared her sorrow when the family dogs died; to Ellen, Charlotte mailed all those needle-work crafts. Their friendship flourished through the post. They generally saw each other two or three times a year as adults, but letters often passed between them once a week. Ellen kept most of the letters that Charlotte wrote her, while those Charlotte received have disappeared. Ellen claimed soon after Charlotte's death that she had close to five hundred of Charlotte's letters, but later, after she had been sharing the letters with various Brontë fans, she fretted she had lost around a hundred. Today about 340 items of correspondence can be traced, including some envelopes with their contents missing.

It all began when Charlotte was fifteen and Ellen fourteen—Charlotte's birthday was April 21, Ellen's April 20—just a few months after they met at Roe Head School. It didn't cease until Charlotte wrote from her deathbed, in very faint pencil, ending with the words "Write when you can." In her first letter to Ellen, Charlotte declined the invitation proffered by Ellen's sister to attend Mr. Murray's lectures on galvanism (electricity created through chemicals, often demonstrated by stimulating the muscles of dead animals). These first schoolgirl notes, brief and stiff—beginning with such formalities as "I take advantage of the earliest opportunity to thank you for the letter you favoured me with last week" and "the receipt of your letter gave me an agreeable surprise"—slowly relaxed and expanded in register and range.[1]

Charlotte learned to be witty or even clownish, like calling dancing "shaking the shanks," and she sometimes signed off with variations on her name, like Charlotte Scrawl or Charivari, probably in this case meaning discordant music, both self-effacing references to inelegant letters. One message she signed, "your affectionate Coz" (cousin), another with a row of CB's getting ever smaller: CB, CB, CB, CB. She took a man's name—Charles Thunder (the Greek word *bronte* means "thunder") or Caliban, the tormented creature from Shakespeare's *Tempest*. Ellen she calls Mrs. Menelaus, a reference to Menelaus's wife, Helen of Troy, whose abduction by Paris started the Trojan War. One note toys with Ellen's name: Helen, Eleonora, Helena, Nell, Nelly. Charlotte's pedantic, bossy side sometimes came out, such as when she pushed for their exchange to be in French: "I beg and implore your reply to be in the universal language." Some messages took a gossipy, chatty tone; others showed an interest in plumbing her own painful mental states. This she did with a developing skill, illustrated in a letter sent in the winter of 1836 about "the melancholy state I now live in, uncertain that I have ever felt true contrition, wandering in thought and deed, longing for holiness which I shall never, never obtain." Penning these letters schooled her in the language of the delicate colorings of the psyche, a searching depth she would master by the time she set out to write *Jane Eyre*.[2]

With her letters to Ellen and others, Charlotte worried about their aesthetic appeal—the handsomeness of the line of text, its spacing and elegance—not so different from how she was anxious about the neatness and fashion of her dress and the way she wore her hair. For many of her contemporaries, caring about one's personal appearance and caring about how one's letters looked went hand in hand. She sometimes ended letters to Ellen with apologies for her "execrable Penmanship" or for "all faults in this wretched scrawl" or, worse, this "most horrid scrawl ever penned by mortal hands." In one postscript she explains that her "paper has I see got somehow disgracefully blotted, but as I really have not time to write another letter, I must beg you to excuse its slovenly appearance—pray let no one else see it—for the writing into the bargain is shameful." In another she comments, cheekily, "Preserve this writing as a curiosity in Caligraphy—I think it exquisite—all brilliant black blots and utterly illegible letters." Charlotte sometimes illustrated her letters, like one she sent to Ellen from Brussels that has an unflattering portrait of herself waving across the sea to an elegant Ellen, who holds the hand of a gentleman labeled "The Chosen" (a man who was courting Ellen at the time). Charlotte's last line reads, "Good-bye to you dear Nell when I say so—it seems to me that you will hardly hear me—all the waves of the Channel, heaving and roaring between must deaden the sound—G-o-o-d—b-y-e CB."[3]

Charlotte developed the idea of the edible letter early on, writing to Ellen in 1836 of their life-sustaining correspondence: "your notes are meat and drink to me." One of her letters to Ellen came out such a jumble that it is more akin to something to eat than to read. "I feel constrained to sit down and tack a few lines together . . . now if the young woman [Ellen] expects sense in this production, she will find herself miserably disappointed. I shall dress her a dish of salmagundiand,—I shall cook a hash—compound a stew—toss up an omelette soufflé . . . and send it to her with my respects." Lucy Snowe, in *Villette*, imagines a letter from the man she loves—Dr. John Graham Bretton—as something to eat, "the wild, savoury mess of the hunter, nourishing and salubrious meat, forest-fed or desert-reared, fresh, healthful, and life-sustaining." Or drink: for the young Paulina, Lucy's friend who is also in love with Bretton, his letter is like clear water from a well to a thirsty animal, a "thrice-refined golden gurgle."[4]

The deliciousness of a letter had to do, in part, with its ability to hold a spiritual or physical portion of the self. Letters might be linked to bodies because, for Charlotte and others of her time, they mattered as palpable things. She has Lucy, for instance, revel in the material feel of her first letter from Dr. Bretton. She gives it a sentience with its white "face" and its seal, a "single Cyclop's-eye of vermillion-red." The address tells of "a clean, clear, equal, decided hand"; the "deftly dropped" wax, of his "untremulous fingers." This is an object that has been intimate with his body: the ink, paper, and wax seal impressed with his initials eloquent with individuality. Just as one might kiss another's closed eye, she presses the seal to her lips. Handwriting especially speaks of the writer's person, as Paulina points out when she begins to receive letters from the same source: "Graham's hand is like himself . . . a clean, mellow, pleasant manuscript, that soothes you as you read. It is like his face—just like the chiseling of his features."[5]

As we've seen with books and boxes, the Brontës and their contemporaries could be literal-minded in their putting of the person (or a part of the person) into various sorts of containers. In an early note, Charlotte asked Ellen to enclose in her next letter a lock of her hair. A pledge of future friendship, this exchange of mementos could also hold a dash of the romantic, even the talismanic. Caroline begs a lock from the man she loves in the already discussed passage in *Shirley*, a snippet that eventually ends up in a locket around her neck. At times, giving one's hair worked as an erotic promise of the body. In Jane Austen's *Sense and Sensibility*, Willoughby cuts a curl from Marianne Dashwood's head, and family members assume this means a solid engagement. When he returns the tress in a rejection letter, she is crushed.[6]

Branwell practiced a similar piece of caddishness when he sent a paring of hair in a letter. After he lost the job as a railway clerk because of discrepancies in the finances under his care, he was hired by the Robinsons, Anne's employers, to tutor their son. Branwell embarked on a secret sexual adventure with Mrs. Lydia Robinson, the thirty-seven-year-old wife of his employer, within a few months of his hiring (more about this in the next chapter). He wrote to his friend John Brown, the Haworth sexton, to tell him about his lover, sending—perhaps as a way of bragging about his conquest—a "lock of *her* hair, which has lain at night" on his breast. "Would to God," he laments, "it could do so legally."[7]

Ellen Nussey doesn't comply with Charlotte's request for a tress, using the mailing expense as an excuse, although she may have felt that Charlotte moved too fast into an ardent friendship. Charlotte, petulant, replies, "I was very much disappointed by your not sending the hair. You may be sure my dearest Ellen that I would not grudge double postage to obtain it but I must offer the same excuse for not sending you any." This little fight couldn't have happened in the same way just eight years after this, when major reforms swept the post office. The cost of sending a letter in the early nineteenth century depended on its weight and distance traveled, and the system was not only prohibitively expensive but also slow and unreliable. A second page or an enclosure, such as a lock of hair, doubled the postage. Adding to the snail pace was the fact that the receiver, rather than the sender, paid the postage to the letter carrier who came to the house door. So, in this case, Ellen's refusal to send her hair could be disguised as a politeness to Charlotte, who would have been the one to pay double postage. Under this system, the arrival of a letter could be unwelcome for no other reason than the receiver's lack of money. Having to turn away the postal carrier with an undelivered letter was a humiliating fact of life for many.[8]

Prank, fan, and hate mail took on an added dimension when the addressee felt obliged to pay for it. After she published her controversial political writing, Charlotte's friend Harriet Martineau received piles of mail consisting of "envelopes, made heavy by all manner of devices, with a slip of newspaper in the middle, containing prose paragraphs, or copies of verse, full of insults." When she published her 1832 *Illustrations of Political Economy*, the postmaster explained that she had to send for her own mail because a wheelbarrow was required.[9]

A letter, with the receiver paying its postage, had better be worth the cost, so felt many a conscientious, or merely anxious, writer such as Charlotte. Letter writing had a certain art to it, made more urgent by payment upon delivery. Manuals proliferated to teach this art, most of them directed at women encouraged to keep up correspondence with their female friends, seen as a conventionally "feminine" expression of their sentimentality. Charlotte, like many letter writers of her time, worked to make her letters vital, sufficiently engaging for the reader to get her money's worth. Writing without much to say could be grounds for anger on the addressee's part. "My letters are scarcely worth the postage," Charlotte excused herself to Ellen, "and therefore I have till now, delayed answering your last communication." Charlotte also apologizes for writing too often: "you will be tired of paying the postage of my letters," she writes to Ellen, "but necessity must plead my excuse for their frequent recurrence."[10]

Keeping one's letter confined to one sheet served as a politeness to the reader, since additional sheets, and even an envelope, added postage. Most personal letters of the early nineteenth century, including Charlotte's to Ellen, consisted of one page folded and sealed so that the address could be written directly on the letter. The return address was often either not included or written on the inside, after the signature. Some correspondents, such as Ellen, cross-wrote to save on postage or on the expense of paper. The cross-writer, instead of using a second page to continue a letter, turned the first sheet horizontally, and wrote over ("crossed") the original text at a right angle. The trick to making a letter like this legible was to carefully space the first page, so that the "crossed" writing could fit in the extra spaces between words. The practice took a very neat hand, and reading it was also something of a skill. Charlotte and their friend Mary Taylor often complained of the difficulty of reading Ellen's cross-writing because she wasn't always neat about it. Anne crossed letters beautifully; one she wrote to Ellen Nussey shows her clever skill. Charlotte rarely cross-wrote, and when she did, it was a chore to read. Some valued cross-writing because the difficulty in reading it made letters more private. A secret message could be "dropt in the secure shade of a crossed letter," one nostalgic writer lamented after crossing went out of fashion. A related but rarer method used sometimes by Jane Austen when writing to her sister, Cassandra, involved filling a page, then turning the top side to the bottom and writing in between the lines. Austen probably did this when she discovered unplanned things still needing to be said after she had filled up the front and back. Or perhaps she deliberately wanted to hide some lines from all but the most dedicated reader. Such letters are so very difficult to read that one suspects some obscurantism. Another means of keeping parts of letters secret, especially when it was customary to pass letters around the family, was to write a line or two at the very top or bottom of a letter. The receiver cut this section off after reading it, then could hand the letter around safely, without the censoring being obvious.[11]

With the official mail so cumbersome and dear, ways of circumventing it mushroomed. So widespread were illicit modes of mail conveyance and contraband letter carriers in the early nineteenth century that more than half of all letters arrived at their destinations through illegal means. Crafty letter senders developed various stratagems for getting around the cost of regular mail. Smuggling a letter in a folded-up newspaper, which passed through the mail postage free at this time, was one oft-used means. Cigars, tobacco, collars, seaweed, gloves, handkerchiefs, music, needlework patterns, sermons, and stockings were all found stashed in newspapers by the post office. Writing a message on the newspaper itself, using a form of invisible ink (milk sometimes served for this purpose), was another way of avoiding delivery costs. Letters traveled in packages, a practice prevalent although against the rules, packages being, illogically, generally cheaper than letters. Charlotte would tuck little notes, on lightweight paper, among needlework presents for Ellen.[12]

One could have a friend who was traveling in the right direction carry one's letter by hand. Charlotte often sent letters to Ellen this way, thus saving her friend the postage. She would sometimes hold a letter, hoping someone she knew could hand deliver it. "I have been waiting a long time," Charlotte explained to Ellen, "for an opportunity of sending you a letter by private hand—but as none such occurs I have determined to write by post." Ellen once had her brother carry a letter to Charlotte when she was teaching at Roe Head. "As I stood at the dining-room window," Charlotte tells Ellen, "I saw your brother (George) as he whirled past, toss your little packet over the wall." Charlotte used this romantic mode of letter conveyance for fictional purposes in *Villette*. As Lucy Snowe saunters in the back garden of the school one night, an ivory box falls at her feet, tossed from a window overlooking the garden. From the box spills a bunch of violets and a folded bit of pink paper. Lucy reads this billet-doux meant for another woman.[13]

One time Ellen's scheme for avoiding postage on a letter to Charlotte misfired. On a visit to Ellen's house, Charlotte accidently left behind her umbrella. She arranged to have it sent to an inn in Bradford. Charlotte asked her local mail carrier to call for it, but he kept forgetting. It sat there for about a month. Ellen had secreted in it a letter for Charlotte, and when it was finally retrieved, she reported to Ellen on the debacle: "Judging by the date of your letter . . . precisely one month and four days intervened between the period in which it was written and that which brought it to my hands. I received it last Monday and till that time it continued to lie snugly enclosed in the umbrella at the Bull's Head Inn."[14]

It was no wonder people felt free to cheat the post, since many of the wealthy posted letters without paying. The Parliament passed bills so that their members' letters traveled postage free. This franking privilege—which meant the members had to sign the outside of their letters—was widely abused. The MPs "franked" letters for others in their family. Much worse, they often lent their signature to a wide circle of acquaintances. Franks were sometimes sold, and officials even partially paid their servants in franks. The fact that those most able to afford to send letters didn't have to pay, leaving those least able to afford it carrying the burden of financing the entire system, stunk of corruption. In response, some localities set up their own system of charging a penny for letters sent and received within their small radius. With Charlotte at home in Haworth and Ellen at her family home in Birstall, near Leeds, they both resided within the Bradford district. Hand-stamped "Bradford Yorks Py Post," Charlotte's notes of the 1830s carry evidence of passing through postal hands during a small window of time and place.[15]

Ripe for reform, the post service changed radically in 1840 when it instituted a countrywide penny post. All letters weighing under half an ounce traveled anywhere in England for one penny. The sender now prepaid postage. Charlotte wrote jubilantly to Ellen in January 1840: "I intend to take full advantage of this penny postage and to write to you often . . . that is as often as I have time." It was primarily the railroads that made this cheap rate possible. The first rail lines opened in the 1830s and expanded speedily; trains carried specially built mail cars, which replaced the horse-drawn mail coach. With the advent of the penny post, the number of letters sent nationwide exploded. Now all but the very poor could afford to correspond.[16]

All sorts of other changes in letter writing resulted, many traceable in Charlotte's letters to Ellen. At first, a one-penny cover, in the form of an official envelope, carried the new national prepayment. A competition for the design, won by the artist William Mulready, led to elaborately illustrated covers, which never took off. More sedate envelopes with a pink, round embossed picture of Queen Victoria's head replaced Mulready's covers. Charlotte occasionally used these envelopes to send her letters. Preprinted envelopes and cheap postage led to a new fashion of sending cards to celebrate Christmas, Valentine's Day, and birthdays. Souvenir stationery was another new idea; one example sold by John Greenwood's Haworth shop in the 1860s had an illustration of the parsonage and text identifying it as the "Home of the Brontës."[17]

What really took off were "postage labels"—what came to be called "stamps"—with the same stylized depiction of the queen. Nicknamed the "penny black," since the first ones were black, they shifted in color to brown then red, a transition that can be followed on Charlotte's letters. The sender moistened the "glutinous wash" on the back of the stamp to adhere it to paper. Arguments made against the adoption of the penny black included the fear that the stamp would spread cholera through saliva. Ultimately, not only would the stamp become the most popular form of prepaying, but also a craze for stamp collecting took hold almost immediately. One lady fancied papering her entire dressing room with used stamps. She took out an advertisement in the *London Times* in October 1842 asking "good-natured souls" to send her their canceled stamps. Some of the stamps on Charlotte's envelopes were cut out, presumably to add to someone's collection, although perhaps for illicit reuse, which was possible if the black cancellation ink hadn't been properly applied. Stamps even served as currency, easily sent through the mail and redeemable at any post office. Charlotte often used them to pay off debts: "I enclose a postage stamp for the 1/2d. you were to pay for me at the Station," she tells Ellen. She even referred to letters synecdochically by their stamps: "let your recklessly lavished 'Queen's Heads' repose for a while" was her plea to one too generous in his correspondence.[18]

Almost as exciting as stamps, envelopes (of the unofficial variety) had been used in the past only by those who didn't pay postage, but now these "little bags," as they were sometimes called, became standard. Charlotte began replacing the large letter sheets that she needed to carry the address and seal along with her message, with smaller ones so they would fit into delicate envelopes, many the size of business cards. Charlotte would occasionally tuck letters written by others alongside her own note to Ellen, so Ellen could find out other people's news firsthand. Charlotte took advantage of these little bags to add a sample of wallpa-

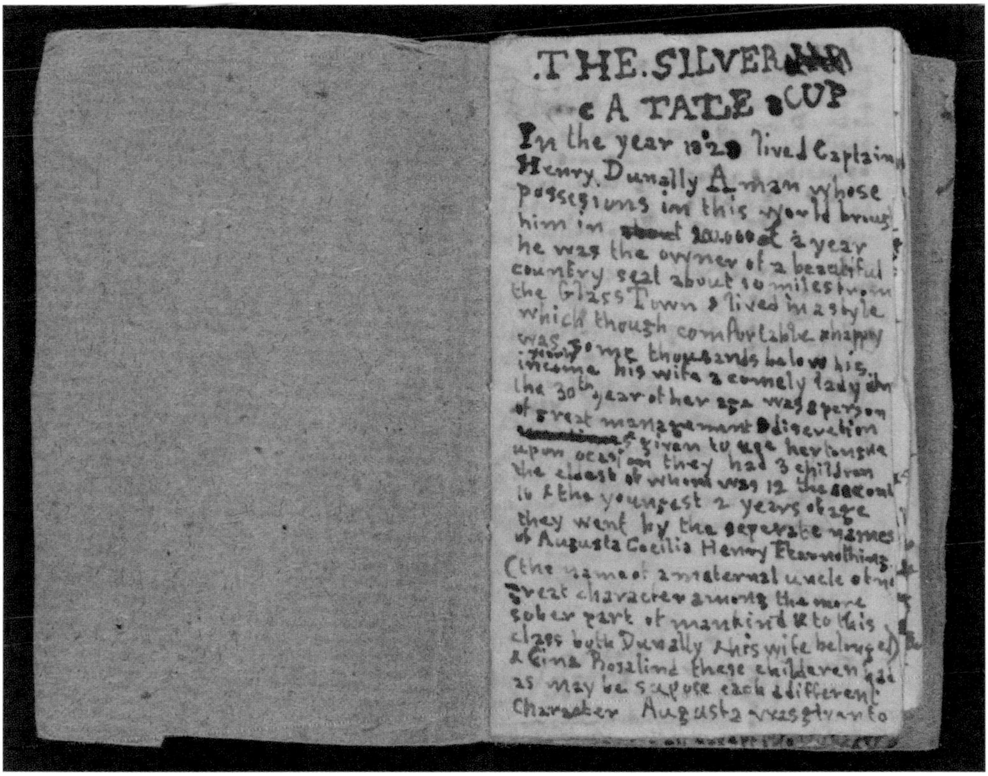

THE SILVER CUP
A TALE

In the year 1829 lived Captain Henry Dunally A man whose possesions in this world brought him in 200.000£ a year he was the owner of a beautiful country seat about 10 miles from the Glass Town & lived in a style which though comfortable & happy was some thousands below his income his wife a comely lady in the 30th year of her age was a person of great management & discretion given to use her tongue upon ocasion they had 3 children the eldest of whom was 12 the second 10 & the youngest 2 years of age they went by the seperate names of Augusta Cecilia Henry Fearnothing (the name of a maternal uncle of great character among the more sober part of mankind & to this class both Dunally & his wife belonged) & Gina Rosalind these children are as may be supose each a different character Augusta was given to

Figure 1: Charlotte's "Blackwood's Young Men's Magazine," October 1829, showing its parcel-paper covers.

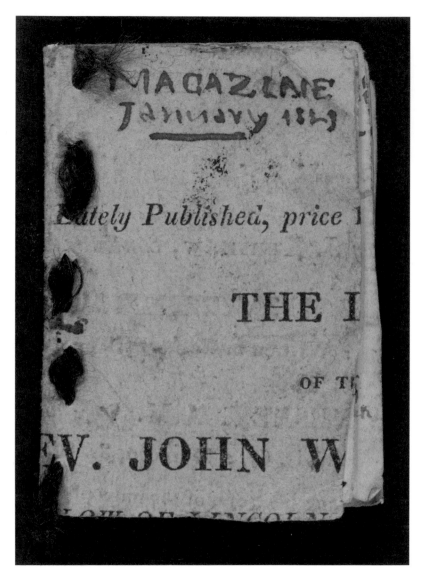

Figure 2: Branwell's "Blackwood's Magazine," January 1829, with the cover made from recycled advertisements and bound with brown yarn.

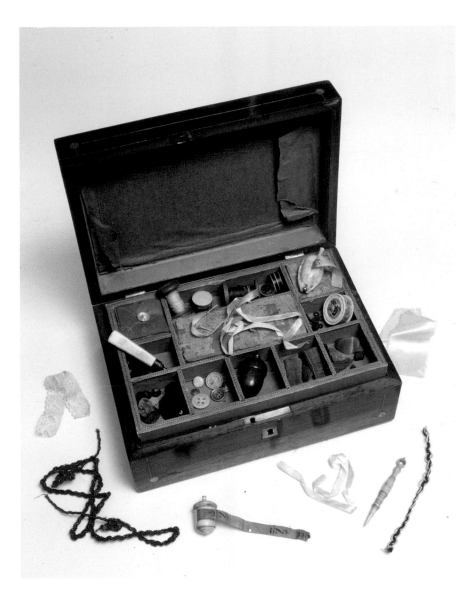

Figure 3: Charlotte's needlework box with some of its contents. Note the cowrie shell measuring tape and the black, round pillbox on the top right.

Figure 4: Detail of Branwell's walking stick.

Figure 5: Photograph of path on the moors that Emily often walked, taken by the author.

Figure 6: Keeper's collar with its warm brass sheen.

Figure 7: Emily's watercolor of Keeper without his collar.

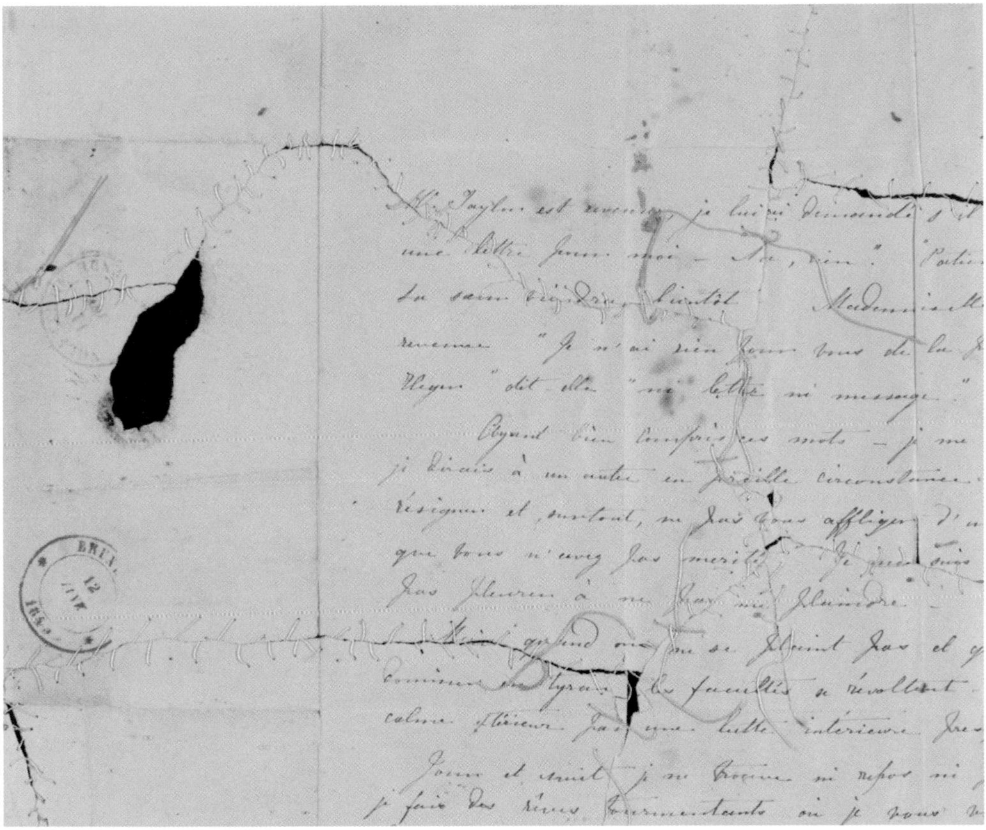
Mr Taylor est revenu, je lui ai demandé s'il
une lettre pour moi – "Non, rien." "Patie
sa sœur viendra bientôt Mademoiselle
revenue "Je n'ai rien pour vous de la
Heger" dit-elle "ni lettre ni message."
Ayant bien compris ces mots – je me
je dirais à un autre en pareille circonstance
résignez et, surtout, ne pas vous affliger d'u
que vous n'avez pas mérité" Je me suis
pas pleurer à ne pas me plaindre –
Mais quand on ne se plaint pas et q
comme un tyran les facultés se révoltent
calme extérieur par une lutte intérieure pres
Jour et nuit je ne trouve ni repos ni
je fais des rêves tourmentants où je vous v

Figure 8: Detail of the letter from Charlotte to Constantin Heger, January 8, 1845, stitched together by wife.

Figure 10: Detail of Charlotte's portable desk with ink stains near where her ink bottle was kept.

Figure 11: Lock of Mrs. Maria Brontë's hair from the framed collection of the Brontë family's hair samples.

per that was being put up in the parsonage, in a letter to Elizabeth Gaskell. In another letter, Charlotte requested of a friend, "When you write again put another violet into the letter." She tucked a pair of baby socks she knit in a note and posted them to the mother of her publisher George Smith. "Any peculant Post-Office Clerk," she scrawled in a postscript, "who shall mistake the contents of this letter for a Bank-Note will find himself in the wrong box." For Ellen, she folded a "scrubby yard of lace" in a letter, worrying again about postal clerks: "I hope such as it is they will not pick it out of the envelope at the Bradford Post Office, where they generally take the liberty of opening letters when they feel soft as if they contained anything." Ellen often replied in kind, putting some "pretty little cuffs" in a letter for Charlotte, which led postal clerks to open it, evidenced by the paper being burned when they melted the wax and by their sloppy attempt to hide it with a "blank seal."[19]

Seals weren't just for keeping out nosy or greedy postmen. Charlotte's relish for them rivaled her fascination with paper. Seals on documents and boxes ensured that any tampering with the contents could be found out from the state of the seal. Sealing something lent it depth to the curious, as if the seal gave it a secret life. Charlotte's love of seals dated back to her early stories, where in one the Duke of Wellington is handed a letter written in blood, with a seal that says, "Le message d'un revenant" (missive from a ghost). In another story, the Marquis of Douro gives the woman he loves a book not just wrapped in the fancy paper mentioned earlier, but also "sealed in green wax, with the motto, 'L'amour jamais.' " A book with a seal reminded Charlotte of the minds of others, which were also "sealed volumes," or "hieroglyphical scrolls, which I can not easily either unseal or decipher." But Ellen's mind, Charlotte told her, opened to her as they became more intimate with their first letters. They brought to light the "turnings, windings, inconsistencies and obscurities" of her nature.[20]

Some seals actually told anyone what they shut up, working as, in effect, anti-seals. When a family member died, Charlotte used black-edged mourning stationery with black seals. When she sent out announcements of her marriage, she asked Ellen to buy her white sealing wax. In the 1840s, Charlotte began sealing her envelopes to Ellen with adhesive wafers made of colored paper with preprinted phrases and mottos. These paper seals with text had their heyday during the ten years when envelopes became widely used but lacked any gumming, one of the many new goods at the Great Exhibition in 1851. Simple sheets of specially shaped paper folded around letters, these envelopes of the 1840s required seals to hold them closed, like the single letter sheet of the past. Envelopes still carried traditional sealing-wax seals (generally made of shellac and vermillion in the nineteenth century, rather than actual wax), but new types of seals met the demand of a growing mass of correspondents. Paper wafer seals came out simultaneously with the penny stamp, sharing the same technology of the "wash" that stuck to paper when dampened. Bought in packets, such as "Cooper's original Gold and Silver Enamelled wafers, second series improved," found in Charlotte's desk, or in round cardboard boxes—Charlotte had a small royal-blue one—paper seals were launched in February 1840, with some picturing Queen Victoria's royal arms joined to Prince Albert's. Used at Windsor a week before the two were married, they made explicit the romance of seals.[21]

Letters put on a public face when posted, signaled by wafers that promoted causes, such as vegetarianism, phonography (a form of shorthand), and temperance, for instance, as on one unusually large seal: "Thousands of women / have been robbed of / their health, rights, / comfort, homes, and / even lives by intem- / perate relations. Tee- / totalism will prevent / all this; therefore wo- / men should promote it." Political progressives, such as chartists, suffragists, and antiwar agitators, had their messages printed on wafers: "The Six Points and no mistake / Complete / Suffrage"; "Where drums beat, laws are silent." One could buy a wafer picturing Byron, Walter Scott, Napoleon (idolized by some Britons, including the Brontës), the Duke of Wellington, or Shakespeare. The principal dance steps of the polka appeared on a series of six hand-colored wafers. Paper seals featured national monuments and historic places, like Westminster Abbey, Tintern Abbey, and an underground railway tunnel. Businesses used seals as advertisements. One of the first was for the Cheltenham and Great Western Union Railway, and the publishers who would bring out Charlotte's novels had their own: "Forwarded by / Smith, Elder and Co. / 65 Cornhill, London."[22]

The palpable whole of the folded, enveloped, addressed, and sealed letter being sent out into the world said something about the letter-writing self. Charlotte's wafers to Ellen—colored blue, mustard, or pink and shaped like diamonds, squares, or rectangles—each had a printed text. Some of the wafers may have perpetuated private jokes or messages between them, and perhaps a sort of dialogue was kept up through wafers, now lost since none of Ellen's letters survive. "Delay not," "To You," "All's / Well," and "Post Paid" related directly to the post. Sentimental mottos showed affection or love, like "Forget / me not," "Farewell," "Remember me," and "Absent / not forgot." Others had sayings in French, like the seal in Charlotte's childhood story: *"L'Esperance"* (hope), *"Si je puis"* (if I can), *"Toujours / le meme"* (always the same), and *"Chacun à son goût"* (Everyone has his taste). A few gave advice—"Be wise today"—and a couple had quasi-spiritual messages, such as "Hope is / my Anchor." "Truth" states one, enigmatically; another trumpets the truism (which isn't very true) that "Time / explains all"—possibly a final comment on Charlotte's worry noted in the letter that the marriage of Ellen's brother to a wealthy woman might not bode well for the future equality of their relationship.[23]

Motto wafers were, by their very nature, flirtatious. They said, don't look into these private contents, yet here is a brief message for you to read—like "Absent / not forgot"—with information about the relationship represented within. They pointed to riches contained inside, sweetening the desire to open them. Charlotte's flirting with Ellen through seals gained another layer when she altered their messages using ink, such as one that appears to have said "*L'Amour*"—it is difficult to make out—which Charlotte effaced with a swarm of little dots. She played at being angry because Ellen secretly put gifts for the Brontë family in Charlotte's trunk when she was leaving Ellen's house: a fire screen for Patrick, a jar of crabapple cheese for Anne, a collar and apples for Emily, a cap for Tabby. "You ought first to be tenderly kissed and then afterwards as tenderly whipped," Charlotte says in the letter.[24]

In contrast, mystery surrounds the wafers Emily kept in round boxes in her desk and paint box. With no evidence that she ever used any—only three letters she wrote have been located, and none of them show traces of carrying wafer seals—their presence has led to fantasies about unknown correspondents. Emily's wafers have an elusive quality to them, as if they hide more than they say, possibly a reflection of her secretive self. Even those with sayings on them like Charlotte's have more ambiguous meanings: "Always ready," "Pray do," "Please yourself," "Read and believe," and "Come if you like." A few feel inappropriate for any situation, like "Come with a ring." Who would she, or anyone, send that to? Thomas Hardy used a similar seal to bring about a major plot shift in his novel *Far from the Madding Crowd*, when Bathsheba Everdene carelessly sends a valentine to William Boldwood, a local farmer, with a seal (in this case, wax) saying, "Marry me." This brings on his obsessive attention, which finally leads to his murder of a rival.[25]

Emily's wafers advertised her interests: a picture of a dog, her beloved animal, standing on a rock has "Faithful" written on the top and "Firm" on the bottom. Another is a rebus: a bear stands against a tree, next to the words "it in mind" (the whole meaning "bear it in mind"). One seems straight out of one of Emily's poems. It pictures a bird in a cage and reads, "I can't get out." A snail scoots along the ground on another, with the words "Always at home," apt for one who relished staying in her shell.

From a white packet in Emily's desk came "Clarke's Enigmatic Puzzle Wafers," "Sold by all Wholesale and Retail Stationers." These seals consist mostly of non-pictorial rebuses, or letters that stand in for words, much like modern-day text messages (pictured here). A few affirm the relationship between writer and reader, like "IOU o but goodwill," "U value me," and "U no secrets I" (there are no

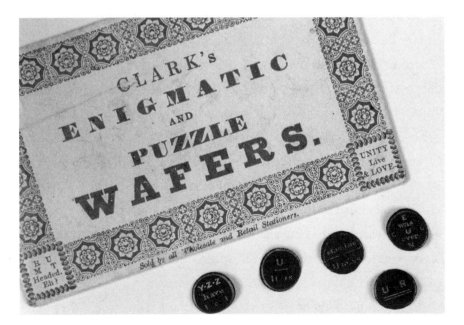

A few of the Rebus wafers from Emily's desk and the envelope they came in. Possible interpretations of these truly enigmatic wafers include, from left to right: "Wise heads have seen ('c') between the lines," "It is beneath you," "You misunderstand me," and "You are above it all." The last one remains unsolved, but it probably ends in "was ever around you."

secrets between you and I). Others flirt, such as "ICUR / temptation" (although since the "temptation" is underneath the "ICUR," this may mean "I see you are above temptation," which could be even more flirtatious). "U No love's lost I" seems rather mean-spirited, unless the Victorians understood this expression differently than we do today. Compliments are given, like "ICURA busy B," "ICUXL" ("I see you excel"), and "URA YZ" (probably "you are a wise head," with the "z" pronounced "zed"). There are the boldly romantic: "UR all price" and "U it is." It's easy to see a poet like Emily, with her queer sense of humor, enjoying these games, although the biggest puzzle is to whom she may have sent these wafers (or any wafers).

Wafers, like seals, could keep contents secret despite being so chatty. The directions printed on one of Charlotte's wafer packets make this clear: "The prepared side of the Wafer should be moistened and pressed firmly on the letter with the finger; when this is done the letter cannot be opened without injury." Charlotte made her letters doubly secure by adding circular paste seals underneath the envelope flaps, cheap replacements for shellac, moistened rather than melted, then stuck on. As these paste seals were usually licked, there was some danger because the coloring agents, part of a recipe that included a batter of wheat or other flour mixed with egg white and isinglass, made them poisonous. (Wafer leavings were sometimes used to kill rats and other vermin.) The Brontë girls kept boxes of these paste seals in their desks, along with seal matrixes with grill patterns of dots, made of metal with ivory handles, which they used to spread and affix these circular paste seals along with the more traditional wax ones.[26]

Charlotte's comment about postal clerks' mistaking socks for money was a personal version of a much wider anxiety about the privacy of letters. Before the penny charge, postal workers exposed letters to a strong light, called "candling," to look for an enclosure, which would double the postage. Worries about personal or political letters being read were even used as one of many arguments for the penny post, since candling would no longer be needed to check for enclosures. Yet a scandal of a larger order swept the post office not long after the institution of the penny post. The discovery that a "Secret Office" of the London Post had been opening and examining mail to the Italian political agitator Giuseppe Mazzini, then living in London, led to a widely publicized backlash in 1844. Home Secretary Sir James Graham, the issuer of the warrant for the mail opening, was widely reviled, especially by the magazine *Punch*. An anti-Graham campaign sprouted up, which included the invention of metal seals, attached by metal "claws," that destroyed the envelope when opened, preventing letters from being clandestinely read and resealed. Anti-Graham slogan wafers became the fashion, such as one with a picture of a fox and this message: "You'll be run down if you break cover" ("cover" another word for "envelope" and the whole a reference to aristocratic fox hunting). A blunderbuss on full cock with the text "I hope the content will reach you" expressed the violent feelings of some about their privacy. More simple ones stated, "Not to be Grahamed."[27]

Around the same time that the anti-Graham campaign was running hot, Charlotte was sending passionate letters to a married man in Brussels, all the time worrying that his wife was intercepting and reading them (as indeed she was). So, while Branwell was actually having an adulterous affair, Charlotte was wishing she could have one. Charlotte and Emily had made this Brussels trip, mentioned in the last chapter, because all of the siblings had to find means to support themselves and to add to the family's small income. This was especially true given that the specter of their father's possible death hung over them. Patrick, now in his sixties, was already past the time's life expectancy. If he died before them, he would leave them with no income, their only savings being a small legacy they expected to receive from Aunt Branwell. Charlotte's attempts at being a governess had been disheartening and worse. About the only benefit of this "slavery," as Charlotte called it, was source material for her character Jane Eyre, who would become the most famous governess of all time. The three sisters had cooked up a plan to open their own school at the parsonage, and Charlotte thought they needed first to polish their skills, especially their French. Aunt Branwell agreed to contribute some money toward their scheme, and they decided to study abroad, where schools were generally cheaper. Belgium was less expensive than France, so Brussels, where Charlotte had some friends at school, was chosen over Paris. As Anne continued to pull in a salary from the Robinsons (tiny though it was), it was Emily, rather implausibly, who went with Charlotte.

While in Brussels, Charlotte fell in love with her professor, Constantin Heger, a married man with five, soon to be six, children. Charlotte called him the "black Swan," his powerful mind offset by a temperament "very choleric and irritable." A "little black ugly being," Heger sometimes had the look of an "insane tom-cat," or a "delirious hyena." From an animal lover, such creaturely attributes would be considered endearing. His anger and impatience with her mistakes as a student appeared especially charming. Heger developed a fondness for Charlotte, and he appreciated her brilliance, yet he didn't reciprocate her ardor. His wife, the director of the school, began to have suspicions and grew cold toward Charlotte. Seeing less of Heger and feeling isolated, Charlotte fell into another gulf of black anxiety, which she re-created in Lucy Snowe's wanderings in an opium trance in *Villette*. Packing up suddenly and returning to Haworth, she sent Heger a series of increasingly distraught letters, of which only four—and none of his replies— survived. While attempting to maintain the language of friendship and the tone of respect due to a teacher, she had trouble hiding her raw emotion and need. After no reply to an especially ardent message (now missing), she wrote begging him for a letter because his words were "one of the greatest joys I know." She longed to be with him someday, and in a postscript she repeated twice that: "I shall see you again." This is a surprisingly bold letter, a baring of wild desire despite (perhaps because of) Victorian codes of behavior. Charlotte acted with a reckless romanticism, more akin to her sister's future character Catherine Earnshaw than to her own Jane Eyre, who will be very careful not to commit adultery with the already married Rochester. To Heger, Charlotte's stormy words probably felt like a threat. He tore the letter into four pieces, threw it into the wastepaper basket, and didn't reply. His wife found the ripped-up letter. Using cut-out strips of white paper of varying sizes and a gum adhesive, she painstakingly pasted the fragments together, making it a mostly legible whole.[28]

Charlotte wrote again a couple of months later, asking if he had received her letter because "for all those six months I have been expecting a letter from you, Monsieur—six months of waiting—is a very long time indeed!" In a postscript she tells him that "I have just had bound all the books that you gave me," including two of his speeches. There is something erotic about this book binding, as if she needed to dress what remained to her of his touch and mind, in order to more fully possess it. This letter he also ripped up and discarded, refusing to send her a response. His wife fished this one out of the bin too, took a needle and white thread, and repaired it, using a loose stitch.[29]

After this, Charlotte's letters became even more rash. In her next letter (pictured at the beginning of this chapter), all her feelings of want tumbled out, uncensored. His neglect has left her "neither rest nor peace" day or night, and nightmares torment her sleep when it does come. She calls him "my master," submits to his possible reproaches for her desperate words, but refuses to resign herself to the loss of his attention; otherwise her heart will be "constantly lacerated by searing regrets." She must tell him how she feels even if "she has to undergo the greatest bodily pains." Her language grows even more abject; she even hints at suicide. "If my master withdraws his friendship," then she will be utterly without hope. Only a tiny morsel of his affection will give her a motive for living. She would then "cling to the preservation of this *little* interest—I cling to it as I would cling on to life." She expects and hopes for nothing more from him than "crumbs," but if these aren't given to her, she will "die of hunger." Heger rent this one into about nine pieces. Again his wife salvaged the torn parts, reassembling them with needle and thread.[30]

Heger responded to this self-abasing cry with a stiff letter in the hand of his wife, to whom he dictated his words, giving Charlotte permission to write once every six months. In her fourth and probably final letter, Charlotte, calmed because of his reply that has "sustained" and "nourished" her, still feels a great privation. A painful endurance must be undergone, she laments, if she can't communicate with him for six months. She has tried to forget him, but can't gain mastery over her thoughts—she is the "slave of a regret, a memory, the slave of a dominant and fixed idea which has become a tyrant" over her mind. If he fails to write her, she warns, she will "pine away." Heger left this letter whole, for reasons unclear, but possibly because he now knew that his wife had read and kept the letters. He absent-mindedly jotted down the name and address of a local shoemaker on its edge, treating it as scrap paper.[31]

It is fitting that the steamiest letters Charlotte ever wrote to a man ended up in the hands of a woman, who used domestic handicrafts—needlework, recycling strips of paper, gumming—to piece them together. Claire Zoë Heger's daughter Louise later explained that her mother kept them because she felt that their inappropriate heat could lead to "misapprehension," and she wanted evidence that the amour was all on Charlotte's side, in case of future accusations. But this doesn't feel like the whole truth. The stitching together of the notes—stored for decades in her jewelry box—has a tinge of obsessiveness to it, as if the troubled relationship between the two women needed memorializing in physical form.[32]

At some point Zoë Heger told her husband that she still had the letters, and when Elizabeth Gaskell traveled to Brussels in 1856 to gather information for her biography of Charlotte, Heger either read passages from the letters to Gaskell or let her read them. Only the tamest extracts appeared in the biography. Madame Heger showed the letters to her daughter Louise many years later, after Charlotte had become famous. According to Louise, this revealing of the correspondence happened after she attended a lecture—she doesn't say by whom—criticizing the Hegers for cruelty toward the great author. After her mother died in 1890, Louise handed the letters back to her father, who must have thought they had long been destroyed because he angrily "flung them into the [waste] basket." Louise rescued them, like her mother before her, but waited until after her father died in 1896 to tell her brother Paul about them. Louise and Paul traveled to London in 1913 to donate them to the British Museum, where curators set each fragile sheet between two glass panes, and then framed them. They built a specially designed box to store them, each frame with its own slot, and the catalog number painted on the side of the varnished wood.[33]

Charlotte probably never knew that Heger ripped up her letters, nor that Zoë reconstituted them, but she did suspect that his wife read them. When Charlotte didn't receive a reply to her first letter, she thought Zoë might be intercepting them and keeping them secret from her husband. She tried various ruses to get around this imagined problem. One letter she sent to the Athénée Royal, where the professor also taught. Others she gave into the care of various friends who were traveling to Brussels, asking them to put them directly into Professor Heger's hands. She even used this excuse to fit in an extra letter to Heger: "I am well aware," she wrote him, "that it is not my turn to write to you, but since Mrs. Wheelwright is going to Brussels and is willing to take charge of a letter—it seems to me that I should not neglect such a favorable opportunity for writing you." In another letter, she makes it clear that hand delivery by her friend Joe Taylor—Mary Taylor's brother—will assure her that Heger will receive it: "a gentleman of my acquaintance will be passing through Brussels and has offered to take charge of a letter to you, as that I shall be certain you have received it." The humiliation of his refusal to reply was compounded by the fact that she expected friends to deliver his letters to her. "Mr. Taylor returned," she wrote bitterly to Heger, "I asked him if he had a letter for me—'No, nothing, Patience'—I say—'His sister will be coming soon'—Miss Taylor returned 'I have nothing for you from M. Heger' she says 'neither letter nor message.' " Involving friends must have made her rejection sting that much more.[34]

She must have known that her fourth letter would be read by Madame Heger as it was a reply to a letter written in the hand of Madame Heger herself. During her last months in Brussels, Charlotte surmised that "her master's" wife knew of her infatuation. In ways hard to parse, Charlotte's passion for Heger wasn't just between the two of them; somehow Zoë made up a third. A complicated mass of emotions probably influenced Charlotte's attitude toward the wife, not just the usual jealousy and feeling of competition for his affections, but also admiration for, even fascination with, this other woman, a worthy adversary.

Charlotte never forgot Zoë Heger. Soon after she arrived back in Haworth, she began writing her first novel, which she initially called "The Master," later changing it to *The Professor*. She based the character Zoraïde Reuter on Zoë. Still thinking of her when she wrote *Vil-lette* a few years later, Charlotte created the more complicated character Madame Beck—the clever but plotting director of the school where Lucy Snowe teaches—with Zoë Heger vividly in mind. (Madame Heger was furious when she read the novel in a pirated edition, immediately recognizing herself.) When Lucy Snowe receives a letter from the handsome Dr. Bretton, she takes care to keep it inviolate from the spying of her employer, Madame Beck, by first folding it in silver paper, then placing it in her "casket," then setting the casket in a box, which she locks, then putting the box into the drawer of her bureau. Despite these precautions, Madame Beck spirits away and reads this letter and another four Lucy receives from Bretton, leaving the ribbon tied around the packet noticeably disarranged, evidence of her perfidy. Here the teacher/student receives letters from the man she loves instead of writing them, as Charlotte did, and the female spy is the outsider looking in on someone else's relationship. This rewriting gives the character most closely identified with Charlotte herself more agency and positive action than the real-life situation, where Charlotte was, in some sense, the outsider trying to pry her way in. Charlotte also gives Lucy the role of the spying third person in a romantic correspondence when she reads the pink note thrown over the wall mentioned earlier.[35]

Lucy, fed up with this "tampering," thinks about other places to squirrel away her letters. She considers the attic of the school as a possibility, but worries about the damp or the gnawing rats. She decides they must be buried, and she goes to a junk shop—"an ancient place, full of ancient things"—and buys a thick glass bottle. "I then made a little roll of my letters, wrapped them in oiled silk, bound them with twine, and, having put them in the bottle, got the old Jew broker to stopper, seal, and make it air-tight"—making this the most elaborate letter "seal" imaginable. She takes this "treasure" and finds a deep hollow in an ancient pear tree in the school's garden. After slipping the bottle in this hole, she puts a slate over it and secures it with mortar, found in a nearby toolshed, finally covering it all up with soil—as if she were mailing them to another world entirely. She calls this a "burial," of the letters themselves and of the grief over her unrequited love that they represent. This sorrowful past must be "wrapped in its winding-sheet, must be interred," in a "newly-sodded grave." The equation of the letters with a corpse is made stronger by a legend that a slab at the base of this tree is the "portal of a vault, emprisoning deep beneath the ground . . . the bones of a girl whom a monkish conclave of the drear middle ages had here buried alive, for some sin against her vow." Lucy herself does some burying alive—of the part of herself that has been vivified by love for Dr. Bretton. Even more than this, Lucy feels herself buried alive, in a life not of her choosing, in a series of jobs she dislikes, and in a society that severely limits her opportunities because she is a woman.

Charlotte's mixing of bones with letters reminds us of mail holding bits of the body (like hair). Her letters to Heger feel this way—as if she has sacrificed some part of herself to write them, has posted a pound of flesh. What ultimately happened to the letters has a flavor of Victor Frankenstein sewing together his creature out of corpse parts, a scenario envisioned by Mary Shelley just twenty-seven years earlier. Yet, even more than Charlotte's letters to Heger, those many messages sent to Ellen evoke the intimacy of personality, gesture, and the fingers and countenance. In fact, this set of letters spanning almost a lifetime could be equally passionate. After Charlotte's ceremoniousness wore off in her early letters to Ellen, she became affectionate and then positively ardent. Receiving a crisply sealed letter from Ellen could bring Charlotte a "thrill of delight." She read some of Ellen's letters "trembling all over with excitement," a visceral bliss she gives to the forlorn Lucy when a letter arrives from Dr. Bretton. Her salutation changed from

"Dear Ellen" to "My dearest Ellen," then to "My *own* Dear Ellen," and her signature from "Believe me to remain / Your affect. friend" to "'Farewell my *dear dear dear* Ellen," and then "Adieu my Sweetest Ellen / I am Ever yours." Charlotte laments when they must be physically separated for too long, wishing she could have "my darling," "my Comforter beside me." She proposes they set up house together permanently, so they would never have to part: "Ellen I wish I could live with you always . . . If we had but a cottage and a competency of our own I do think we might live and love on till Death without being dependent on any third person for happiness." Charlotte courts Ellen, as if they were on their way to becoming lovers, using the kind of language a Victorian man would use in wooing a woman: "My darling, I have lavished the warmest affections of a very hot, tenacious heart upon you—if you grow cold—it's over." When Vita Sackville-West, herself bisexual and having an affair with Virginia Woolf, read Charlotte's letters to Ellen in 1926, she said they "leave very little doubt in one's mind as to what Charlotte's tendencies really were. Whether she knew it herself is another matter. But they are love letters pure and simple."[36]

Charlotte and Ellen enjoyed sharing a bed, like so many girls of the time, a practice started when at Roe Head School. Charlotte's rest had an especially deep quality with Ellen by her side. "I do miss my dear bed-fellow. No more of that calm sleep," Charlotte adds in a postscript to a letter to Ellen where she admits, "I am afraid of caring too much for you." Delicate matters were best discussed between the sheets or while they were curling their hair before the fire. Just about the time Charlotte was falling in love with Heger in Brussels, she wrote to Ellen wishing she could talk with her, face to face, on a thorny topic not specified in the letter. She hoped that "one day perhaps or rather one evening—if ever we should find ourselves again by the fireside at Haworth or Brookroyd with our feet on the fender—curling our hair—I may communicate [it] to you." Conversation over difficult matters and curling of hair became so synonymous, the latter was a shorthand version for the former. Charlotte entices a friend to visit by promising "a series of quiet 'curling-hair times.' " Later, after her sisters died, Charlotte would have Ellen at Haworth to comfort her. The two would talk, and Charlotte would stroke Ellen's head and lean over her, once saying, "If I had but been a man, thou would have been the very ticket for me as a wife."[37]

We can never know if Charlotte and Ellen had a sexual relationship—there is certainly no proof that they did—and perhaps it doesn't matter. Their correspondence attests to a fervent love that included romantic, and perhaps even erotic, feelings. It's likely that Charlotte had heard of women who took women as lovers or "wives," such as fellow Yorkshire-woman Anne Lister, or perhaps even knew some.[38]

However it might be characterized in the twentieth or twenty-first century, Charlotte and Ellen's ardor, although heartfelt and true, followed conventions of the time. Victorian women were expected to have devoted female friends. These attachments showed their mastery of what the Victorians felt were the virtues of their gender: their openness to emotion and deep sentiment. In her history of Victorian female friendship, Sharon Marcus explains that it wasn't until the twentieth century that a fear of the homosexual developed. In the nineteenth century a larger range of acceptable ways flourished for women to be with other women. Women kissing each other on the lips, walking with their arms around each other's waists, sleeping curled up together in the same bed, and forming lifelong partnerships, sometimes described by contemporaries as "marriages," were all viewed as "natural" expressions of femininity. Some women did, of course, develop erotic and sexual liaisons with other women—what we would today call lesbian relationships. Yet the majority of these meaningful bonds between women wouldn't fit into our category of "lesbian," although none of our categories really fit. Marcus charts, through studying hundreds of diaries and letters, the freedom Victorian women felt to be passionately attached to other women, to be competitive with other women for the affections of especially attractive female friends, and to be appreciative of the physical beauty of other women. Women could practice with their female friends an amorous freedom condemned in their relations with men to whom they were not married, which were carefully monitored and circumscribed.[39]

Charlotte's novel *Shirley* is more about women smitten with each other than anything else, even though her two heroines ultimately marry men. Charlotte manages to fit two highly charged same-sex connections into the novel. The tender adoration Shirley's governess, Mrs. Pryor, showers on Caroline, Shirley's best friend, bears the guise of an obsessive infatuation since neither the characters nor the reader are informed until the last quarter of the book that the older woman is actually Caroline's long-absent mother. Mrs. Pryor goes so far as to suggest that they set up their life together, in a passage that almost mimics heterosexual marriage proposals in many a Victorian novel. "With you I am happier than I have ever been with any living thing . . . your society I should esteem a very dear privilege—an inestimable privilege, a comfort, a blessing . . . I hope you can love me?" Her dearest wish is to take a house of her own, hoping Caroline will "come to me then." When Caroline falls ill, her confinement in bed means Mrs. Pryor can encircle Caroline in her arms and draw her to her heart. "I shall hardly wish to get well," Caroline remarks, "that I may keep you always."

Shirley, in turn, has a fellowship with Caroline that fuels the plot with a vitality missing from the heterosexual romances. Charlotte builds Shirley (usually a man's name at that time) into a "masculine" character, based on the Emily that would have been if "placed in health and prosperity." Shirley thinks of herself as an "esquire" and "Captain Keeldar," because her parents "gave me a man's name; I hold a man's position," she explains. "It is enough to inspire me with a touch of manhood . . . I feel quite gentlemanlike." Her governess fears that when Shirley disdains needlework and whistles, people will feel "you affected masculine manners." Shirley tells Caroline of her pleasure in knowing "that my quiet, shrewd, thoughtful companion and monitress [Caroline] is coming back to me: that I shall have her sitting in the room to look at, to talk to, or to let alone, as she and I please." Caroline feels "twined" with Shirley, a "sustenance and balm" too rooted to be shaken by quarrels or passions for others. "I am supported and soothed when you—that is, you only—are near, Shirley."[40]

When the two women spend the night in the same bed together, Caroline discovers that the man she loves has asked Shirley to marry him. In staying awake and talking "the whole night through," they work loose the knot: Caroline then knows that there is no love between Shirley and Caroline's beloved. The consolation and ease of girls occupying the same bed is a theme Charlotte returned to throughout her writing life. There is the scene in *Jane Eyre* of Helen dying in Jane's arms at Lowood school. In a final, unfinished novel called *Emma*, a student's reward for studiousness is sharing a bed with the headmistress.

What results from the nocturnal conversation in *Shirley* are the marriages of these two friends to two brothers, thus linking them forever as family. Charlotte probably drew on her closeness with Ellen for this plot twist; Ellen's brother Henry actually proposed to Charlotte. Not being in love with him, Charlotte said no, but one thing made her want to accept. "Now my dear Ellen there were in this proposal some things that might have proved a strong temptation—I thought if I were to marry so, Ellen could live with me and how happy I should be." In these cases, marriage happened or almost happened as exchanges between women, with their bond more essential than the heterosexual couple's.[41]

When it came to gender manipulation and play as in *Shirley*, Charlotte stood on home ground. In her early stories, she almost always wrote from the point of view of Charles Wellesley, continuing to speak as a man in her first novel, *The Professor*. She savored stepping into masculine identities and names in letters, and when visiting Ellen, she liked to be called "Charles" by the household. She used the ambiguously gendered pseudonym Currer Bell for all her novels. Even when she brought women into the center of her stories, as with Jane Eyre, she continued toying with gender. Rochester turns into something more interesting than merely an impenetrable, privileged man when he dons the clothes and character of an elderly gypsy woman. In *Villette*, Lucy Snowe performs as a male dandy in school theatricals, flirting with Ginevra Fanshawe with a real zest.[42]

Taken as a whole, Charlotte's eye on exchanges between women in her fiction ranged far and wide. Rivals for men's affection are a standby, as in *Jane Eyre*, where the snobbish Blanche Ingram courts Rochester, who, it turns out, is already married to Bertha Mason. Jane's connection to Rochester's wife, the "madwoman in the attic," has been brilliantly decoded by the feminist scholars Sandra Gilbert and Susan Gubar. They see the women as psychological doubles or alter egos, with Bertha as the angry, sexualized, rebellious side of Jane, acting with a rage not available to a governess, forced to suppress such feelings. Women in Charlotte's novels speak and act for other women.[43]

Not surprisingly, it was an engagement with a man that caused one of the few gaps in Ellen and Charlotte's correspondence. When Charlotte decided she would marry Arthur Nicholls, Ellen became so jealous, it almost ended their friendship. Ellen, who never married, managed to overcome her sorrow at losing first place in Charlotte's affections, but their correspondence never fully recovered. Arthur found their let-ters "dangerous as lucifer matches" because of their wealth of personal detail. Fearing they might fall into the hands of strangers, he insisted that Ellen must "distinctly promise to burn my [Charlotte's] letters as you receive them"; otherwise he will "read every line I write and elect himself censor of our correspondence." This shocking threat—that Arthur would read and alter Charlotte's letters to her best friend—feels like a violation. Ellen sent a promise to Arthur to "pledge herself to the destruction of Charlotte's epistles" if he promised to leave their letters uncensored. Ellen didn't keep her promise because he continued to cur-tail the intimacy of their correspondence. Ellen knew Arthur looked over Charlotte's shoulder as she wrote to her, because Charlotte would add that information to the letter. Ellen must have felt a little like Char-lotte did when she tried to send those letters directly to her professor, circumventing spousal prying eyes. Charlotte submitted to Arthur's domineering behavior with a surprising passivity. Possibly she found some frisson in this "manly" pushiness, a style her heroines admired. The independent Shirley prefers her husband to be "a master": "One whose control my impatient temper must acknowledge . . . A man I shall find impossible not to love, and very possible to fear." This she finds in her former teacher, who vanquishes and restricts her, turning her into a "chained denizen of deserts."44

Ellen claimed that the hundreds of letters Charlotte had received from Ellen, stretching over the many years of their attachment, were burned by Charlotte at Arthur's request and that he destroyed any left after her death. But since he maintained that he never saw any of the older letters, it's impossible to know what happened to them. Ellen mutilated some of Charlotte's letters herself. She cut Charlotte's signature off some to send to fans requesting autographs, sometimes taking lines of text along with it. She blacked out names and censored some of the ardent words and phrases when she contemplated their publication. Patrick also cut up Charlotte's letters to satisfy relic hunters. Some he snipped apart completely, sending their fragments all over the globe. The Brontë scholar Margaret Smith, who painstakingly researched her three-volume collection of Charlotte's letters, reconstituted some of these sheets. A June 9, 1849, letter, for instance, was scissored into many pieces. Smith located five fragments of the letter in as many places: the Morgan Library in New York; the private collection of Mrs. Karen Bicknell; the Harry Ransom Center at the University of Texas; Trinity College, Dublin; and the Brontë Parsonage Museum in Yorkshire. Smith's painstaking work, one might say, was another act of fellowship between women, faithful and sealed with meticulousness.[45]

Some of Charlotte's letters to Ellen will probably always retain a sense of mystery. On one envelope to Ellen sent on August 28, 1847, Charlotte sealed the back flap with a wafer that says, "Look Within." She then took her pen and put a line through "Look," adding two dots over the "L." She wrote an "S" before "Within," making it "Swithin," underlined it, and added three dots underneath the "Swi." The letter contained in this envelope has gone missing, and what she meant by the altered wafer remains obscure. Perhaps it is a reference to Saint Swithin's Day, which falls on July 15? Traditionally, that day's weather will hold steady for the next forty days. July 15 came on clear and warm, and while some of the days in the next forty had occasional rain and thunder, they were mostly fine. Ellen visited Haworth at the end of that July, and all four women—the "Quartette," Ellen liked to call them—spent long hours on the moors. They saw a parhelion (an optical phenomenon that makes the sun appear multiplied) while on a stroll on July 21. Perhaps the strange sun led them to talk of forecasts and superstitions about reading the future weather. August 24 would have ended the Saint Swithin's Day period, and Charlotte sent the note with the altered wafer a few days later.[46]

Yet August 24 was momentous for Charlotte for altogether different reasons. She put a package on a train containing the manuscript of *Jane Eyre*, posting it to the publishers Smith, Elder and Co. She added stamps to offset the cost of carriage, not being able to prepay at the rail station. Despite Ellen's dearness to her, Charlotte did not share her writing life with her. She did not tell Ellen she wrote books until after *Shirley* had been published, long after Ellen had guessed its and *Jane Eyre*'s authorship. Perhaps Charlotte's demand on her letter seal that Ellen *not* "look within" had a subtle hint of her undisclosed secret. This part of her life she only truly shared with those other important women, with whom she had thorny, yet essential relationships: her sisters.

CHAPTER SIX

The Alchemy of Desks

Graham would endeavor to seduce her attention by opening his
desk and displaying its multifarious contents: seals, bright
sticks of wax, pen-knives, with a miscellany of engravings . . .
—CHARLOTTE BRONTË, *Villette*

It was charlotte's poking around in Emily's private writing space, in the autumn of 1845, that led to the sisters' first appearance in print. While Charlotte practiced being out in the world with her writing, taking risks by unbending in letters, Emily penned poetry for herself alone, not sharing it with Anne either, even though the two still wrote Gondal stories together. Emily, now twenty-seven, and Anne, twenty-five, even pretended to be characters from their fantasyland, "escaping from the palace of instruction" while on a train to York at the end of June. Yet Anne notes in her diary paper, written a few weeks after this trip (dated July 31, 1845), that Emily is "writing some poetry." "I wonder," Anne goes on, "what it is about?"[1]

Based on the manuscripts of Emily's poetry that still exist, her writing process went like this: she composed poems on scraps of paper, some of them scratched on corners torn from letters, handwritten essays, or snippets of light-brown cardboard. Many of the odd bits of paper came from notebook pages divided into halves, quarters, or smaller portions. With some of these leaves, it appears she tore down the page to fit snugly around the already penned poem, leaving no margins. She drafted verse in the tiny script Charlotte and Branwell used for their magazines, often loading numerous short poems onto minuscule fragments, in one case crowding eight separate poems onto a sheet measuring just three by two and a quarter inches. She seemed to pack her crabbed words onto a sheet too small for her purposes, cramming in more until her verse fell off the edge. She composed one 1844 poem about death titled "At Castlewood," and with a Gondal setting, on part of a sheet of black-edged mourning stationery, in use from their Aunt Branwell's recent death. After its last line she wrote, "My task is done."[2]

Emily sometimes illustrated her poems with landscapes spouting volcanoes, furry or springy creatures that look like extraterrestrials, snakes with wings, and birds in flight. On one she drew a picture of a person sitting in a chair, looking out a window onto some moors, probably a self-portrait. Others have various symbols, like diamonds and horseshoes, that comprise a private language, its meaning now obscure.

Later she made fair copies of this host of little leaves in a notebook, revising as she transcribed. The notebook's non-chronological order made some sort of sense to her, and it fulfilled her need to see the poems together as a body of work. A few years on, she decided to revise and rearrange the best ones and to add some new poems, in two fresh notebooks, one for the Gondal poems and another for the others. This meant tearing sheets out of the first notebook and discarding them once they were rewritten (and generally revised) into one of the new notebooks, or merely crossing them out in the first notebook if they shared a leaf with a poem not deemed worthy to be copied into a later notebook. One, "Gondal Poems," has a red paper cover retaining its original price of 6d and a title page that mimics a published book, decorated with twisting vines. These notebooks stood as Emily's version of publication, final copies with just herself as an audience.[3]

Emily likely stored her poetry scraps and notebooks in her portable desk, along with letters, stationery, seals, ink, and metal nibs—all of the latter were found there after her death. The desk locked, and she may have kept it that way, with a key she carried on her person. All three of the Brontë sisters had these portable writing desks (Charlotte's is pictured at the beginning of this chapter). Branwell must have had one too, bigger than his sisters'—women's desks were made more "delicate" than men's—but it has not been located. Emily called them "desk boxes," as in her 1841 diary paper, which begins, "It is Friday evening, near 9 o'clock—wild rainy weather. I am seated in the dining-room, having just concluded tidying our desk boxes, writing this document."[4]

On the page next to her writing, Emily sometimes drew portraits of herself using her banged-up rosewood desk, her sheet (the one she was actually writing on just then, visibly pictured) propped on the ink-stained, purple velvet that covers the writing slope. When closed, the desks became rectangular cases, not much larger than shoeboxes. Divided on a slant and hinged together, when opened the lid and bottom lay flat, forming a continuous sloped surface for writing and reading. Even when unfolded, the desks were small, so they were sometimes called lap desks, although they were also known as table desks. In the portrait already mentioned of Emily in her little bedroom (pictured here), she is sitting on her wood stool, penning a diary paper on her desk as it rests on her lap. Keeper is stretched out on the rug near her and Flossy on the bed. In another picture of herself composing, she scribbles on the writing slope as it sits on a table. Another, drawn on the same page, has her standing at the window, gazing out, with the desk open on the table, a page sitting on it, ready.[5]

No pictures of Charlotte using her desk exist, but the nature of its service can be surmised from the desk itself. Ink bottles sat in slots at the top of the opened desks, and one of Charlotte's still has dried ink crusted on the bottom. The brown-velvet writing slope, stained like Emily's with ink, is especially blackened on the upper right-hand corner, where Charlotte dipped her pen into the bottle, the ink having dripped as she moved the pen to the page. The slopes on these desks opened to reveal storage areas. Charlotte squirreled away in these nooks all sorts of oddments. A braid of Anne's hair, tied with a blue ribbon and stuffed in a little envelope, cut by their father when Anne was thirteen, found a place there. Charlotte also stored in it hand-drawn patterns for collars, cuffs, and wallpaper, pointing to the use of the desk for domestic work and artwork along with writing. Needlework and desk boxes were more than close cousins—letters and papers were stored in both, as were sewing patterns and bits of cloth. Even the paper for manuscripts showed this lack of separation: in the center of a paper pattern for a coin purse, Charlotte penned a little poem about long-lasting love, titled "I can never forget."[6]

Given the Brontës' penchant for tiny text, it is fitting that they would have miniature desks to make and store their specks of scribbling. These wood boxes have an affinity with the tin box, about two inches long, where Emily and Anne kept their folded diary papers. In

OF EMILY BRONTË'S DIARY.

turn, they put the tin box into one of the desk boxes. Arthur Nicholls, Charlotte's husband, who inherited many of their things, turned it out from the bottom of a Brontë desk in 1896 to show an early biographer. Writing boxes went into trunks when the sisters traveled. Seemingly part of their process of composition, the folding and putting of texts into containers, and then those containers into other ones, carried over to the manuscripts of their novels. Sections of Charlotte's fair copy of *The Professor*, for instance, show signs of being folded in two or four, so it is likely that it underwent a boxing process of some sort. Emily bought another tin box in 1847 in order, her biographer Edward Chitham thinks, to hold the manuscript of *Wuthering Heights*.[7]

Charlotte has her character Lucy Snowe mirror this practice. The letters she receives from the man she loves, while not of her own writing like the Brontës' texts were, still need, compulsively, to be encased in many layers, as explored in the previous chapter. First they are wrapped in silver paper and put into a casket. The casket then goes into a locked box, all of which is hidden in a drawer. When that doesn't keep out the prying eyes of Madame Beck, there is the oiled silk bound with twine, then the bottle stoppered and sealed, and finally the burial that includes a slate and cement. Given this scenario, one can imagine the kind of excavation that had to happen for the Brontës to get their writing into print.

The sisters' predilection for hiddenness was shared during this time. Victorians favored special boxes for all sorts of activities. They not only relished the practice of keeping things boxed up but also had a penchant for putting these boxes into other ones. Characters in many a Victorian novel can be found sedulously putting things into things. The novelist George Eliot, who herself had a box for storing lace that contained "false" drawers opening out in strange and secret ways, gives an illustration of this common ritual in her book *Mill on the Floss*. The character Mrs. Pullet draws a bunch of keys from her pocket, choosing one to unlock a wing of a wardrobe. From among layers of linen she extracts a door key. Moving to another room, she unlocks another wardrobe. After she takes out sheet after sheet of silver paper, a bonnet is disclosed.[8]

Despite seeming to be specially made for them because of their fairy littleness, the Brontë desk boxes were unremittingly average, of the sort ordinary middle-class women possessed. With their basic inlays and simple designs, they were nothing like the dreamy desk that Charlotte imagined in an early story, constructed of satinwood and containing a diamond pen, gold inkstand, and a vase to hold letter wafers. The penny post made such desks nearly ubiquitous, used for writing all those letters and for storing materials for correspondence, like stamps, wafers, and the new-fangled envelopes. Keeping apace with innovations in the post office, desk boxes became cheaper, some even made of papier-mâché. George Eliot had a black one of these, decorated with mother-of-pearl. Florence Nightingale also owned a black papier-mâché desk, with a still life painted on the top that includes dead birds. A gift from well-wishers in Derbyshire, near where she grew up, it has a plaque affixed on the front reading, "Presented to Florence Nightingale on her safe arrival at Lea Hirst from the Crimea / August 8 1856 / as a token of esteem by the inhabitants of Lea, Holloway, and Crich."[9]

Some desk boxes of the day had so many parts and uses and could be so transformed by hidden springs, levers, and buttons that they seemed straight out of fairy tales. Department stores, where one could also buy needlework boxes, sold desk boxes of all sorts, as did jewelers and cutlers, like Thomas Lund's 1820s "Cutlery Warehouse" at 56 and 57 Cornhill, London, which advertised "Portable Writing Desks, Dressing Cases, and Morocco articles of every description." In 1830 a maker named Michi of 4 Leadenhall Street, London, advertised mahogany desks in nine sizes. Ladies' desk boxes, sometimes simply called "stationery cases," could be purchased pre-stocked with luxury items such as rose-scented paper and wafers, called "Papier d'Amour," and even colored and perfumed inks. One shown at the Great Exhibition by Eliza Byam of Soho Square had many roles to play: "Compound stationery case: traveling, writing, working, dressing and refreshment case; lady's carriage companion." Some portable desks had mirrors added to the top, thus doubling as vanity cases; others had fire screens, to keep the heat off the face of the writer while penning letters. One type of lady's traveling desk worked also as a needlework table, with a pleated bag for storing items in process, but it also featured an adjustable reading stand, with a hinge so it could be stowed, and a pullout writing slide. Elizabeth Gaskell had one of these multi-use, portable desks, much fancier than what the Brontës used. An upright box with doors, one of which opened to disclose a steep writing slope, it included a wooden support for a timepiece and a forest of dividers, cubbies, and drawers. No wonder Lewis Carroll's unsolved puzzle, asked by the Mad Hatter in *Alice's Adventures in Wonderland*, gained such traction: "Why is a raven like a writing desk?"[10]

The plot device of the locked desk as personal space safeguarding secrets was a favorite of many Victorian novels, like Anne's *Tenant of Wildfell Hall*, in which the abusive husband holds his wife prisoner in her own home. After reading her plans to escape him in her diary, he takes the keys to her writing desk, thus spiriting away a significant portion of her privacy. In William Makepeace Thackeray's *Vanity Fair*—Charlotte's favorite novel—the clever, scheming governess Becky Sharp has a desk box, her "private museum," where she hides all the tokens of her adultery: love letters, cash, and jewels given to her by rich lovers. When her husband forces open her desk, their marriage is over. The character Amelia Sedley, who gave Becky this desk, puts, in the "secret drawers" of her own writing desk, the gloves left behind by the man she loves. Another character, the spinster Briggs, has similarly hidden away in her old lap desk the "lock of yellow hair" of her "hectic young writing-master" from twenty-four years before and his letters, "beautiful in their illegibility," further underlining the equation of desks and the recesses of the heart. In a potential mix of fact and fiction, Mary Shelley, traveling with her portable desk earlier in the century, was rumored to have stored there that book containing her husband's heart."

In another jumbling of desk and body, Charlotte eroticized the contents of her character Shirley's desk. Louis Moore, standing in Shirley's drawing room alone, thinks over how much he adores "all her little failings," how she "enchains" him hopelessly. He notices she has left her desk open, with the keys hanging in the lock, even though here are "all her repositories . . . her very jewel-casket." He dwells on the charm of what he finds there: "a pretty seal, a silver pen, a crimson berry or two of the ripe fruit on a green leaf, a small, clean, delicate glove." These things, "her mark," lead him to exclaim, "Why does she leave fascination in her footprints?"

The Brontë sisters probably took their desk boxes with them to their teaching and governess jobs. Anne described a horrid situation with a desk in *Agnes Grey*, likely based on her own experience. Her charges, brats all, find the most outrageous possible abuse to visit on their mild-mannered governess. One yells to the other, "Mary Ann, throw her desk out of the window!" Agnes explains that "my precious desk, containing my letters and papers, my small amount of cash, and all my valuables, was about to be precipitated from the three-story window." In *Jane Eyre*, the moneyed and snobbish complain about the "nuisance" of governesses, and how the children took joy in driving theirs, "the poor old stick," to extremities. One pliable governess would "bear anything; nothing put her out . . . we might do what we pleased" such as "ransack her desk." Lucy Snowe's employer in *Villette* sneakily has the keys to Lucy's desk and workbox copied so she can nose around in them whenever she wants. Such violations were all the more hateful since the interior of the governess's desk provided one of the few private spaces at a job that was lived, except for sleeping, almost always in public. "A private governess has no existence," Charlotte wrote to Emily (whom she calls here "Lavinia") from her first governess job. Charlotte viewed these duties as little more than wiping "the children's smutty noses" or miscellaneous "drudgery," and her charges as, variously, "fat-headed oafs," "riotous, perverse, unmanageable cubs," "small, petted, nuisances," or "pampered spoilt and turbulent," so it comes as no surprise she felt a governess needed all the privacy she could get.[12]

Another precious desk was Jane Austen's mahogany one, its writing slope covered in leather, that she took along when traveling. When she stayed at the Bull and George Inn in Dartford on one trip in 1798, the desk, given to her by her father and now at the British Library, was accidently placed in a chaise whose luggage was bound for the West Indies. It was saved just in time when she sent off a horseman to stop the carriage. "No part of my property," Austen remarked, "could have been such a prize before, for in my writing box was all my worldly wealth." She probably kept her money in the secret drawer in the bottom right-hand corner, which opens with a hidden bolt set into the top of the writing slope. Such concealed recesses became dear to the Victorians, some desks had three or four of them tucked away, and mechanisms for opening these drawers included stiff springs released by catches, themselves concealed by wooden covers. While the Brontës couldn't afford desks with hidden compartments, they did admire such boxes, like an ivory casket in an early story by Charlotte that opens "by means of a secret spring" and holds a piece of paper recording a scandalous secret: two female friends were so intimate that they decided to switch babies and raise their friend's child as their own.[13]

Dickens's portable desk, now at the New York Public Library, is more than twice as large as one that belonged to Charlotte Brontë, which sits next to it in a display case. Charlotte's is a plain Jane, while Dickens's has elaborate inlaid brass and a manly writing slope that could never fit on a lap. It has secret drawers in a hidden section opened by first unlocking the whole desk, then unlocking the top part of the slope. A long wooden panel, part of the pen tray and ink bottle compartment, is next removed by nudging it up, which releases it from a catch, causing it to pop out, owing to a tense brass strip that works as a spring. Behind this are three shallow drawers, discreetly tucked away with pale-green ribbon pulls. The brass plate on the top engraved "CD / Gads Hill" marks this expensive desk as a luxury item associated with Dickens's country mansion and his wealth more generally.[14]

Another novelist known for his mobile equipment was Anthony Trollope, who wrote a good deal of his many works on a "tablet" while commuting by train to his day job at the post office. Perhaps it was this desk—where he, like Austen, kept all of his money when traveling—that was smashed into pieces by a porter at a railway station in America when Trollope went there in 1861 to write a book about the area and its people. "I shall never forget my agony as I saw and heard my desk fall," Trollope recalled, as he watched the porter toss it seven yards to where it landed on the hard pavement. "I heard its poor weak intestines rattle in their death struggle." The experience almost made him convinced that the country, full of savages, was irredeemable. When he traveled by ship, Trollope had carpenters build special desks in his cabins. A later writing box must have been quite large, because on one trip "some wretch had pitched the desk down like a ball," shattering a bottle of ink. It tinted not only "all my beautiful white paper" but his three shirts stored on top "to keep things steady." And then there were the one hundred loose cigars: "I have not yet tried how cigars, bathed in ink, smoke;—but I shall try."[15]

Also portable in the sense that they could be moved to different parts of the house (along the lines of today's laptop computers), depending on which room was quietest or warmest, or best lit, such desks belonged even to those who never traveled outside the home. Characters in Victorian novels often carried lap desks from here to there and back again, or had servants do it for them, reflecting actual practice. The slope often moved rather than the person. In Anne's *Tenant of Wildfell Hall*, Mr. Hargrave "sent for his desk into the morning room," where the ladies sewed and read. When the heroine can't sleep, she "got my desk and sat down in my dressing-gown to recount the events of the past evening." A man sick in bed needs to write a note canceling an appointment. He asks his guest for help, who responds, "Most willingly I consented, and immediately brought him his desk."

The Brontë desks stayed mostly inside the parsonage as the winter of 1845 came on. All the siblings found themselves unemployed. Not long after Anne left her job with the Robinsons, Branwell was fired (from the third job in the last five years), probably because his employer figured out what he was up to with his wife. Branwell tried to blunt the agony of a broken heart with alcohol, or as Charlotte put it, he kept "stunning or drowning his distress of mind." His beer, gin, and, perhaps, laudanum habits were partially funded by the wealthy Mrs. Robinson, who sent him money, probably to keep him silent. He also tried writing as a way to block out "almost killing cares," he called them, mostly poems with suicidal themes. In one a corpse floating on water is envied, with its untroubled calm and the "healing balm" of its cold oblivion. He even started a novel, a reworking of an earlier Angrian tale, about—what else?—troubled love.[16]

Charlotte, meanwhile, attempted to launch the school project she had been planning for so long, aided by the small legacies each of the girls had inherited from their Aunt Branwell. A school at the parsonage would keep them all home, a state they desired above all else. The three had a prospectus printed, and enlisted the help of their friends to spread the word. But no one sent their children, probably because of Haworth's inaccessibility. "If you were to persuade a Mamma to bring her child to Haworth," Charlotte explained to Ellen, "the aspect of the place would frighten her and she would probably take the dear thing back with her instanter."[17]

As the sisters filled their days with the usual walking, chores, reading, and writing, they felt the smallness of their house. Emily, especially, needed to carve out pockets of privacy in the crowded rooms. In the fall of 1845, she was working on a Gondal poem that praised the cultivation of inwardness. So, as Charlotte poured out her soul to Heger and sent flirty letters and seals to Ellen, Emily labored over "Julian M. and A.G. Rochelle," later retitled "The Prisoner." A young woman jailed in a dungeon-crypt figures out how to be happy by feeding on inner visions, which rise up when "winds take a pensive tone and stars a tender fire" and then can "kill me with desire." Needing no fellowship, or even any freedom of movement, her imagination is enough for her to slip her bonds. Around the same time Emily was recording this poem into the Gondal notebook in October, Charlotte "accidently lighted on" it, rather ironically given that it is about lone inspiration. One wonders where Charlotte was snooping when she found it. Did she discover it by peeking into Emily's desk? If Emily kept her desk locked, then Charlotte's "accidental" discovery seems something worthy of Madame Beck from *Villette*. Charlotte snuck away with the notebook and read it "alone and in secret." So excited by the poems' "peculiar music," Charlotte confessed her transgression to

Emily. Emily was furious, not being a person "on the recesses of whose mind and feelings, even those nearest and dearest to her could, with impunity, intrude unlicensed," as Charlotte explained the incident and her sister's reaction. Emily sternly berated her for this "unwarrantable liberty," this exposure of her private world by her nosy sister.[18]

Their relationship continued to grow knotty as they became adults, Charlotte's need for intimacy increasingly clashing with Emily's deeply reserved nature. Profoundly entwined emotionally and spending their days at such close quarters, the two couldn't avoid explosions, like the one over Emily's private notebook. Charlotte found Emily's impenetrability baffling, and she couldn't help but push against it. It was likely Charlotte's need to understand Emily that led her to read Emily's poetry notebook, perhaps by penetrating the recesses of Emily's desk.[19]

Charlotte tried to assuage her sister's anger: it took many hours. Anne helped, taking a conciliatory role as she often did, by bringing Charlotte some of her own poems to read. This led Charlotte to campaign for publication, something she had long been pondering. Days were spent trying to convince Emily to publish. "By dint of entreaty and reason," Charlotte later wrote, she "at last wrung out a reluctant consent" to publish the verse of all three in one volume. It is curious that Emily agreed, given her reluctance to let even her sisters read her poems, although she insisted they write under the ambiguously gendered pseudonyms that still retained their initials: Currer, Ellis, and Acton Bell. " 'Ellis Bell' will not endure to be alluded to under any other appellation," Charlotte explained to her later publishers when they found out the real identities of the sisters, "than the 'nom de plume' . . . it is against every feeling and intention" of "him."[20]

Such pen names were nothing new to the three, who had been writing under similar ones, about the lands of Gondal and Angria, since they were children. They started with those toy soldiers, which they snatched up, made into their alter egos, then further transformed into writing personas. The most recent versions of the writing soldiers—of the genies, kings, and queens—the Bell disguises had something in common with script too small to read, closed up in boxes, and sealed or locked away, all forms of keeping a vital portion back. Although it was Emily's drive for secrecy that led to their adoption of these alternate identities, Charlotte also had an "ostrich-longing for concealment," as she called it, even after the public began to figure out that Currer Bell was some obscure clergyman's daughter called Charlotte Brontë. A need to pass invisible among others lasted throughout her lifetime, in equal measure with a relish for adulation.

Their volume of poetry provoked many rejections. They finally managed to convince the minor firm of Aylott and Jones to bring it out, if the authors paid the expenses of thirty-one pounds and ten shillings, close to a year's salary for most governesses. The slim book, entitled *Poems by Currer, Ellis, and Acton Bell*, appeared in May 1846, bound in green cloth with a geometric design on the front surrounding the title, and the price of four shillings printed just under it, an unwelcome touch of the commercial. Poems by the three traded off at points and at other times appeared coupled.

The book sold only two copies. Yet it served the purpose of nudging open a window of possibility. Now published authors, even if only in a very small way, they felt some confidence about sending out their novels, which were well under way when their poetry volume came out. The tension between Charlotte's pushiness and Emily's resistance possibly provided the true impetus for publication and even for the writing of their novels. Without this complex form of collaboration, with its anger and strife, their great masterworks might never have been published, or even written.

The collaborative nature of the creation of their novels had a peripatetic quality. Composing on their own during the day—sometimes at their writing desks but also on tables and in bed—they paced together around the gate-legged dining room table after nine o'clock most evenings, talking over their plots and characters and reading passages aloud for feedback. This habit of nocturnal exercise and thought indoors dated back at least to Charlotte's time with Miss Wooler at Roe Head School, and she would continue it alone even after her sisters died. These writing "workshops" helped drive them to finish their first novels in less than a year. The masses of fiction they had been churning out since childhood also worked as steady preparation for their burst of effort now.[21]

Charlotte came to these evenings with pages of what would become *The Professor*, her short novel written from the point of view of one William Crimsworth, a dry and dispassionate man. Anne was working through her largely autobiographical story of a governess's life, *Agnes Grey*; and Emily, the gothic dreamscape of *Wuthering Heights*. The two former works had a good deal in common, being realistic, unadorned tales about ordinary Victorian working life. Even though Charlotte reused part of an old story for its first few chapters, *The Professor* strikes one as the production of a sober adult. *Wuthering Heights* came, contrarily, straight out of the land of Gondal. Charlotte expressed her misgivings about the otherworldly passions of *Wuthering Heights* during their nighttime pacing, as she would do publicly after Emily's death. "In its storm-heated and electrical atmosphere," Charlotte later grumbled, "we seem at times to breathe lightning." This was a result, she felt, of her sister's mind being "too exclusively confined" to the terrible and tragic, something that Charlotte hoped would have changed if Emily had lived longer, giving her mind the chance to grow "like a strong tree, loftier, straighter." She described the reactions of the "auditor" of Emily's work "when read in manuscript"—surely Charlotte herself—

who, "shuddering under the grinding influence of natures so relentless and implacable, of spirits so lost and fallen . . . complained that the mere hearing of certain vivid and fearful scenes banished sleep by night, and disturbed mental peace by day." When the "auditor" told "Ellis Bell" this, "Ellis" wondered what was meant and suspected the complainer of "affectation." Emily surely did some criticizing of her own, probably about the lack of fire in *The Professor*.[22]

Charlotte, for one, saw the importance of hammering out her novels in close fellowship, even one troubled by competition among fierce natures. Composing a novel after her sisters died meant fabricating "it darkly in the silent workshop" of her own brain. She couldn't even put into words "how much I hunger to have some opinion besides my own, and how I have sometimes desponded and almost despaired because there was no one to whom to read a line—or of whom to ask a counsel. 'Jane Eyre' was not written under such circumstances." In fact, despite Charlotte's reservations about *Wuthering Heights* and her attempts to convince Emily to make it less relentless, she was deeply under its influence when she wrote *Jane Eyre*. To Emily's novel she owed the heavy doses of passion, insanity, and imprisonment.[23]

Other aspects of the composition of these first novels are more difficult to reconstruct. None of Anne's or Emily's novel manuscripts exist, either in drafts or as fair copies, presumably going the way of the Gondal saga. Anne composed most of her poetry in an ordinary cursive hand, without the pictures and doodles of Emily's drafts, giving them a saner quality, as if she had always been ready to meet a public, unlike Emily, who never was. Anne also copied her verse into notebooks, some hand bound, much of it written while at her governess jobs, likely on her writing slope. When she wasn't working on her poetry, she probably locked the manuscript in her desk to keep it away from the ill-behaved children of her employers. Later, when Anne settled into living at home, caught up in the mood of writing her second novel, Charlotte observed her "continually sitting stooping either over a book or over her desk—it is with difficulty one can prevail on her to take a walk or induce her to converse."[24]

Since the servants reported seeing Emily often scribbling away while at her housework, the process of composing on odds and ends, as for her poems, likely continued with her novel. Charlotte's friend Mary Taylor once said, when Charlotte told her about the endless tales of Angria and Gondal, that it was like the siblings were "growing potatoes in the cellar." "Yes! I know we are!" Charlotte replied. Emily never really emerged from that cellar, it might be said, and Anne only ever descended a step or two into it. Charlotte went all the way down, but she could also go all the way up to the attic.[25]

Emily found pens troublesome. Her fight with her pens is apparent on her stained writing slope and also on her manuscripts: Blots dropped onto the page, penetrating through to the other side and interfering with the poem on the verso. She dug her nib into the paper; her pen ran out of ink as she wrote. Her nib would become clogged with sediment from the dregs of the ink bottle, and she cleaned it by dragging it along the page. Her blotting paper has holes in it from hasty nib clearing. Pen-wipers were the more tidy means to clean excess ink off nibs. Charlotte had handmade ones, typical craft items made by women and given as gifts. Her brown, green, and blue pen-wiper with a beaded edge probably came from the needles of Ellen, sent in a package with sickbed items for Anne when she was dying of tuberculosis.[26]

Emily grappled first with quill pens, made from goose feathers, that the siblings dipped into those ink bottles to write the Gondal and Angria tales. They began using wooden holders with detachable, metal nibs by the time they started their novels. Emily and Charlotte had wood pens and nibs, first patented in 1831 by Joseph Gillott, a Birmingham button maker, in their desk and paint boxes, alongside quill ones. Simpler and faster to use than quills (although the evidence points to Emily still struggling with them)—and much cheaper—nibs in holders grew in use after the penny post made correspondence an ordinary part of most Victorians' days. Charlotte may have also used a pen of gutta-percha, a type of latex made of tree sap, since nibs for one were also in her desk.[27]

Writers of the time liked to imagine pens as having lives of their own—thinking, dreaming, and talking—while sitting expectantly in desks among their cohorts, seals, paper, and ink. Stories gave them a chatty agency, like the anonymous *Genuine and Most Surprising Adventures of a Very Unfortunate Goose-Quill* and "The Adventures of a Pen," by one J. Hunt. The latter pen gets passed around from writer to writer, most of them frivolous and less honest than the pen himself. He rubs shoulders in a sailor's pocket with a pocket dagger, a comb, and a snuff box, and at one point a "celebrated Beau" uses him to "make rebuses for the ladies." When he can't bear to be used to write immoral words, the pen finds his ink freezing up with horror in his nib.[28]

Charlotte didn't always use a pen (of any sort) or her writing slope when composing her novels. For early drafts, she used pencils, like the stubby ones cut to points with a knife found in her various boxes, including her desk. (One, with "Pitman's Phonographic Pencil" printed on it, advertises a form of shorthand created by Isaac Pitman, who traveled to nearby York and Leeds and elsewhere to promote phonography in the 1840s.) With such pencils, she wrote on scraps of paper in her miniature hand, placed "against a piece of board, such as is used in binding books, for a desk," according to Gaskell, who saw some of Charlotte's early drafts. This way, she could position the paper near her face, a necessary position because of her shortsightedness (although she did, eventually, wear spectacles, one pair still stored in her desk). Harriet

Martineau made a similar observation, remarking that Charlotte's first drafts were penciled into "little square paper books, held close to her eyes." Emily may have used a similar method, which would explain the ripped-off cover of a hardbound book with pencil doodles of men's and women's faces found in her desk—a perfect hard surface for scribbling in odd places. For Charlotte, this was sometimes in bed. With her early novels, she occasionally worked late at night when insomnia struck, so the extra portability of these boards and pencils—no need for an ink bottle, for instance—meant that another writing space could be made: lying down, tucked in. Using an ink pen and her slope, she then made a neat, clean copy, to be posted out to publishers. In her desk she stored a hand-ruled sheet of paper, likely put behind the pages of her fair copy, helping to keep her lines of text perfectly straight.[29]

Very little had, in fact, changed since Charlotte snipped out and stitched that miniature magazine long ago. The fundamentals of production since the early days of Gondal and Angria remained in place. Here again the sisters collaborated, with Charlotte and Emily still deploying a secret script on small sheets or paper booklets. All three altered their identities (and genders), and they even sent off the manuscripts in brown parcel wrapping, of the same sort used to bind their little books. Instead of the address being concealed inside, now it went exposed, written out for the postman to act on. Granted, the three now coveted an audience larger than the family. Yet this readership within the family remained an essential component; these were joint projects among the "Bell brothers."

During the long labor of reaching this expanded circle of readers, the three works were initially linked up, despite their great differences. In April 1846, Charlotte wrote to Aylott and Jones, informing them that the Bells were completing three works of fiction, and asking if they were interested in them. They were not. Charlotte, continuing to act as secretary for all three, wrote to Henry Colburn, a prominent London publisher, requesting "permission to send for your inspection" their manuscripts. This was the beginning of July, so the fair copies of all three works must have been freshly written out and polished by midsummer. At this point, Charlotte proposed to Colburn that the works be published together, even calling them a "M.S. of a work of fiction in 3 vols." She knew that the three-volume format, or the "three-decker," was the easiest to sell, and the tales they had written were each far shorter than three volumes. The three-decker had become popular largely because subscription lending libraries had so much power in dictating what was published. While the bulkiness of the Victorian novel emerged in part due to a widely held idea that novels ought to represent a comprehensive social world, with multiple plots and characters, a form at which Dickens especially excelled, the three-volume structure became standard because it made more money for the lending libraries. Such "libraries," actually lucrative businesses, were so widely patronized that they had a tremendous influence on fiction. They especially liked three-volume novels, since three subscribers could be lent different parts of a novel at once, and pressured publishers into limiting their purchase of novels of other lengths. While Charlotte tried to get around this by presenting the Brontë novels as fit to be published together, Emily must have miscalculated the length of *Wuthering Heights*, which grew to be fit for two volumes, although never for three.

Having no luck with Colburn, the works were "perseveringly obtruded upon various publishers for the space of a year and a half," Charlotte said, their fate repeatedly "an ignominious and abrupt dismissal." At some point Charlotte began going at it alone, with *The Professor* plodding "its weary way around London" on its own. Either because of thriftiness, or because the "chill of despair" at times invaded her heart, Charlotte reused the brown parcel that wrapped the manuscript, just scoring out the address of the publisher who rejected it and writing the new one underneath. By the time it reached Smith, Elder and Co., who would eventually publish all of her novels, the paper cover had the directions of three or four other publishing houses crossed out, which didn't make the new addressee optimistic about its contents.[30]

As the three monitored the comings and goings of these parcels, trailing hopes and disappointments, they watched their father lose his sight to cataracts, a terrible thing for the still-vigorous old man. Advised to try surgery, they found a doctor in Manchester who had become known for his high rate of success with this type of eye operation. Charlotte went there with Patrick in August, and on the day of his surgery she received another rejection of *The Professor*, at their lodgings on Oxford Road, probably forwarded by Emily and Anne from Haworth. Instead of despairing, she did the opposite, immediately starting to write *Jane Eyre*. She must have brought her desk with her to Manchester, well stocked with paper scraps, paper booklets, a board, and pencils. More than any of her other novels, this one surged unfiltered out of her imagination, a spontaneous overflow of passion. While her father recovered, she spent the five weeks in Manchester drafting the first few chapters about the angry, abused orphan.

When Charlotte and Patrick returned to Haworth at the end of September, his sight was slowly coming back and she still had the story streaming out of her. She gave herself up to it just like she had with the Angrian adventures. "I'm just going to write because I cannot help it," she had written years before, but this feeling of helplessness in the face of compulsive creativity could have been written during the early autumn of composing *Jane Eyre*. Once Jane meets Rochester, "on she went," Harriet Martineau tells us, from Charlotte's spoken account, "writing incessantly for three weeks; by which time she had carried her heroine away from Thornfield." If this was literally true, Charlotte wrote seventeen chapters, some three hundred pages, in three weeks. When she was in such a state, she would wake up after a night's sleep, and the "progress of her tale lay clear and bright before her, in distinct vision," Gaskell recounts. She became possessed, the characters and events in the novel more present than the real life happening around her.[31]

About seven months after starting *Jane Eyre*, Charlotte was close to completing it. She began making a fair copy (now at the British Library) of early chapters in March 1847 and polished it off by August. In July, Emily and Anne had finally found some success with their first novels, although it was, at best, a mixed accomplishment. The publisher Thomas Cautley Newby agreed to shepherd their novels into print, in the three-decker format, with *Wuthering Heights* taking up the first two volumes, *Agnes Grey* the last. Yet they again had to pay out of their own pockets: the hefty sum of fifty pounds, more than a year's salary at one of their previous teaching jobs. Newby promised to repay them once enough copies were sold, but he never did, even though they sold well enough to earn back their money. Both Emily and Anne died without realizing any profits from their novels. Charlotte, meanwhile, couldn't find anyone to take *The Professor* on any terms whatsoever. She did receive an encouraging rejection from Smith, Elder and Co.; they requested she send the manuscript of any future novel she might write. This she could do easily enough, since *Jane Eyre* was so close to completion. She put *Jane Eyre* on that train in August. In a couple of weeks they had accepted it and offered to pay her one hundred pounds for the copyright, a common way at the time of paying authors, although it had the drawback of preventing Charlotte from receiving royalties.[32]

The ease of *Jane Eyre*'s composition meant she didn't need to use a tool she would later employ on her manuscripts: scissors, kept in either the desk box or the workbox. With other novels, including *The Professor* when she went back to revise it, she practiced some literal cutting and pasting, as can be seen on the manuscripts themselves. She would snip out, with great care and craft, part of a page (written on one side only), then paste on another partial sheet of paper, sometimes blank and other times with new text. In a couple of cases, she tore the page rather than using scissors, as if with urgency or emotion. This paper craft descended directly from the handmade books of her childhood, not to mention other crafts—needlework and quilling on that tea caddy for Ellen. Not only did she master storytelling, but the manuscript as a tangible entity also needed her skills: its paper and ink, its cutting, pasting, and wrapping.[33]

Charlotte was lucky with her publishers, but her sisters, especially Anne, were not. Smith, Elder and Co. rushed Charlotte's book into print, while Newby let Anne's and Emily's novels languish, not printing them until a couple of months after *Jane Eyre* appeared, and probably only doing so because of the runaway success of this other work by a "Bell brother." In plum bindings, with cheap paper, and with advertisements for other books bound at the very beginning titled "New works by popular authors in the press and published by Mr. T.C. Newby," the three volumes abounded with errors and affronts to the authors. Probably the most galling for Anne was that the title page of the first volume read "Wuthering Heights. A Novel by Ellis Bell, in three volumes," not even mentioning *Agnes Grey*, which filled the third volume. Yet Anne didn't let this discourage her; she even used Newby again for her second novel, despite his shabby treatment of them. While Charlotte blazed through *Jane Eyre*, Anne had begun working on *The Tenant of Wildfell Hall*, probably starting in early 1847. Showing heavy influences from *Wuthering Heights* just as *Jane Eyre* did, *Tenant* didn't, however, follow the lead of Emily's novel; rather, Anne's new novel criticized its central principles, turning the passionate, handsome man, who could have been a Heathcliff, into a drunken, abusive husband.

Jane Eyre also received some revision in *Tenant*, the two novels probably under discussion at the same time during those evening colloquies. Anne's heroine also finds herself in a country mansion with a mysterious man, like Jane with Rochester, and she must flee and find her way. But Anne sucked all the romanticism out of the situation, all the depth out of the shadowy man, presenting the cold, hard facts of a woman in an abusive relationship during a time when the laws overwhelmingly favored the husband.[34]

Another influence on Anne's novel was Branwell, who provided a model for the drunken dissolution of Arthur Huntingdon. Some have argued that Emily and Charlotte drew on Branwell's brokenhearted despair for their depictions of men in love, such as Heathcliff and Rochester. While they may have woven some of his characteristics into their heroes, the influence could have been only partial and indirect. Branwell appeared pathetic to his sisters, as Charlotte makes clear in letters to Ellen that are full of resentment for his lack of restraint and his emotional and financial drain on the family. His hopeless mental state and drunkenness were nothing like the strong-willed determination of Heathcliff and Rochester, Byronic types that Emily and Charlotte had brought into their fiction since they were young girls.

Emily may also have been bringing a new novel to these nocturnal sessions. No draft of a second novel exists, but many have speculated that after Emily's death Charlotte destroyed whatever beginning Emily had made. Charlotte's belief that *Wuthering Heights* had been too shocking, coupled with her wish to protect her sister's reputation, all support the argument that she burned work she felt was disturbing to notions of Victorian propriety. A letter and an envelope from Newby found in Emily's desk go a long way toward proving the existence of a partial draft of a second novel. Among reviews of *Wuthering Heights* clipped from papers, receipts for clothing from Brussels merchants, a program for a concert in Brussels, and some Belgian coins—evidence that Emily may have taken this desk to Europe—the note and envelope, addressed to Ellis Bell and with a blob of red sealing wax, have generated much speculation. Dated February 15, 1848, the message refers to a second novel by Ellis then in progress. While it has been suggested that this referred to Anne's *Tenant*, and that Newby was confusing Acton with Ellis, something he was known to do, it could also have been accurately addressed to Emily.[35]

If Emily had been drafting a new work, its pages of minuscule script would probably have been kept in her writing desk. There is something ghostly about this absence, a haunting that lingers around this box, a little like the strange bed in *Wuthering Heights* mentioned already. In that "large oak case," the dead Catherine's presence imbues her books, with their scribbled marginalia and musty smell. Her name carved in the wood itself is like an autograph on a manuscript, carrying a fragment of selfhood. Emily can also be felt in her desk box: in the hand-ruled pages found there, probably to guide the fair copies of her manuscripts; the blotting paper with ink stains; pieces of chalk browned with age; fragments of lace; an ivory seal; and an empty cardboard box that Emily marked with her initials: EJB, once containing pen nibs made by Caldwell, Lloyd, and Co., an Edinburgh publisher and stationer.

For a Brontë enthusiast, each leftover in these desks, no matter how enigmatic and insignificant, seems to shine out with meaning. Another wisp of paper in Emily's desk illustrates the charmed life of these remnants, the sense that they hold stories. A comic adhesive wafer stuck to a fragment of envelope pictures a man drowning, with the caption "High-water at the Isle of Man and *Bury*-Head." Emily added another caption in ink: "Likewise at Bolton Bridge on Thursday June 20th 1844." All four siblings were home on this Thursday, and they may have been playing a word game called High Water at Bolton Bridge, which was about thirteen miles from Haworth. Or perhaps someone fell into the River Wharfe and "buried" her or his head briefly, which struck Emily as humorous and worth preserving? It is tempting to imagine that this scrap could somehow be related to the lost manuscript of a second novel, a temptation that takes one onto the path of wild speculation, a trail many Brontë lovers (including me) feel compelled, at some point, to trod.[36]

"Reading" the contents of Emily's desk as evidence of any sort is complicated by the fact that Charlotte had it for years after Emily's death, and that it passed through numerous hands after Charlotte's death. Who knows what sort of fussing Charlotte did with the contents of the box, especially given her controlling nature? Some of the items stored there actually belonged to Charlotte herself: a letter to her from a Belgian friend; an empty envelope, on which she inscribed, "Diploma given to me by Monsieur Heger, Dec 29—1843." Yet, after all, this mingling of objects somehow suited the situation of these women, whose novels partook of a similar type of mingling of ideas and experience. Stashing someone else's personal effects in one's desk pulled them closer to one's body and self. "I find I have stolen a pencil-case of yours," Charlotte once wrote Ellen, after a visit. "I put it away with my pen in my little box." Going through someone else's desk could be irritating to the desk's owner, but it could also be seen as an act of love, as Charlotte depicts in *Villette* when the professor regularly rifles the contents of Lucy Snowe's desk, leaving behind the scent of his cigar smoke as evidence, a gesture of nosy affection.[37]

One of the most eloquent testaments to the effect on Charlotte of her three siblings' deaths, which happened within eight months, is the chaos of her manuscript for *Shirley*. Charlotte began it around the start of 1848 and probably discussed it with her sisters in the evenings along with *Tenant* and, perhaps, Emily's second novel. She finished the fair copy of the first volume at the start of September 1848, and it has a moderately tidy appearance. She started the second volume and had mostly finished it when Branwell and then Emily died. "I try to write now and then," Charlotte wrote her publishers about four months after Emily's death. "The effort was a hard one at first. It renewed the terrible loss of last December strangely—worse than useless did it seem to attempt to write what there no longer lived an 'Ellis Bell' to read." A couple of months after Anne's death, she picked up the manuscript again, beginning with the chapter called "The Valley of the Shadow of Death." The parts of the "clean copy" written after Anne died show her usually neat handwriting uneven and confused. Alterations and deletions multiply, with cut-away and pasted-in passages breaking up many leaves. A text of grief, it makes material a sorrowful mind.[38]

CHAPTER SEVEN

Death Made Material

Long neglect has worn away
Half the sweet enchanting smile
Time has turned the bloom to grey
Mould and damp the face defile

But that lock of silky hair
Still beneath the picture twined
Tells what once those features were
Paints their image on the mind.

—EMILY BRONTË, UNTITLED POEM

Iғ ᴛʜᴇ ʙʀᴏɴᴛ̈ᴇs' things feel haunted in some way, like Emily's desk and its contents, then the amethyst bracelet on the previous page made from the entwined hair of Emily and Anne is positively ghost-ridden. Over time the colors have faded, the strands grown stiff and brittle. Charlotte may have asked Emily and Anne for the locks as a gesture of sisterly affection. Or, the tresses were cut from one or both of their corpses, an ordinary step in preparing the dead for burial in an era when mourning jewelry with hair became part of the grieving process. Charlotte must have either mailed the hair to a jeweler or "hairworker" (a title for makers of hair jewelry) or brought it to her in person. Then she probably wore it, carrying on her body a physical link to her sisters, continuing to touch them wherever they were.[1]

Illness had started in the parsonage earlier in the year of 1848. Branwell rallied for a time after his forced exile from the woman he loved had led him to drink heavily, applying for jobs on newly opened rail lines and returning to writing poetry, even starting a novel. Then Mr. Robinson died in May 1846. At first Branwell was elated: now he could be with his beloved, who would be free to marry him after a period of mourning. But Mrs. Robinson had higher ambitions than the former tutor of her children, now unemployed, penniless, and steadily becoming a drunk. She devised various stratagems to keep him away but at the same time to pacify him so he wouldn't cause a scandal. She sent her servants to him with excuses and often even with money. Branwell became emotionally overwrought. He stopped eating and sleeping for days, "too wretched to live," he exclaimed. When the fact that he would never be with her sunk in—she soon married a wealthy relative—he turned drinking-himself-to-ruin into a full-time job. He only slowed when he ran out of money. While his sisters busied themselves with bringing out their poems and completing their novels, he was killing himself. As he undermined his health and his sanity, suffered fainting fits, delirium tremens, and hallucinations, he caused dangerous accidents, such as one night when he set his bed on fire. Anne, passing his room at the right moment and seeing the fire, rushed in and tried to put it out. Not succeeding, she fetched Emily, who hauled him out of bed and into a corner, dragged the bedclothes into the middle of the room, and doused them with water from the kitchen (a mishap possibly reworked for *Jane Eyre*, with Emily becoming Jane, and Branwell, Rochester). In his last surviving letter, Branwell begged his friend John Brown to oblige him by contriving "to get me Five pence worth of Gin in proper measure."[2]

At some point in 1848, Branwell contracted tuberculosis, which made quick work of his weakened constitution. His death caught everyone by surprise. At the very end, he seemed to repent of his "godless" ways, Charlotte felt, "praying softly in his dying moment." After the terrible death struggle, in which he flinched and jerked so violently he was almost on his feet, he fell back into his father's arms, and his face took on a "marble calm." He died on Sunday morning, September 24, 1848, just thirty-one years old. "I felt as I had never felt before that there was peace of forgiveness for him in Heaven," Charlotte found, looking upon his countenance. Charlotte hardly regretted his death, since he was now "at rest," but Patrick was inconsolable, calling out, "My son! My son!"[3]

Rather surprisingly, given that he didn't die in a particularly holy way, Charlotte interpreted Branwell's demise as a "good death," an idea that Protestant evangelicals like the Brontës had borrowed from Catholic tradition, and one that had become widespread since evangelical revivals in the late eighteenth century. If God called away the chosen one to a more peaceful place—a paradise full of rewards—then death should be seen as a happy event. Emily put such ideas into the head of the servant Nelly Dean in *Wuthering Heights*, an average Victorian evangelical and believer in the "goodness" of death. Catherine Earnshaw died "as quietly as a lamb!" Nelly exclaims. "She drew a sigh, and stretched herself, like a child reviving, and sinking again to sleep."

The heavenly realm could even be seen on the countenance of one going there, or having recently arrived there, many believed. Nelly finds in Catherine's corpse "perfect peace," an "untroubled image of divine rest . . . a repose that neither earth nor hell can break." Gazing on the dead body leads her to "feel an assurance of the endless and shadowless hereafter." A radiance or holy light emanated from the faces of the dying and came directly, many were convinced, from the place of light where the dead had gone. Deathbed scenes with such signs became favorite devices of Victorian novelists, especially Dickens, whose little Paul Dombey, in *Dombey and Son*, dies illuminated by a "golden light," which seems at first to come streaming through the window, but then shines on his head from the face of his mother,

who is already in heaven. The remains of Little Nell in *The Old Curiosity Shop* appear "fresh from the hand of god," and when children die
in *Oliver Twist* the cares of a cruel world pass off the face and "leave
heaven's surface clear." To catch such evidence of grace, families
watched at the side of their dying, kept diaries that detailed final days
and moments, and listened for last words of wisdom. Some of these
accounts were published, such as the celebrated *Clear Shining Light*, a
diary of Sophia Leakey's death from tuberculosis in 1858, written by
her sisters. "Surprise and rapture" suffused her face just before death,
and she exclaimed, "Yes, it is heaven . . . it is lovely, glorious!"[4]

Postmortem art thrived. In the corpse, the faithful found consolation
that a vitality still flickered somewhere, evidence that needed fixing,
copying. The ancient practice of recording the deceased's appearance
in drawings, paintings, or death masks went through a renaissance in
the nineteenth century. Branwell sketched his aunt's head just after her
death, with her cap neat and her face at rest. The Brontës had no death
(or life) masks made of themselves, but other authors of the time had
their features documented after their deaths, to be fashioned into masks
or busts. When Dickens died on June 9, 1870, his daughter Katey
watched his face smooth and then radiate a "beauty and pathos." The
artists John Everett Millais and Thomas Woolner traveled out to Dickens's estate together the next morning. Millais made a pencil sketch of
the still features; Woolner spread an oily mixture over the face, then
covered it in a thin layer of soft plaster, which conformed to all the
crevices and grooves that a worried life had written there. When the
cast had dried, he lifted it off and used it to shape a bust. Ordinary Victorians had masks made of their loved ones too, then hung them on the
wall of a bedroom or parlor, or displayed them in boxes with glass tops.
Locks of hair had a special status as souvenirs, since they were "the
very things themselves," as Elizabeth Gaskell puts it in a story about

a woman who looks through miniatures of the dead but finds touching their hair more poignant because it is "a part of some beloved body which she might never touch and caress again, but which lay beneath the turf, all faded and disfigured, except, perhaps, the very hair, from which the lock she held had been dissevered."[5]

Emily died a few months after Branwell—possibly catching his consumption—and just a year after the publication of *Wuthering Heights*. Her death looked nothing like her character Catherine Earnshaw's "escape into that glorious world." It started in October 1848, with the east wind "blowing wild and keen over our cold hills," and with Emily plagued by a persistent cough and an obstinate pain in her chest. "She looks very, very thin and pale," Charlotte fretted to Ellen. Emily irritably refused sympathy or even any mention of her illness. She continued all of her daily work, spent no extra time in bed, and was fully resolved to deal unflinchingly with her own suffering. She worsened as autumn grew on, becoming feverish and short of breath. Charlotte demanded repeatedly that Emily see the local physician, but this only made Emily angry. She wouldn't let any "poisoning doctor" come near her. Charlotte and Anne often paused in their sewing or writing to listen to Emily's step fail as she climbed the staircase, to hear her labored breath forcing frequent pauses. They couldn't discuss it in her presence, let alone assist her; her usual wall of reserve was now strengthened by stoicism. Becoming more "piteously wasted," as the days went by, she struggled to draw breath. Charlotte "incurred her displeasure" by again urging the necessity of calling in a doctor, but Emily, intractable, insisted that "Nature shall be left to take her own course."[6]

By the end of November, any exertion caused her breathing to become a rapid pant. "Day by day," Charlotte later said of this dark period, "when I saw with what a front she met suffering, I looked on her with an anguish of wonder and love." Or, put another way, "on herself she had no pity." In her desperation, Charlotte wrote to a Dr. Epps, trying to describe Emily's illness in order to receive advice, but the effort proved difficult because Emily would not explain her symptoms. Charlotte, not able to accept how close Emily was to death, retained a fragile hope that she would finally rally. Only later did Charlotte see Emily's death as of a piece with her life: "Never in her life had she lingered over any task that lay before her, and she did not linger now . . . she made haste to leave us." Emily persisted, on the evening before she died, in the nightly ritual of feeding Keeper and Flossy herself, but she staggered on the uneven flagging of the floor and fell against the passage wall.[7]

On the morning of her death, Emily got up and dressed herself, with "the rattle in her throat" and "dying all the while." Attempting to untangle her hair, she dropped her bone comb in the fire. She watched it burn, too weak to retrieve it. A servant, Martha Brown, came into the room and pulled it out, a few of its teeth having been consumed by the fire. Emily then went downstairs and attempted to sew while Charlotte, who had no inkling Emily would die that day, sat writing to Ellen that "moments so dark as these I have never known." As noon came on, a terrible change approached. Charlotte finally understood what was imminent when, after a long hunt on the moors for a spray of heather, she presented the flower, Emily's favorite, to her, but Emily no longer recognized it. Collapsing on the black, horsehair-stuffed sofa in the parlor, Emily whispered to Charlotte, in between gasps, "If you will send for a doctor, I will see him now." Dr. Wheelhouse was called in, but it was no use. After a "short, hard conflict," Emily, aged thirty, was "torn from conscious, panting, reluctant." She died at two o'clock on December 19, of tuberculosis.[8]

William Wood constructed her coffin, recording in his account book that it was just five feet, seven inches long and sixteen inches broad—the smallest he had made for an adult, he claimed. The family purchased white gloves for funeral attendees, some of whom kept them as mementos. Buried underneath the church floor, Emily no longer felt "the hard frost and keen wind," Charlotte thought, finding some comfort. Black-edged memorial cards were ordered from Joseph Fox—a "confectioner," the cards say—who dropped a year from her age and a diaeresis from her name: "In Memory of Emily Jane Bronte, who died December XIX, MDCCCXLVII, Aged Twenty-Nine Years."[9]

The day after the funeral, Charlotte wrote to Ellen on mourning stationery, with a black seal, her handwriting rough with emotional distress and desolation: "There is no Emily in Time or on Earth now . . . She has died in a time of promise—we saw her torn from life in its prime." A postscript scribbled at the top of the letter, an afterthought written just as she was sealing it up, pleads with raw emotion: "Try to come—I never so much needed the consolation of a friend's presence." In other letters she rang the changes on this belief that Emily was "torn": "from us in the fullness of our attachment, rooted up in the prime of her own days in the promise of her powers . . . like a tree in full bearing—struck at the root." She asked with great bitterness, in another letter, "And where is she now? Out of my reach—out of my world, torn from me."[10]

When Charlotte looked at Emily's face in death, did she believe in an afterlife written there? Her question about Emily's posthumous location—"And where is she now?"—implies that she had doubts. In fact, Charlotte's words held a touch of heresy. Heaven, as pictured by sermons and consolation letters of the time, contained loved ones waiting for those still down below, in a place so familiar it varied little from a middle-class suburb. The dead maintained an active existence—growing, continuing good works in their physical selves, and watching over the living. Charlotte wrote such letters herself, at times able to imagine such a place. "Certainly she is happy where she is gone," Charlotte consoled Ellen when Ellen's sister Sarah died, using characteristic language of the day, "far happier than she was here—when the first days of mourning are past you will see that you have reason rather to rejoice at her removal." Charlotte's publisher William Smith Williams wrote to her of Emily's state of existence just after her death as pure and exalted. She looked down with "heavenly serenity" at those who mourned her, he wanted Charlotte to believe. Patrick often aired such ideas in letters, such as one to the mother of a little girl who "closed her eyes, on time, and open'd them in eternity, I doubt not in an Eternity of glory and bliss." When his own wife died, her "soul took its flight to the mansions of glory," he told a friend.[11]

We don't have Anne's reaction to her siblings' deaths, but she was the most devout of the Brontë children and believed in the doctrine of universal salvation—that everyone would be elevated eventually to heaven, even if some had to spend a little time in purgatorial fires. She grew ill not long after Emily's death, with the same symptoms, but was as patient and tractable with doctors and their remedies as Emily was unyielding. She drank loads of cod-liver oil and carbonate of iron, which made her nauseous, then she agreed to be treated by hydropathy (dousing in cold water) and with Godbold's Vegetable Balsam. She wore the cork innersoles that Ellen sent, to keep off the cold of the parsonage's flagstone floors. By March, Anne was clearly dying. Insisting on traveling to the seaside in May, she convinced Charlotte and Ellen Nussey to take her to Scarborough. Here her life rapidly ebbed. On the day she died, she asked if they might be able to get home if they started right away. But there was no possibility of reaching Haworth in time. She died in Scarborough, on May 28, 1849, aged twenty-eight. And that is where Charlotte buried her, making her the only family member not interred in the vaults under the floors of the Haworth church.

Even more than with Branwell's death, Anne's affirmed Charlotte's sometimes troubled faith in an afterlife. Charlotte shared the view, common among friends and family, that Anne was a sort of saint going to paradise. Anne sank "resigned—trusting in God . . . deeply assured that a better existence lay before her." Anne's quiet, Christian demise struck Charlotte as the opposite of Emily's stern end, and she even developed a narrative about how Anne, from childhood, seemed always prepared for an early death, whereas Emily turned "her dying eyes reluctantly from the pleasant sun." Ellen's description of Anne's dying moments made concrete her saintliness and closeness to God: Anne "without a sigh passed from the temporal to the Eternal. So still, so hallowed, were her last hours and moments it was more like a translation than a death." [12]

Unlike Anne's, Emily's religious beliefs will always remain a mystery. Perhaps she constructed her own faith out of the philosophy and spiritual thought picked up in her reading. A small clue might be found in Emily's reaction to Mary Taylor, Charlotte's freethinking friend. Mary, on a visit to Haworth, mentioned that someone had asked about her religion and she had replied tartly, "That is between God and me." When Emily, lying on the hearthrug, heard this, she exclaimed, "That's right." [13]

Wuthering Heights is full of characters who believe in different kinds of postmortem lives, from Nelly's conventional heaven to Catherine's dream about being kicked out of heaven and landing, to her delight, on the paradise of the earthly moors. Country folk report seeing the ghosts of Catherine and Heathcliff. A young shepherd claims his sheep refuse to be guided because the dead lovers flit across the road. Others "swear on the Bible" that Heathcliff "*walks.*" Catherine promises Heathcliff that "they may bury me twelve feet deep, and throw the church down over me; but I won't rest till you are with me—I never will!" He believes her, having always had a "strong faith in ghosts."

The strangest notion about death in the novel gives the corpse itself a value, as if in the afterlife the body still mattered. When Heathcliff slips into Catherine's room to see her body, he finds the curl of Linton's light hair in the locket around her neck. He throws it to the floor, replacing it with a hank from his own black head. Many who sent tokens down into the grave with a loved one imagined a sort of life down there, as if the dead might be able to see or care about such things. John Callcott Horsley, a popular Victorian painter, wrote in his diary about a little red-velvet bag he hung around his wife Elvira's neck after her death in 1852. It contained locks of his and all their children's hair, which she had cut herself when she found out she was dying, labeling each with the person's name and the date it was snipped. Like Horsley and his family, both Edgar Linton and Heathcliff want a synecdochic fragment of their bodies to persevere in the place where Catherine is going. They dearly hope that their hair will act as tenuous filaments stretching across the permeable boundary between life and death.[14]

Letters and manuscripts might have meaning to the dead. Horsley also included letters to his wife in a pine box settled next to her body, and the poet John Keats asked to be buried with letters from Fanny Brawne, the woman he had hoped to marry. He received these letters from her when he was dying, but he was too distraught to open them, so they went into his coffin sealed and unread, along with a lock of her hair and a purse made by his sister. In another gesture of adding pages to a coffin, the Victorian poet and painter Dante Gabriel Rossetti buried the only copy of his recently written verse with his young wife, Elizabeth Siddal, who had committed suicide. An act of atonement for the part he felt he played in her death, the interment of his notebook turned out to be only temporary. When he wanted to publish the poems years later, he had her coffin opened and the sodden, wormy book pried away from her body. Sometimes texts were added to coffins for practical reasons.

A Victorian woman had promised that when her close friend died she would bury with her letters from a son who had predeceased her. But the woman forgot, when this friend indeed died, to include the letters in her grave. Luckily, a local postman died soon afterward, and the woman buried the letters with him, assuming that he would deliver the letters to her friend in his next existence.[15]

Many still believed in grave goods—belongings included with the corpse in case they might be needed on the other side—a mixture of early Christian and even earlier pagan ideas that still lingered. Pennies, combs, jewelry, and medicine bottles were nestled next to bodies. Confusions about what happened to the body in the afterlife—whether the soul stayed in the grave with the body until judgment day, for instance, or was judged right at death and then reunited in heaven with the body—led many to feel that the dead body must be as whole as possible upon burial. The ancient custom of holding onto lost teeth and including them with one's corpse, to have a full set after death, survived well into the mid-nineteenth century. Violent protests against human dissection grew, in part, out of this thinking that the body would be raised to heaven.[16]

Catherine's corpse, buried with his hair in her locket, has, for Heathcliff, a secret life on which he dwells longingly. Finally needing to press his flesh against hers, he digs up her grave, not once but twice. When her husband, Edgar Linton, dies and his grave next to Catherine is being dug, Heathcliff gets the sexton to remove earth off of her coffin lid so he can open it. Preserved in the peaty soil, her face is yet hers, and Heathcliff thinks he'll stay there with her for good. The sexton has "hard work" to stir him, but tells him her face would "change if the air blew on it." So, instead, Heathcliff strikes one side of the coffin loose and bribes the sexton "to pull it away, when I am laid there, and slide mine out too . . . by the time Linton gets to us, he'll not know which is which!" His yearning for Catherine even after her death includes her body; he wants to find her "resting her darling head on the same pillow as she did when a child," and it doesn't matter if his heart is "stopped and my cheek frozen against hers." What he unearths are not so much "remains" as Catherine herself, and what he desires most is not that their spirits meet in heaven, as a good evangelical would, but that their bodies dissolve into each other, in the earth.

Finding a measure of eroticism in bodies—or parts of bodies—joined in the grave wasn't new to the Victorians. The seventeenth-century poet John Donne, for instance, wrote two poems about corpses wearing their lovers' hair as bracelets, emblems of the two being, at last, together. In "The Relic," the speaker fears that a gravedigger will disturb the "bracelet of bright hair about the bone" that might allow the lovers to "meet at this grave, and make a little stay." Victorians also saw the appeal of the grave as a kind of marriage bed. In Victorian poet Alfred Tennyson's 1842 "Locksley Hall" (which Emily knew well, as she did Donne's poems) the speaker thinks it "Better thou wert dead before me . . . Better thou and I were lying, hidden from the heart's disgrace, / Roll'd in one another's arms, and silent in a last embrace." The Victorian writer Algernon Charles Swinburne says in a poem that he (or an alter ego) wishes he were dead with his lover today, "Lost sight of, hidden away out of sight, / Clasped and clothed in the cloven clay . . . Made one with death, filled full of the night."[17]

Emily, alert to intensities of longing, created Heathcliff with these desires in mind. He pines for his body to meet Catherine's in the grave and make just such a little stay. But she also has a presence above ground, he believes, which draws so near that he can't sleep or eat from yearning for her. When he tries to sleep in her box bed in order to find her, he is "beaten out of" it, for the moment he closes his eyes, she is "either outside the window, or sliding back the panels, or entering the room . . . and I must open my lids to see." He finds her in all things, especially those everyday objects around the house, as if her spirit has infused ordinary matter. "I cannot look down to this floor, but her features are shaped on the flag!" Inanimate things seem to come alive, to gain a certain strangeness, because they feed on an afterlife. There is not only the fir branch knocking on the window that becomes Catherine's girlish hand, but also the windows that "reflected a score of glittering moons" and two old balls in a cupboard, one marked "C" and the other "H," with the bran having fallen out of the latter. Through such things, Catherine begins drawing Heathcliff into death, which he comes to believe is a place just a few feet away. He has to remind himself to breathe, his heart to beat, he is so devoured by anticipation. This desire is fatal: he quickens to death. His corpse, which Nelly finds in Catherine's box bed, works as a sort of parody of the "good" death, on his face a "frightful, life-like gaze of exultation" and a sneer on his lips. The servant Joseph interprets this as proof that the devil has made off with his soul.

This belief that an afterlife shimmered through objects (and animals) was another holdover from ancient folk customs. When death approached, furniture and other possessions might respond. Clocks stopped at the moment of their owner's death, and mirrors needed to be covered in case evil spirits came to reside in the reflected image. Things nearby had to be manipulated so that all would go well: windows and doors would be left open so that the spirit or soul could easily slip out. Black hangings and clothing protected the living from evil forces let loose by death's presence. Related worries haunt Catherine Earnshaw when her mind is weakened by illness at the end of her life, such as her confusion at seeing her face in a mirror, which she takes as her double, traditionally a sign of one's imminent death. Finding pigeon feathers as she picks apart her pillow, she remembers that they prevent an easy death, according to tradition. "No wonder I couldn't die!" Among these charmed tokens—clocks, mirrors, feathers—the hair of the dead held a special place. Enlivened by the spirit world too, the hair of others worn on the body strengthened the connection between the living and the dead.[18]

Part of the body yet easy to separate from it, hair retained its luster long after the rest of the person decayed. Portable, with a shine like certain gems or metals, hair moved easily from being an ornamental feature of the body to being an ornament worn by others. By the 1840s, hair jewelry had become so fashionable that advertisements for hair artisans, designers, and hairworkers ran in newspapers, and magazines printed a sea of articles on the minute particulars of the fad. The London jeweler Antoni Forrer, a well-known professional hairworker in the 1840s, had fifty workers fully employed at his Regent Street store. At the Great Exhibition, around eleven displays of the art garnered glowing reviews, including pictures embroidered in hair of Queen Victoria, the Prince of Wales, and the Hamburgh Exchange. A tall vase "composed entirely of human hair" and a "horn filled with artificial flowers in human hair, representing the horn of plenty," were other impressive exhibits. Hairwork kept women's hands busy at home, another one of those many domestic arts, like needlework, quilling, shellwork, and taxidermy. Fashion magazines discussed the homecraft of hairworking and included jewelry patterns, instructions, and tips. Hair wreaths, set into shadow boxes or under glass domes, also had their day, as did the use of hair in drawing and painting. One industrious woman copied a Rembrandt using only hair in a cross-stitch. Charlotte brought the device of a "cambric handkerchief with a coronet wrought upon it in black hair" into more than one early story, a means of signaling that the male owner has a secret lover who embroidered it with her own hair.[19]

The hairwork process—involving boiling the hair to clean it, then weaving it on specially designed round tables (which could be mail ordered) with a series of weights that were attached to the strands of hair—was described in instructional manuals, such as Mark Campbell's popular 1865 *Self-Instructor in the Art of Hair Work*. The tight weave of the bracelet with Anne's and Emily's hair, pictured at the start of this chapter, was likely achieved this way, although in this case probably by a professional, who then attached the ends of the hair to the metal. A bracelet made of Anne's hair, from locks given to Ellen Nussey by Charlotte after Anne's death, has a slightly different weave, and Ellen may have made it herself. By the time Ellen died, she had at least three hair bracelets, four hair brooches, a hair ring, and a couple of loose locks, much of it hair from the Brontë family.[20]

A coil of hair stowed in the case at the back of a watch was an easy *aide-mémoire*. Sergeant Troy, in Thomas Hardy's *Far from the Madding Crowd*, tucks away Fanny Robin's golden plait, then marries Bathsheba Everdene. She witnesses, with much misgiving and jealousy, Troy steal a look at the forbidden cutting in his gold timepiece. Jewelers of this time added compartments to jewelry, in the front or back of a ring or brooch, for instance, to hide hair. The locket containing hair, a staple in the Brontës' writing, also usually represented stormy love. A cross with gems, "the centre stone of which was a locket enclosing a ringlet of dark-brown hair," is worn by a beautiful lady in an early story by Charlotte, to profess her love for a duke who, though married to someone else, gave her his hair. In a poem by Emily, someone's dual loves are encased in a "locket fair / Where rival curls of silken hair / Sable and brown revealed to me / A tale of doubtful constancy." Another locket tells the same tale, in *Wuthering Heights*, when the servant Nelly Dean finds Edgar Linton's wisp of light hair on the floor where Catherine's body is laid out. She opens the locket and entwines it with Heathcliff's black curl. The Brontës themselves possessed a number of jewelry pieces with compartments that snapped open, such as a tiny locket with one glass side, making visible an anonymous circle of hair. Simple jewelry like this was increasingly mass-produced by the end of the 1850s, becoming affordable to most Victorians, who individualized the ornament by adding a curl. A brooch of Charlotte's containing Anne's hair has this inexpensive, standardized quality.[21]

Forming tendrils of endearment among the living, the hair in the lovers' lockets and the tress Charlotte begged from Ellen had nothing to do with death. In truth, the amethyst bracelet pictured at the head of this chapter doesn't have the hallmarks of a mourning piece. Mourning jewelry is usually enameled in black or fashioned of black material such as jet, and often has engravings like epitaphs, such as a gold brooch at the Victoria and Albert Museum that has two interleaved curls of different colors and textures and is inscribed, "Sir Marc Isambard Brunel, Died Decr 1849. Aged 80. Sophia Brunel, Died Jany 1855, Aged 79." Symbols of death, like weeping willows or women in classical robes grieving over urns or tombstones, also appeared on mourning pieces, with parts of the scene—the willow branches or clouds in the sky— sometimes made of tiny cuttings of hair. The elderly ladies in Elizabeth Gaskell's *Cranford*, for instance, prove the hold on them of their dead friends and relatives by their many brooches decorated "with mausoleums and weeping-willows mostly executed in hair." Such jewels seemed themselves like little tombs, the hair standing in for the corpse. When discovered today at an antique shop, a piece of anonymous hair jewelry can feel like an unmarked, but still visible, grave. Whose bodily shred lies here? Who treasured it enough to encase it?[22]

In corners of the Brontë archives, hair marking all sorts of relationships can be found—close to fifty curls or hairwork associated with the family are deposited in various libraries and museums in Europe and the United States. One especially strange, poignant work created initially out of a sense of devotion to the living became, all too soon, a collection of fragments of the dead. Attached to a dark velvet–covered backdrop are seven snippets of hair, some taped and others sewn, each labeled by hand with the name of a member of the Brontë family and the date it was cut (see color photograph). Reputedly gathered by Sarah Garrs, one of the Brontës' nursemaids, when she left their employ, all the locks are dated 1824, except Patrick's. Dated 1860, his hair was probably sent to Garrs when they were in touch toward the end of his life. The cuttings represent all of the family members—including their sister Maria and their mother—but one. The hair of their sister Elizabeth seems never to have been collected, for reasons unknown.[23]

The intimacy of hair worn, especially when exposed and brushing the skin of the wearer, is missing in this framed and glassed-in group on the wall. This desire for a physical connection with the dead has its roots in the wearing of saints' hair in amulets—traveling reliquaries common during the Middle Ages. There was little need to visit relics in a sacred place when one could find the miracles, health, or good luck thought to emanate from them so readily at hand. The sapphire amulet Charlemagne gave his wife in the ninth century, one of the earliest and celebrated of such talismans, held, it was believed, the Virgin Mary's hair and fragments of the cross on which Jesus was crucified. Even long after the Reformation reached Britain in the 1530s and many of the saints' relics were destroyed, the practice still could be found, in modified form. For instance, Royalists, believing Charles I had a divine right to rule and had been martyred, wore rings containing his hair after he was beheaded in 1649. Some of the snippets had been dipped in pools of his blood from the scaffold. For Protestant Victorians, the hair of a loved one, substituted for relics of the saints or royals, connected them to heaven, with its blessing of immortality.[24]

Yet a dash of paganism, persisting into the nineteenth century, also added magic to hair's religious aura. Special materials or gems had protective qualities, according to ideas stretching back to antiquity, and wearing them guarded against hard luck such as illness, slander, and the "evil eye." Rings with "toadstones" (believed to be from the head of a toad, but actually the fossilized tooth of a now extinct fish) warded off poison and kidney disease, for example, and rubies aided in holding onto land and status. Since a caul—the membrane still in place around an infant at birth—was believed to protect the possessor from drowning, it was sometimes worn in jewelry, as with an early nineteenth-century pendant at the British Museum containing both braided hair and a caul.[25]

Victorian hair jewelry radiated similar powers for many, carrying the foundational safeguard of love, often so strong it could outlast the grave. Some thought hair had an animal magnetism, an invisible fluid permeating the world and allowing bodies and objects to interact even when far apart. Hair could draw the absent donor's "fluid" or presence toward the possessor of the curl, creating a link between the two beings. In an early story, Charlotte has "two locks of soft, curly hair, shining like burnished gold," magically lead her character out of the "land of the grave" and back to where he most yearns to be: with the two young princes who gave him the hair. In another story, a coffin is opened, a lock of hair is cut from the corpse, and "with magic ceremonies," which involve throwing it into a fire, it is formed into "a little locket or brooch in which a small portion of hair appeared under a very rich diamond." This talisman protects the son of the dead man from all misfortune: the loving hand of the father hovers around his strands of hair. In *Villette*, Paulina calls the locket she wears containing the hair of her father and husband intertwined an "amulet," which she believes will " 'keep you two always friends. You can never quarrel so long as I wear this.' "[26]

Strewn liberally across novel plots of the day, hairwork meant all sorts of things, like in Elizabeth Gaskell's *Mary Barton* when the dying prostitute Esther is redeemed after she kisses a locket containing her dead daughter's hair just before she herself expires. Men's (and sometimes women's) watch fobs made of hair became so ubiquitous they marked middle-class respectability, such as the "hair guard" Bradley Headstone in Dickens's *Our Mutual Friend* wears, a means for this working-class man to establish his middle-class credibility. Helen, the heroine of Anne's *Tenant of Wildfell Hall*, has a small gold watch with a "hair chain," a conventional touch establishing her steady character, leading the reader to trust her despite her status as a runaway wife. Contrarily and a little scandalously, Charlotte writes in "Caroline Vernon" of an illicit love affair made material by the man going to the theater wearing a "watchguard" composed of his lover's "long streaming tress," "the black braid across his chest," prominently displayed for all to see. Romantic intrigue blossoms through other hair jewelry, like Edward Ferrars's ring in Jane Austen's *Sense and Sensibility* "with a plait of hair in the center." Edward claims it is the hair of his sister, Fanny, but Elinor Dashwood (in love with Edward) and her sister Marianne think it might be Elinor's hair, a secret profession of Edward's love for her. When they discover it belongs to the love of Edward's youth, the vulgar and obnoxious Lucy Steele, all hope of romance seems to be ruined.[27]

Deep drama in Victorian tales springs from coils of hair: they provide clues to identity, stand at the heart of mysteries. The first hint to the orphaned Oliver Twist's parentage in Charles Dickens's novel comes from a "little gold locket, in which were two locks of hair and a plain gold wedding ring" engraved with the name "Agnes," with a blank space for the surname and the date of Oliver's birth. In Charlotte's story "The Secret," a lady orders a ring from a jeweler "with a crystal stone" for "a little braided chestnut-coloured hair." Central to a complicated blackmail plot, the ring is made in order to replace the authentic one, originally given by a wife to her husband when he left to fight in a war. The wife later marries a wealthy aristocrat after hearing of her husband's death by shipwreck, but she keeps her first marriage secret. Imposters use the fraudulent ring to try to blackmail her by claiming her first husband is still among the living.[28]

Charlotte craftily preyed here on an anxiety that one's mourning jewelry might not contain the hair of the loved one. Rumors and scandals about unscrupulous makers of mourning ornaments replacing hair mailed to them with someone else's hair of the same color were discussed at length in women's craft and fashion magazines of the day. Women sold their hair for such purposes—also for wigs and hairpieces—and hairworkers found this bought hair easier to work with because it was usually thicker, longer, and healthier. The "false" piece of jewelry took on the qualities of a disturbingly anonymous "grave" if the fraud was detected or even merely suspected. "Why should we confide to others the precious locks or tress we prize," a writer for the magazine *Family Friend* asks, "risking its being lost, and the hair of some other person being substituted for it, when we may ourselves weave it into the ornament we desire?"[29]

Scraps of hair and other remnants of the dead showed up in ghost stories, a subgenre dear to Victorians. Following other writers of the time—especially Dickens, whose characters are often haunted by the past, like his Ebenezer Scrooge—Emily and Charlotte built plots around the haunting of houses. Read in a certain way, *Wuthering Heights* is a traditional ghost story, the entire narrative unfurling in response to the question, posed at the beginning of the novel: Who is the girl-waif who torments Lockwood in his nightmare in the strange box bed? Wuthering Heights, "swarming with ghosts and goblins," influenced

Thornfield Hall, in *Jane Eyre*, which also seems to be troubled by some demon or goblin that lights fires, rips wedding veils, and bites flesh in the dead of night. In *Villette*, Lucy believes she sees the specter of the long-dead nun, supposedly buried at the foot of the pear tree, glide past her numerous times. While these apparitions are explained away in both of Charlotte's stories, others remain supernatural, such as in the passage when Jane at Moor House hears Rochester call out to her from hundreds of miles away, an instance of something akin to animal magnetism or romantic telepathy. Unlike her sisters with their gothic proclivities, Anne, the steady realist, didn't write about ghosts; her houses are troubled only by human cads, flirts, and abusive husbands.

Charlotte believed in supernatural occurrences and omens, as did many of her contemporaries. Besides her stories being riddled with them, she once told Mary Taylor that she sometimes heard ghostly voices, like when a disembodied voice said one night, "Come, thou high and holy feeling, / Shine o'er mountain, flit o'er wave, / Gleam like light o'er dome and shielding." A contemporary with faith in the haunting of material objects like hair was Queen Victoria. Even before her husband's sudden death in 1861, the queen was alive to the capability of things to soak up experiences and memories. She and her husband adored souvenirs, and few events were too insignificant for commemoration. A visit to their beloved Highlands in Scotland in 1844 led to the commissioning of an inkstand that included pebbles they had picked up on a stroll in Blair Atholl and teeth taken from deer Albert had shot there. Not only did the prince have necklaces, studs, pins, and waistcoat buttons made of stag teeth, engraved with the date and place he killed them, he and the queen had jewelry made of the baby teeth of their children, with inscriptions stating where and when they had been pulled or had fallen out. The queen also had her babies' legs and hands carved in marble before their small roundedness disappeared as they aged. Albert gave her a charm bracelet with nine hearts, each holding the hair of one of her children.[30]

After her husband died, the queen had his bedroom left exactly as it was at the terrible moment of loss, and every day she had fresh clothes laid out for him and hot water put on his nightstand. The glass used for his last dose of medicine remained next to his bed, and his blotting book lay open on his writing desk, his pen resting on it—all frozen to lament his absence. She would hold one of his nightshirts as she slept, and she kept a cast of his hand nearby. Not only did she commission a death mask, but she also had a tomb effigy fashioned, the face modeled on the death mask. She sent a pile of his hair to Garrard, the royal jewelers, who made at least eight pieces incorporating his hair, such as a gold pin with an onyx cameo of the prince, his hair kept in a box at the back. The queen's half sister, Princess Feodora, gave her a bracelet set with tresses from the heads of family members, mixed in with Albert's. The queen's eight-year-old son wore "a Locket with beloved Papa's hair."[31]

The queen believed that Albert still lingered in spirit form. "I feel now to be so acquainted with death," she wrote to her daughter soon after he died, "and to be much nearer that unseen world." She conducted séances in order to communicate with him, certain that her "adored Angel" hovered near, watching over and guiding her. Spiritualists like the queen believed that the dead usually chose everyday things through which to "speak" to the living: knocking or "rapping" on tables or walls, or moving heavy objects, such as levitating the séance circle's table. Spirits played on musical instruments with invisible hands, believers reported, or guided the medium to write down messages, which was called passive or automatic writing. The most difficult task mediums performed involved "materializing" a spirit. The medium, usually tied to a chair behind a curtain, caused a form of the deceased person to emerge—a spirit, supposedly, but one solid enough for the audience to "prove" its existence by touching, grasping, or kissing it (it was often the medium herself, escaping her bonds and wearing a disguise). Believers theorized that the wispy forms consisted of a kind of "ectoplasm," a type of mesmeric fluid or force. In the 1870s, the celebrated medium Florence Cook "materialized" a spirit called "Katie King," who cut off locks of her hair and handed them to audience members as souvenirs from the afterlife. Harriet Beecher Stowe told George Eliot that she spoke with Charlotte Brontë's spirit during a séance in the 1870s.[32]

Photographers claimed to capture images of ghosts with their cameras, in pictures that usually showed mourners with a white, wispy form floating nearby, like an emanation from their sorrowful thoughts. Some of these "spirit photographs" pictured ectoplasm or other types of fluid, sometimes seeping out of the orifices of mediums. It hardly mattered that these photos and performances were hoaxes; a widespread faith in spirits, which peaked in the 1860s and '70s, remained unshakable until the beginning of the twentieth century, feeding the collecting of relics and souvenirs. One Thomas Wilmot claimed in 1894 to catch an image of the "angel" Charlotte Brontë, called up by a medium, in a photograph that pictures a woman reaching toward the viewer.[33]

But all of this was after the Brontë children died. They didn't take up spiritualism; it barely existed during all but Patrick's lifetime. Neither did they take up photography, which was invented in the 1830s but not widely available until the 1850s, and even then it was quite expensive and usually required a visit to a photographer's studio. Patrick was the only family member known to be photographed, although a glass negative that may be of Charlotte in 1854 surfaced in 1984 in the archives of the National Portrait Gallery, but its authenticity remains controversial.[34]

Photography would gradually replace memorializing the dead with hair keepsakes. Along with this new technology, many historical changes led to the disappearance of hairwork. The spread of secularization starting around the end of the nineteenth century meant that doubts about the existence of an afterlife grew. Dying and the corpse began increasingly to represent meaningless loss rather than paradise and continuity. In medicine, revised theories about bacteria, germs, and disease led doctors to attribute death to specific physical causes rather than divine interference. God had not caused the death, rather the disease had, making it more difficult to believe that the body (and its hair) served as a window to heaven. Death began to feel more like failure than triumph, a defeat of the physician's skill, a collapse of the patient's will. Yet the true blow to the belief in the beautiful corpse came with World War I. The death of hundreds of thousands of young men (over four hundred thousand British soldiers died in the First Battle of the Somme alone) led to the widespread desire to distance the physicality of death. Mass graves came to replace personal ones as the war worsened and many had to be buried where they fell, or sometimes they couldn't be buried at all because they lay in no-man's-land or their bodies had been exploded into tiny fragments. About half of the bodies of British soldiers were never found. Alongside this growing distaste for the corpse and hair mementos came new technologies for creating keepsakes of the dead. Cameras and film became so cheap by 1900—when Kodak brought out the Brownie—that most of the population could own a camera and take snapshots regularly. Instead of crystallizing a moment by cutting a lock of hair, one could hold it in amber with a photo. Voice recordings, moving images, even typewriters were all means of holding onto the dead without the leavings of their actual bodies, or even of their writing as a remnant of their hand moving across a page.[35]

But this shift in feeling happened decades after Charlotte died, on March 31, 1855, just before she turned thirty-nine. No photograph was taken of her corpse, another type of death souvenir Victorians favored. The servants Martha Brown and Hannah Dawson (the elderly Tabby Ackroyd had died just before Charlotte) laid out her body in the bedroom that her mother had died in many years before. They cut off a long tress of her dark brown hair to keep. She had promised it to them, they said, during her lifetime. Later, when Charlotte's husband was despondent because he had forgotten to gather some hair on her deathbed, Martha and Hannah split the tress with him.[36]

Ellen Nussey arrived soon after Charlotte's death, to pay her last respects to her closest friend. She spread evergreen branches and flowers on Charlotte's "lifeless form." She, along with Charlotte's husband, Patrick, and many townsfolk, saw Charlotte's small coffin interred alongside her mother, aunt, and four of her siblings. Patrick still held onto his faith in heaven despite having lost all of his children. He wrote of his daughter's demise: "our loss we trust is her gain."[37]

After the funeral, Ellen went home with a few curls: some she wore in jewelry, others she later gave away to favored friends and Brontë fans, such as John James Stead, who eventually donated his to the British Library. Arthur Nicholls had a gold ring made with his initials, a snippet of Charlotte's hair tucked away behind a little door.[38]

CHAPTER EIGHT

Memory Albums

The violet's eye might shyly flash
And young leaves shoot among the fern

—EMILY BRONTË, UNTITLED POEM

Our hills only confess the coming of summer by
growing green with young fern and moss in secret
little hollows.

—CHARLOTTE BRONTË, IN A MAY 1851 LETTER

WHEN CHARLOTTE WAS working on her final novel, *Villette*, in 1851, she made a trip to London. Her real identity had begun to leak out into the larger world after the publication of *Shirley*, and she had started on a career of being "lionized," as she put it. Trips to London meant meeting famous people eager to make the acquaintance of the author of *Jane Eyre* and, if less so, *Shirley*. The Great Exhibition at the Crystal Palace had just opened when she arrived in May. She visited the giant fair full of objects of all sorts—hair pictures, elaborate traveling desks, needlework boxes, machines for making gummed envelopes—again and again, finding that "its grandeur does not consist in *one* thing," as she told her father.

> But in the unique assemblage of *all* things—Whatever
> human industry has created—you find there—from the great
> compartments filled with Railway Engines and boilers, with Mill-
> machinery in full work—with splendid carriages of all kinds—
> with harnesses of every description—to the glass-covered and

velvet spread stands loaded with the most gorgeous work of the goldsmith and silversmith—and the carefully guarded caskets full of real diamonds and pearls. . . . [I]t is such a Bazaar or Fair as eastern Genii might have created.

She admired a special alarm bed that pushed the sleeper awake and onto the floor at the set hour, which she thought the somewhat lazy author William Makepeace Thackeray should be made to use. By her fifth visit, though, she began to tire of the fair somewhat, finding it bewildering and feeling it left one "bleached and broken in bits." She may have had this multifarious collection of things in mind, or the love the Victorians had for things in general, when she considered at first calling *Villette* "Choseville," meaning "thingville" in French.[1]

Charlotte probably also saw on one of those visits another invention, which rivaled the alarm bed: a glass container created by Nathaniel Bagshaw Ward, a London doctor. A mostly self-sustaining environment for ferns, the Wardian case (generally about the size of an average aquarium) required only a small amount of upkeep to maintain an ideal habitat. At the Great Exhibition, Ward displayed two cases that he claimed had been closed for many years—miniature worlds thriving almost magically. Ward's boxes with their living interiors must have been especially striking when set in the gorgeous glass and steel structure of the Crystal Palace, built in Hyde Park: little glass cases within one giant one. In fact, the designer of the Crystal Palace, Joseph Paxton, had been producing glass houses for nurseries for much of his career, and he based the Crystal Palace on these smaller dwellings for plants. Wardian cases could soon be found in most fashionable women's parlors, alongside needlework, taxidermy, and other decorations made or tended by hand. Bought at nurseries, conservatories, and glass manufactories beginning in the 1840s, fern houses spread in the 1850s into average middle-class homes. Often sitting on stands, or placed on tables, like today's aquariums, Ward's cases also projected out of windows. Some of these vibrant cells came in the shape of the Crystal Palace itself, as souvenirs of the origins of their popularity. Charlotte would surely have been drawn to these living cabinets, since ferns had already become, for her, markers of dreamy places and memories. She also had an affinity for the contemporary practice of boxing-up, as we have seen, taking something potentially wild, whether it be natural specimens, hair, or dead and stuffed animals, and putting it in a container, album, or book or under a glass dome.[2]

Wardian cases were part of a "fern craze" that reached its heyday in the 1850s and '60s. "Your daughters, perhaps, have been seized with the prevailing 'Pteridomania,' " the writer Charles Kingsley commented in 1855, taking the Greek word for fern, *pteris*, derived from *pteron*, meaning feather or wing, to give the fad a title. Ferns began to replace flowers and other plants as the most desired greenery for gardeners and the most exciting specimens for amateur naturalists on hunts in the countryside. For craft-minded women, ferns became the most treasured plant to press and collect in albums and books, or to affix to white paper in order to be framed and hung on the wall. Pteridomaniacs sent birthday and greeting cards that not only had ferns depicted on them, but often included pieces of real ferns. A favored motif in decoration, fern shapes appeared on plates, glass, curtains, and wallpaper, as well as in needlework and lace. The Brontë household, for example, had a white ceramic water jug with a raised pattern of fern leaves winding around its exterior. The ghostly shadow of ferns emerged on objects when an actual fern frond set on a surface was sprayed with india ink or another dye or paint. Then the plant was carefully removed, creating a piece of "fern ware." Also called "splash-work" or "spatter-work," this fern pastime became popular with young girls, who would use a toothbrush wet with ink drawn along the teeth of a comb to do the spattering.[3]

Fern madness led to some types of ferns coming close to extinction from over-harvesting in parts of Britain and brought talk of passing "fern laws," so they wouldn't go the way of the wolves. In the second half of the nineteenth century, parents named their girls, and sometimes boys, Fern, and people called their houses "Fern Bank, Fern Cottage, Fern Hollow, Fern House, Fern Lodge, Fern Villa, Fernbank, Ferncliffe, Ferndale, The Fernery, Fernielee, Fernlea, Fernleigh, Fernmore, The Ferns, Fernside, or Fernwood," as the historian Sarah Whittingham enumerates. On these houses, ferns were usually carved into the window frames, keystones, or stone capitals.[4]

The Brontës were early fern lovers, beating the fern cultists by more than a decade. For them and others with a literary turn, walking out to look at and gather ferns, or other forms of "botanizing," brought to mind the Romantic poets, especially the close study and interest shown by Dorothy and William Wordsworth in hidden, tender plants that sprout in dark, damp places, like ferns. Dorothy collected ferns on her walks around their Dove Cottage and planted them in their garden, and her brother wrote of them in poems and prose, including of "Fair Ferns . . . Sole-sitting by the shores of old romance." One of Ward's favorite fern cases was designed after a window in the ruin of Tintern Abbey. He may have had in mind William Wordsworth's famous poem, written while looking at the abbey, when he designed it—both the poem and the fernerie grew out of a love of contemplating the decayed and ruined, the remains of the past that brought on a sweet sense of melancholy. Since ferns grew in shady places, they had an association in the popular imagination with old walls, hollow trees, ruined chapels, tombstones in churchyards, and other places lovely because desolate. Mourning jewelry occasionally had fern carvings, as did gravestones. Ferns were sometimes "skeletonized," or had their fleshly parts removed, and then bleached to make mourning arrangements, called "phantom bouquets," often preserved under glass domes with pictures or relics of the departed. Some Wardian cases took the shape of a gothic cathedral, while others had tiny ruins set up in them. Outdoor gardens and ferneries also mimicked castle and abbey remains, the ferns magnifying the atmosphere of ancient loneliness. One George Glenny took blood-stained moss gathered by a friend at one of the battlefields of the Crimean War of 1854 and trained it to grow on an "old ruin" in his Wardian case.⁵

The fern craze developed out of a larger gothic revival in art, architecture, and design, with the art critic and professor John Ruskin as its most celebrated spokesman. The medieval gothic style, Ruskin and his followers felt, developed from an organic creativity with form, as if it grew straight out of the busy soul of the craftsman, compared to the stiff, clean surfaces of styles like the neoclassical. Ferns were the plant version of the gothic, with their intricate detail and coiling stems. Ruskin believed that the hand of God could be found in the "spirals of springing ferns," their representation in art a way of celebrating God in nature. Ruskin painted watercolors of ferns and advocated for fern designs on gothic-influenced architecture, most famously on the capitals of the Oxford Museum of Natural History, carved with recognizable fern species. Charlotte admired Ruskin's books and was reading volumes of the *Stones of Venice* (published by her own firm of Smith, Elder and Co., which sent them to her) during the months before her marriage, including his famous chapter titled "The Nature of the Gothic."⁶

No Wardian case appears to have graced the parlor of the Haworth parsonage, but the Brontës found ferns growing just outside their windows, the poor moorland soil ideal for numerous species. In Emily's poems the plants and their wild plots evoke seclusion, solitude, and the grave, usually desired places in her world—sites of comfort and concealment. In a Gondal poem, fern leaves "sighing wave" over a character's grave, "like mourners." A wildly rushing mountain spring in another poem has its source in "fern and ling." "Ferny glens" in a third beckon the poet (or her alter ego) on her walks, being part of her "own nature," as is the "wild wind." Emily's feelings for ferns mirrored those in the popular consciousness, with their gothic gloominess infused with a sense of consolation. Writers on ferns saw them as part of a linked chain, starting with the boggy landscapes in which they grew, the peat that ferns and other plants (moss especially) became, which was burned to warm the home and make the hearth glow. Peat under enough pressure became coal, and Victorian fossil hunters wrote excitedly about finding fern imprints on coal, evidence of plants growing eons ago.[7]

Yet somehow, in a curious paradox, ferns represented both this ancient decay and the fresh green grotto, the glimmering stream. Ward's case originated out of a desire to create a rustic garden at his house in Whitechapel, London. He tried to build a rockery in his backyard, fed by trickling water and covered in ferns and mosses, but the smoke and fumes from surrounding factories killed the plants. One day he captured a moth in a glass bottle and happened to add some "moist mould." Covering it with a lid, he found to his delight that a fern sprouted up in the perfect moistness, and he surmised that the delicate plants needed protection from the "noxious gases" of the factories in order to thrive. Even indoors, plants were difficult to grow because of fumes from open fires and gas lighting (increasing in use since the 1850s), so Ward embarked on many experiments that involved guarding plants from interior pollutants, assisted by a friend who owned a nearby nursery. His inventions were instrumental in the development of the "aqua vivarium," or aquarium, and the terrarium, a term not coined until the 1890s. Sealed ferneries in Victorian parlors brought "some shadow of the green country lanes and lovely scenes, so refreshing even in the remembrance," one writer enthused, "into the close atmosphere of a city."[8]

Charlotte had all of these associations in mind when Jane Eyre ends up in Ferndean—"fern valley"—Manor with Rochester, after she has passed through a succession of houses and institutions: Gateshead, Lowood, Thornfield Hall, and Moor House (also called Marsh End). Gateshead, where Jane is a child living with the Reeds, needs entering then leaving behind, like one would any gate at the head of a path. Lowood, the charity school to which Mrs. Reed sends her, represents an unhealthy environment because it is "low," a place of potential sickness according to the Victorian theory of "miasma"—a belief that fevers could emerge out of certain damp, vapory environments and be carried on the air. The "forest-dell" of Lowood, a "cradle of fog and fog-bred pestilence," brings the typhus that kills off so many girls, already weakened by bad food and insufficient clothing, results of the "low" or unethical culture of the poorly run school. Thornfield, where she is the governess to Rochester's ward, pricks, fraught with romantic attraction and dangers. Moor House, where she stumbles upon her cousins, has much going for it with its bracing altitude and its boggy spots, which bring peat fires rather than pestilence. The pebbly bridle path that leads to it winds between fern banks. But Rochester isn't there, and St. John, who has a certain perilous magnetism for Jane, is.

Jane finally reaches and then ends her days in the ferny valley, which has a soft give compared to the thorns of Rochester's other house, a masculine place where women pace, fret, and descend into madness. Ferneries and fern hunts served in many Victorian novels as settings for romance and assignations. "Ferns, and picnics, and love tales, go so well together," opined one fern expert, "that perhaps the fact may account for some of the 'pteridomania' now so common a complaint."

Part of the fern's allure came from its association with a state of "fascination," from the Latin verb *fascinare*, meaning "to enchant." Victorians drew on an established tradition of giving flowers and other plants symbolic meaning, called the "language of flowers." The daisy represented innocence, for instance, while the common thistle meant misanthropy, and the poppy consolation. One greeting card from a "language of flowers" series had a maidenhair fern frond attached to it. The card was labeled "Fern—Fascination" and had printed on it:

> This little spray of Maidenhair,
> Will, better far than words, declare
> That by the charms of your art;
> Your modest mien; your loving heart;
> "I'm fairly fascinated."

This fern species was given its name by country folk because it reminded them of women's pubic hair.[9]

When Ferndean is first introduced to the reader, it has miasmic potential, representing the rot and darkness of ferny places. It would have been safer if Rochester had concealed his mad wife Bertha at the old manor house at Ferndean, a place more secure from prying eyes than Thornfield because "even more retired and hidden." But he had "a scruple about the unhealthiness of the situation, in the heart of a wood," he tells Jane, because the "damp walls" would soon have killed her. After Bertha burns down Thornfield, a crippled, chastened Rochester moves to Ferndean, and Jane comes there to nurse the widower. "Deep buried" in a heavy wood, Ferndean begins at this juncture to pick up some of the more heartening emotions attached to ferns. Jane first arrives on foot at the start of evening, descending into further shadows, "so thick and dark grew the timber of the gloomy wood," and almost losing her way in the "sylvan dusk," like a girl in a fairy tale. The next day, when the two are together, they take a walk and find "cheerful fields" with a "sparkling blue" sky. Even in the woods they encounter "hidden and lovely" corners. After the two marry, they people the spot with their children. Still, some of the atmosphere of the ferny graveyard lingers. The novel ends with a letter from St. John, who is dying in India, which brings the idea of death back to Ferndean and lets it linger as the story concludes.

Ferns brought to mind fairy tales for many Victorians, openings into supernatural realms. Fairies were often pictured dancing in ferny settings, and they left behind rare ferns as tokens of their presence. To make oneself invisible, one need only gather fern seeds, according to an old proverb, revived in Victorian fern lore. Some still believed in a folk tradition that the moonwort fern provided a cure for "lunacy" (so called because mental illness was once thought to be related to the moon) when picked in the light of a full moon. Charlotte clusters these images around a young Jane in the famous passage in the potentially haunted red room at Gateshead. Jane looks into a mirror, but, with a hint of Catherine-like madness, she sees staring back at her a tiny phantom, "half fairy, half imp," who comes out of "lone, ferny dells in moors," appearing before the "eyes of belated travellers." The fairy side of Jane, which retreats for many chapters, peeks out again when she first meets Rochester, riding out of the darkness with the gytrash bounding before him. He teases her after his fall by calling her a fairy who bewitched his horse. When the two finally withdraw to Ferndean, they find comfort, like in a peaty fire, but also the thrill of the gothic, with its murk and magic. This is the eroticism of ferns.[10]

Charlotte gathered and pressed the ferns for the album pictured at the start of this chapter during her honeymoon in Ireland. She had known the man she married for many years. The twenty-six-year-

old Arthur Bell Nicholls, three years Charlotte's junior, became
Patrick Brontë's curate in May 1845, after he had completed his ordi-
nation as a deacon. An Irishman like Patrick, Nicholls had received
his bachelor of arts from Trinity College, Dublin. Charlotte found
him a "respectable young man," but she was pining for Heger, her
unavailable "master." Rumors floated about that Nicholls courted
Charlotte, but she quickly quashed them, telling Ellen that a "cold,
far-away sort of civility are the only terms" on which they had ever
been. The curates of the area saw her, she claimed, as "an old maid,"
and she regarded them as "highly uninteresting, narrow and unat-
tractive specimens of the 'coarser sex.'" She paid these curates in
kind by portraying them in *Shirley* as a pack of dunderheads, Nicholls as Mr. Macarthy, an Irishman somewhat unhinged by the local
Dissenters and Quakers. After word spread about the true identity
of the author of *Shirley*, local Haworth people began to read it and
Jane Eyre, then told the author herself what they thought of the
books. Nicholls read them both, and he found the passages about the
curates in *Shirley* so hilarious that he gave "vent to roars of laugh-
ter," as Charlotte described it, "clapping his hands and stamping on
the floor." He read them aloud to Patrick and "triumphed in his own
character."[11]

At some point Nicholls began falling in love with Charlotte. The
situation was fraught: she had grown famous, he continued as a lowly
curate with a tiny salary. But he had also been there as a witness to
Branwell's fall, and he had officiated at Emily's funeral. By 1851, Charlotte reported to Ellen that Nicholls, before leaving for a vacation in
Ireland, had invited himself to tea at the parsonage and "comported
himself somewhat peculiarly for him being extremely good—mild
and uncontentious." In the letter to her father where she describes her
visit to the Great Exhibition in London, she includes Mr. Nicholls in

her hope that all at home are well. Starting in 1852, Nicholls visibly pined for Charlotte, staring at her, holding her gaze, and treating her with a feverish restraint.[12]

He finally steeled himself to propose. After tea one day, Charlotte had withdrawn into the parlor while her father and his curate talked in the study. Charlotte heard Nicholls get up as if to go, but instead he tapped on the parlor door. He entered and stood before her, "shaking from head to foot, looking deadly pale, speaking low, vehemently yet with difficulty." Charlotte felt a strange shock at seeing the usually cool man overcome by passion. He told her that he had suffered for many months, that he could no longer endure it, and that he craved for some hope. She promised she would give him a response the next day, and led him out of the room. Then she went and told her father, who was so furious at Nicholls's presumption that he seemed on the edge of a fit or stroke, with the veins starting out on his forehead and his eyes suddenly bloodshot. Charlotte considered her father unjust—he applied to Nicholls various strong "epithets"—yet she also didn't feel in love. She sent him a note of rejection.[13]

Patrick refused to speak to Nicholls, seeing the match as a degradation for Charlotte. Nicholls, for his part, hardly ate, he became restless, ill, and so deeply unhappy that he believed he must leave his situation. He applied to become a missionary in Australia. Charlotte pondered all this, reckoning Nicholls to be one "whose sensations are close and deep—like an underground stream, running strong but in a narrow channel." Needing a break from the impossible turbulence at home, she slipped away to London, ostensibly to see *Villette* through the last stages of printing. Returning a few weeks later, she found Nicholls still lingering about, not able to tear himself away. She regarded his dogging her up the lane after the evening service—and all his dark, gloomy looks—as pitiful. As spring came, Nicholls remained inconsolable and so alone in his heartbreak that Charlotte fancied "he might almost be *dying*" for love of her. Touches of tenderness for the outcast and unhappy man became unavoidable for Charlotte. Nicholls found another curacy, and as he officiated at his last church service in Haworth, he gazed on Charlotte in the audience and lost command of himself, becoming pale and beginning to shake. Only with difficulty could he "whisper and falter through the service," and women in the audience who understood what was going on began to weep. "I could not quite check my own tears," Charlotte wrote to Ellen. Patrick didn't attend, but when he heard about it he called Nicholls an "unmanly driveller." Yet, up until the last, Nicholls let Anne's spaniel Flossy come to his rooms, and he and the dog went out for long walks.[14]

On the night before Nicholls left, he came to deliver some papers to Patrick and to say good-bye. Charlotte heard them from another room, listening as Nicholls left the house and then paused in the garden. She felt compelled to go out and say a few words of farewell. She found Nicholls, believing he would never see her again, "leaning against the garden-door in a paroxysm of anguish—sobbing as women never sob." She tried to comfort him, but took care not to give any hope. Still, Charlotte's attitude toward him had begun to shift. His well of passion for her must have reminded her of the heroes she wrote about. Nicholls was something of a Rochester figure, with his masculine physique—not conventionally handsome—and his devotion to one, plain woman. Nicholls had no ancient fortune or name though, no great gloomy mansion, no mad wife in his attic. He was a real-life lover. In short: Would this be enough for Charlotte?[15]

This was not Charlotte's first marriage proposal, nor even her second. There was the one from Ellen Nussey's brother, mentioned already; a proposal from an Irish clergyman she had met briefly when he was visiting Haworth in 1839; and another from James Taylor, the managing clerk at her publishing house. This latter proposal came in 1851, not long before Nicholls began mooning over her. Taylor's offer was flattering to Charlotte, but she had a kind of physical distaste toward him.

After Nicholls moved away, he began secretly corresponding with Charlotte. Matters progressed, and he made some sly visits to Haworth, without Patrick's knowledge. After six months of this courtship, Charlotte told her father all, insisting that he agree to Nicholls's courting her more formally. Patrick finally submitted, but only with great bitterness. Nicholls began openly visiting the parsonage. Charlotte accepted Nicholls's renewed proposal, and he returned as Patrick's curate. Charlotte told her friends she wasn't really in love, though she had "esteem" and affection for the steadfast, devoted man. She wished he had more brilliance and finer talents; she worried that he wasn't her intellectual equal. She mainly felt gratitude, perhaps not the best foundation for a marriage. Elizabeth Gaskell made an astute comment about the impending nuptials and Charlotte's intended: "I am sure Miss Brontë could never have borne not to be well-ruled and ordered well!" she remarked. "She would never have been happy but with an exacting, rigid, law-giving, passionate man."[16]

Charlotte had much to do before the wedding: she was "very busy stitching" green and white curtains for Nicholls's study, which used to be the "peat room" that Emily sometimes kept animals in. She had to buy a border for the tablecloth and sew it on and purchase her wedding dress—a white, book muslin "with a tuck or two." She refused the pricier silk tulle that friends favored, although she wore a lace mantle over it, embroidered by Ellen. Her white bonnet trimmed with green leaves brought to mind a "snow drop," according to townsfolk. Like Jane Eyre, she took care that her veil was neat and inexpensive, not wanting to "make a fool of herself." Wedding cards with both "card" envelopes and "postage envelopes," all to be sealed with white wax, had to be bought and then sent out.[17]

At eight o'clock on the morning of June 29, 1854, Charlotte and Nicholls married in the Haworth church. Only a handful of people were invited. Patrick declared at the last minute he wouldn't attend, claiming illness, but one wonders if it was resentment that kept him in his bedroom. Charlotte's teacher at Roe Head, Margaret Wooler (one of the models for Miss Temple in *Jane Eyre*), gave her away instead, rather fittingly. Ellen played the role of bridesmaid, and a few of Nicholls's friends attended, one of them officiating. After a brief wedding breakfast, Charlotte changed to a gray-and-lavender silk dress, with velvet trim at the neck, and they left immediately on their honeymoon in a carriage and pair to the Keighley train station, then on to Wales and Nicholls's Ireland.[18]

They passed through busy cities and towns, like Dublin and Banagher, where they stayed with Nicholls's family, but they generally sought, in Charlotte's words, "wild and remote spots." It was at Killarney, in the south of Ireland close to the coast, where Charlotte collected the ferns that made up her album. She wasn't the only one to hunt ferns there: it was a thriving tourist spot for Victorian "fernists"; even Queen Victoria visited with Albert in 1861 and gathered a few ferns for her garden. Killarney was known for its more than fifty species, especially the tall royal fern and the Killarney fern. A "filmy fern" with transparent leaves originally found in Yorkshire in 1724, the Killarney sprouted on the edges of waterfalls and streams and could also be found in caves (now rare because of Victorian over-harvesting). Ward planted a Killarney fern in one of the cases he displayed at the Great Exhibition, and one appears to be represented in Charlotte's album (although it's not easy to tell since the ferns weren't labeled). The intrepid Mary Taylor sent Charlotte some exotic fern fronds from New Zealand, which may have ended up on these pages. Charlotte didn't leave behind an account of her "botanizing," so we don't know if she carried a vasculum—a rounded tin case with a handle for preserving specimens—or a collecting press, which held sheets of absorbent paper.[19]

The adventures of zealous fern seekers appeared in magazines, including an account in *Punch* of a Miss Netley on a search in Devon, "seldom out without an Alpine-stick and a basket, as if she were going to market." "Splendid ferns everywhere," she exclaimed. Ferns often took enthusiasts to edges of cliffs or fast-flowing rivers, and accidents were numerous, as in 1867 when a Miss Jane Myers fell 170 feet after bending down to gather a fern on the edge of a cliff at Craighall in Perthshire, Scotland, and died. Charlotte may have been ferning when she had a potentially perilous accident near Killarney. As she crossed the Gap of Dunloe—a pass between high cliffs—on horseback, having ignored the recommendation of their guide that she dismount because of the boulder-strewn path, her horse slipped, trembled, and, suddenly going "mad," reared and threw her onto the stones under its hooves. Nicholls, not noticing for a moment that Charlotte had fallen, grasped the horse's bridle while it plunged and stamped around her. Convinced she would die, she worried about leaving behind her husband and father. But then Nicholls saw her on the ground and let go of the horse, which immediately sprang over her. Helped up, Charlotte was miraculously unhurt. When recounting the story to a friend, she mentioned "a sudden glimpse of a grim phantom," probably a reference to death, but also to local folk tales and legends about the gap and its environs. A "Phantom of the Lake" supposedly haunted the area: the specter of O'Donoghue Ross, a chieftain who had been thrown from his horse and, taking this as a sign of impending death, began practicing the "black arts" in order to assume strange shapes. He appeared to travelers every seven years, the legend went, riding on his horse. This was an aptly ferny adventure for a honeymoon, with its gothic, fairy tale overtones and hints of romance. A superstitious person might take Charlotte's accident in the way O'Donoghue did his, since not only would Charlotte die within the year, but what would have saved her was deemed by many a "black art" (more about this later).[20]

Having gathered the ferns, a collector such as Charlotte would then dry the fronds for herbariums, which included not only albums, but also portfolios or individual leaves kept in cabinets or boxes. For albums, the ferns would be attached to the pages by, for example, sewing the stalk to the thick paper, or threading ties through small holes to affix parts of the fern stem. Charlotte's "fern book," as these albums were sometimes called, has black leather binding and gold trim. A band was cut out of each of the heavy pages that make up the album, and the stem of the fern was stuck into it. Some sort of clear paste—flour paste, gum arabic, isinglass, mucilage, and starch were all recommended by manuals on how to make fern albums—was then used to affix the tops and edges of the fronds. A sense of sinuous movement, of wind feathering the intricate frond, now all stilled, lingers in the ferns' positioning on the pages. Albums specially made for receiving fern specimens, such as "The Fern Collector's Album," had preprinted descriptions of common ferns on one side. The other side had a frame in which the plant could be added. Those unwilling to do any work themselves could purchase printed books already containing pressed ferns—like William Gardiner's 1850 *Selection of British Ferns and Their Allies*, with each plant surrounded by decoration and botanical information—at shops catering to tourists in spots haunted by fern lovers.[21]

Victorians were prolific album compilers, creators of all manner of curated collections arranged in the little museum of the volume. Albums, along with Wardian cases, were part of the Victorian enthusiasm for collecting, containing, classifying, and organizing, especially when it came to saving the past by placing it into some sort of permanent system. An ancient ancestor of the Victorian album was the commonplace book, typically a place to copy favorite quotations, to record one's reading and intellectual activity. These compilations of notes survived throughout the Victorian period and continue in various forms up to today (with notebooks and journals). Arthur Nicholls kept a commonplace book, where he stored poetry and prose extracts and drew a family tree of the Bells, his maternal relatives. Many functioned as private *aide-mémoire*, while others were receptacles for basic information, holding hand-copied recipes, patterns for embroidery, or sketches. Usually private, occasionally they were made as gifts, especially as educational tools for children, or treated as heirlooms, like the poet Felicia Hemans's commonplace book, which ended up in the hands of, rather appropriately, Elizabeth Barrett Browning. In the beginning of the nineteenth century, when newsprint became cheaper, commonplace-book makers began to include clippings from printed sources, often alongside their own handwritten recordings, beginning the compiling of books of "scraps," later in the century called "scrapbooks."[22]

Albums functioned also as social spaces for gathering traces of friends, families, or the famous. The autograph album, a relative of the commonplace book, had a semi-public character, often displayed in the drawing room to be paged through with visitors. The lucky hostess could prove her stellar social position by the illustrious guests who had contributed a poem, sketch, or signature. Those not able to muster famous friends bought or begged for autographs to paste into their albums. The strips of handwriting that Patrick mailed to Charlotte's fans, created by cutting up her letters to him, often went into autograph albums, as did the signatures Ellen cut off of letters from Charlotte. Mary Jesup Docwra, from Kelvedon, in Essex, sent a letter to Patrick in 1858 pleading for some of Charlotte's handwriting. She put the note he sent in reply—"Dear Madam, The enclosed is all I can spare of my dear Daughter Charlotte's handwriting. Yours, very respectfully, P. Brontë."—in her album with marbled covers, along with the snipped sample, so small that it holds only the words "my book—no one" and then, on the line below, "ious than I am to." When Harriet Martineau became a famous writer, she complained about the "importunity about albums" and being "despoiled of the privacy of correspondence" with her friends "by the rage for autographs." Surely the most exciting Brontë autograph is a small letter containing all three of the sisters' signatures, signing as "Currer Bell," "Ellis Bell," and "Acton Bell." It was requested by a Frederick Enoch—probably one of the two people who bought their volume of poetry—through their publishers in 1846, a year before any of their novels appeared in print. Enoch and his contemporaries found an emotional charge in a signature; it captured and relayed selfhood for them, something like what the photograph would do.[23]

One needn't be someone of note to be asked to contribute to an album. Many women (and occasionally men) appealed to people in their circle to contribute to their friendship album or "souvenir." In 1845, Charlotte, not yet famous, copied a poem in German from memory into a Miss Rooker's album and one in French—"Le Jeune Malade," by Charles Hubert Millevoye—into Ellen Nussey's, glossing it with the fact that the poet himself died young and that she considered the poem the most poetical of all French verse. When Branwell was on his drunken path of self-destruction in 1846, he stayed in Halifax where his friend J. B. Leyland lived. Mary Pearson, the daughter of a local innkeeper, asked Branwell to contribute to her album on more than one occasion, and his verse and sketches mirrored his troubled state of mind. He copied out some of his own poems and lines from Byron's verse and did some sketching, including of a man with a desolate face, captioned

"The results of Sorrow." A churchyard with a tombstone inscribed "I IMPLORE FOR REST" makes up another entry. He also penciled a portrait of himself and, on the same page (pictured here), drew a man kneeling and weeping, with a sinking ship in the background.[24]

A school album at Roe Head, begun in 1831, bristles with the talents and whimsy of the young pupils. Bound in dark leather, heavily embossed with the image of a reclining woman in classical robes surrounded by flowers and pink watered silk on the inside covers and endpapers, the album was purpose-built by De La Rue and Co., London, as a friendship album. Most of the schoolgirls wrote or painted on the leaves, which had paper "frames," either printed directly onto the page or constructed so that drawings could be inserted into them. Some pages carried blank music staves to be filled by the purchaser. A handwritten "Prologue" begins with "Whoever with curious eye this book explores / Must add some contribution to its stores," and states some rules, such as no "profane" wit. On the first leaf is a "ruined church" sketched in pencil by Charlotte's friend Mary Taylor, who also contributed a very accomplished watercolor of a castle on another page. Charlotte drew a picture of St. Martin's Parsonage, Birmingham (copied from a David Cox drawing), on leaf 7, in pencil, and other girls rendered landscapes, flowers, and religious scenes. Original poems cover some pages, including one clever verse called "On being desired to write in an album," signed "H.H."; quotations from the Bible and Milton decorate other pages. One unsigned watercolor depicts an open album similar to the one in which it is contained, a witty commentary on the potential endlessness of album culture.[25]

Mementos of shared communities (school, parlor, neighborhood), such albums functioned something like photograph albums would later in the century. An especially gorgeous friendship album, bound in green morocco with a label on the spine that says, "Souvenir D'Amitié," was compiled between 1795 and 1805 by Anne Wagner, whose niece was Felicia Dorothea Browne (later Hemans). Inscriptions and quotations written by friends and family were embellished with watercolors, braids of hair, collages, paper cutouts, and portrait silhouettes, often by Wagner herself. On one page a brown braid is attached to the paper with pink ribbon, with this verse next to it: "Close as this lock of hair the ribband binds / May friendship's sacred bonds unite our minds / Yrs. Sincerely, Eliza Brooks, Liverpool, June 15th -95." Charlotte brings a similar album into *Shirley* with Caroline Helstone's enamel-covered souvenir book. Caroline cares so deeply for her friends, she wants to memorialize moments of affection. She takes a few flowers from a bouquet as she gives it to her dear friend Cyril Hall. Pressing them into her small album, closed with a silver clasp, she pencils in the date and these words: "To be kept for the sake of the Rev. Cyril Hall, my friend." Cyril slips a sprig into his "pocket Testament," penning her name next to it. Affinity was also expressed by creating an album as a gift. Margaret Stovin, an important botanist and early expert in ferns, gave two fern albums in 1833 to her friend Miss Walker that evoke her local walks searching for rare breeds. Stovin also created an album of pressed flowers and plants, collected in Derbyshire, for her young friend Florence Nightingale.[26]

Meant to be touched, albums functioned not just as visual feasts, especially when they held matter once alive or things that appear to emerge from the pages, as if they might spring out or walk off. Seaweed, skeletonized leaves, and pressed flowers thicken one early Victorian album. The anonymous compiler also cut out pictures of colored birds from cards and decorated them with real feathers. The "fever" for stamp albums was followed closely by a popularity for collecting valentines, Christmas cards, and postcards—personal ephemera crying out, many felt, to be arranged in a narrative form in an album. Travel or tourists' albums filled with souvenirs mapped adventures. Lady Emilia Hornby, for example, visited the battlefields of the Crimean War, gathered wildflowers, and pressed them into an album, creating a portable battleground memento. Novelists used obsessive album keeping in their plots to show characteristics like melancholy sentimentalism, as in Wilkie Collins's 1875 *Law and the Lady* with Major Fitz-David, who treasures an album of ornamented, vellum pages, bound in blue velvet with a silver clasp. Locks of hair, "let neatly into the center of each page," carry inscriptions. Each page represents a "love-token" from a female lover, each inscription a reminder of the end of the affair. The first page "exhibited a lock of the lightest flaxen hair, with these lines beneath: 'My adored Madeline. Eternal constancy. Alas, July 22, 1839!' " Charles Dickens, in *David Copperfield*, satirizes this saving of the minutiae of memory by having fashionable girls put the finger and toenail parings of a Russian prince in their keepsake albums.[27]

Moments of experience, friendship, and love could, through albums, be celebrated and controlled. Unlike with a box, case, or cabinet, the album provided a means to order objects not only on a page but also within the chronology of the volume. The keeper of the album sat down with a visitor to leaf through it together, often accompanying the turned pages with narration. A story emerged, told in part by the sequence of the leaves, a kind of autobiography in objects. Queen Victoria had the resources to affix the story of her life—or attempt to—onto the pages of a series of themed albums. She started as a young girl by making a seaweed album. Later she had many series of keepsake albums assembled, mostly collections of mounted watercolors she commissioned. Numerous "animal albums" pictured her pets, for instance, and in the "Souvenir Albums" she kept a chronological record of places she visited, ceremonies she attended, and other events needing memorialization. The question arose, did it really happen if it wasn't put into an album?[28]

Yet Charlotte made a collection of ferns only. Her album reminds us of Ferndean and the complicated eroticism between Rochester and Jane in that place of ferns, leading us, perhaps, to some inkling about why she married Nicholls. One wonders, in considering the oral performance that often accompanied the sharing of albums, if she ever showed her ferns, and, if so, what sort of chronicle she gave. Perhaps it prompted a travel narrative—the parts of Ireland they covered and what they saw there. Or was it too personal to show outside of the family? The gathering and pressing of these ferns coincided with what was probably Charlotte's first sexual experience with a man. What she made of it can never be known: she left no record of her feelings. She did write some enigmatic lines to Ellen just after returning from her honeymoon, maybe referring to her sexual life with her husband. She begins by explaining that the six weeks of her married life have changed "the colour of my thoughts." She believes that married women who "indiscriminately urge their acquaintances to marry" are "much to blame." She now knows what a "solemn and strange and perilous thing" it is "for a woman to become a wife."[29]

Even so, from the evidence of Charlotte's letters, she grew to have a deep fondness for her husband. His "kind and ceaseless protection" especially appealed to her, and she remarked that his attachment made her "own attachment to him stronger." Part of this may have had to do with his physical self, his touch, caress, and kiss. They went on long walks together on the moors most days. After they had been married many months, Charlotte called him "my dear boy," feeling that he became ever "dearer." When she began to succumb to her final illness, she found him "so tender, so good, helpful, patient." She adds, "My heart is knit to him."[30]

Even before her death, but especially after it, Charlotte was herself "collected" in albums, as we have seen with her autograph. Because the parsonage, moors, and Haworth became so associated with the three Brontë sisters, the place was often represented in scrapbooks. A souvenir album created around 1859 has a section devoted to the anonymous compiler's visit to Haworth. On one page, two glued-on ivy leaves from the area decorate a carefully arranged collage that includes a snippet of paper with Patrick's shaky signature on it and a drawing, clipped from stationery or a magazine, of the parsonage and surrounding cemetery, which includes the caption "The Home of Charlotte Brontë." Some collectors filled albums with postcards of the Haworth area; others, when photography became cheaper and more portable, with photos they took themselves, such as those in a now unbound album titled "Views taken during 1903," which feature many famous Brontë sites.[31]

Piles of "Brontëana" scrapbooks from the later nineteenth century sit in archives, largely forgotten today. Album makers cut out reproductions of the painting George Richmond made of Charlotte, which often appeared in articles and books, as a kind of replacement for her absent photograph, and glued them to their pages. One Matilda Pollard filled a pink album in 1894, which she entitled "Scraps," with newspaper cuttings related to the Brontë family, going back to 1888. A Miss Brown of Haworth, probably related to the Brontës' servant Martha Brown, took a dark-green volume with "Album" embossed on the front and a picture of a dog sitting near a man's hat and walking stick, and filled it with newspaper cuttings, many Brontë related. Thrifty scrap-album assemblers would reuse printed books they no longer wanted, pasting cuttings on top of print. William Scruton and J. Hambley Rowe, for instance, clipped images of places important to the Brontë story and pasted them into *The Temple Dictionary of the Bible*, removing some of the original pages so the thickened ones would fit between the boards. Horsfall Turner took *The Stock Exchange Year-Book 1898* and pasted in Brontë cuttings from newspapers and magazines. Given Charlotte's attraction to remnants, paper, texts—remember those tiny handmade volumes she and her siblings created as children, often with recycled scraps as covers—she probably would have found this attempt to represent her in a paper museum apt. Could a rustle of life be found again by turning over the leaves? Or does such an album present merely the dead shadow of what was once there?[32]

CHAPTER NINE

Migrant Relics

Arranging long-locked drawers and shelves
Of cabinets, shut up for years,
What a strange task we've set ourselves!
How still the lonely room appears!
How strange this mass of ancient treasures,
Mementos of past pains and pleasures;
These volumes, clasped with costly stone,
With print all faded, gilding gone;
These fans of leaves, from Indian trees—
These crimson shells, from Indian seas—
These tiny portraits, set in rings—
Once, doubtless, deemed such precious things;
Keepsakes bestowed by Love on Faith,
And worn till the receiver's death,
Now stored with cameos, china, shells,
In this old closet's dusty cells.

—CHARLOTTE BRONTË, "MEMENTOS"

"I PURCHASED OF THE proper person the whole lower sash of the window of the bedroom of Charlotte Brontë," wrote Charles Hale, a Boston journalist and politician traveling in Europe while recovering from ill health, in a November 8, 1861, letter to his mother, penned mostly while at Haworth and finished at the house of his friend Elizabeth Gaskell. After Patrick's death in June 1861, renovations on the parsonage were started by the new incumbent, a John Wade. Pilgrims like Hale could carry off fragments of the actual parsonage house itself. "This is the window at which she was most fond of sitting," Hale boasted. He also brought away woodwork from the interior, which he combined with window glass to make picture frames, so he could look at photos through the "same medium" as Charlotte when she gazed out at the "dreary landscape." His photos, Hale went on, "will be surrounded with wood that was about her as she sat there." He met the local carpenter, William Wood, who told him of Emily's bravery in breaking up a dogfight; the sexton's wife showed him the "little wickerwork doll's cradle mentioned in one of the books"; the sexton pointed out where the family dogs were buried in the garden; and he sat in Charlotte's pew in the church where Patrick served. Hale also got his hands on the "wire and crank of Mr. Brontë's bell-pull," which Patrick had "used daily for forty-one years." Finally walking back to Keighley to catch the train to London, he was so laden with loot that William Wood went along to help carry it.[1]

Coveting parings or slivers of literary "shrines," Victorian tourists who thronged such sites were not so different from religious pilgrims of the past. At the Lord's tomb, Christ's legendary place of burial and resurrection, believers tapped oil from lamps burning outside. Dirt and little pebbles gathered from the ground were set into reliquaries. Such substances, called *eulogiae*, stored within themselves the blessings of the holy place and could even be ingested: tokens from the Holy Land made of compact soil were crumbled along the edges into water, then swallowed as a kind of sacred medicine.[2]

Similarly, Victorians wanted to imbibe the authors who had blessed them with their words. The writer Thomas Hardy plucked violets from John Keats's grave in Rome, as did scores of others. The mulberry tree said to have been planted by Shakespeare in Stratford was stripped for souvenir trinkets, as was the thorn tree that Robert Burns stood under as he parted from Margaret Campbell, the inspiration for many of his poems and songs whom he called "Highland Mary." Visitors to Burns's birthplace bought needle-cases, trays, cups, "fancy boxes," and other souvenirs guaranteed to be made of wood that grew nearby. A residue of grace permeated the surroundings of genius and might be a portable substance, lambent with ghostly presence.[3]

Even land associated with fictional works, rather than the authors of those works—like *Wuthering Heights* and its moors—glowed richly, as if fiction and real geography were somehow contiguous. When visiting the moors—doubly meaningful with fictional and authorial associations—tourists picked sprigs of heather to add to letters, or to press into books, especially *Wuthering Heights* or Gaskell's biography, which many brought along as a kind of guidebook. Some literature lovers wanted to be buried close to or in such sites, like Alloway Kirk, immortalized in Burns's "Tam O'Shanter," where fans arranged for interment. It was almost as if one could be buried inside a favorite story or poem, to be resurrected there and to live there always.[4]

Those later women writers who came to Haworth, like Virginia Woolf on her moor-wandering trip in 1904, also felt the pull of personal objects. What she found "most touching," even more so than the manuscripts and letters displayed in the museum, were the "little personal relics of the dead woman." It struck her forcefully that Charlotte's shoes and thin muslin dress had outlived her, even though the "natural fate of such things is to die before the body that wore them." Because these material remnants, "trifling and transient though they are, have survived, Charlotte Brontë the woman comes to life." Sylvia Plath made a short list in her journal of what she found in the "rooms of memorabilia," which included "Charlotte's bridal crown of heirloom lace & honeysuckle" and "Emily's death couch." She goes on, "They touched this, wore that, wrote here in a house redolent with ghosts."[5]

Charlotte had herself felt this almost-religious reverence for her heroes, this desire to touch what they had touched, to peer through the same medium. There were all those stories she wrote as a girl about the Duke of Wellington and his kindred. As an adult she idolized the novelist William Makepeace Thackeray, even dedicating the second edition of *Jane Eyre* to him, which caused many to speculate that the novel was in part based on his own life—his wife had gone insane and, like Bertha Mason, had to be confined and restrained from self-harm—and that "Currer Bell" had been Thackeray's own governess. Her admiration for Napoleon led her to write a school essay in Brussels about his solitary death on Saint Helena, "exiled and captive—bound to an arid rock." Professor Heger, noting her deep respect, gave her a mahogany chip of Napoleon's outer coffin, which had been broken up after being replaced by an ebony sarcophagus following his exhumation and re-interment in Paris, some twenty years after his first burial on Saint Helena. Charlotte recorded the scene of giving, perhaps with an attention to provenance, or in some slightly mystical gesture similar to her inscriptions in books, and then wrapped the descriptive page around the nugget. On August 4, 1843, at 1:00 p.m., Heger walked into her classroom, she wrote, and gave her the "relic," which he brought to her from his friend Mr. Lebel. She went on to explain that Lebel was the secretary of Prince Achille Murat (Napoleon's nephew) and that the Prince de Joinville traveled with Napoleon's remains from Saint Helena. Lebel wrote directly on the wood in French, attesting to its authenticity. This stray oddment needed these announcements on and around it; otherwise it could easily have been cast off as detritus. It is in the stories surrounding and encasing it—as with those specks called thorns from Christ's crown cradled in crystal, gold, and gems—that the object comes alive with meaning.[6]

Unlike Napoleon's demise and the afterlife of his body, Charlotte's death was so quiet that most of her friends didn't even know she had been dying until well after she was interred in the church vaults. Only her husband, father, and a few servants witnessed her illness and final breaths. None of the obsequies at Napoleon's end—multiple ends— were practiced at Charlotte's (despite the cult that developed around her possessions): no piece of coffin was sawed off, no death mask molded, no fragment of the pall detached. No body part was reputedly snipped off and eventually sold—as was rumored to have happened to Napoleon's penis—just those simple locks of hair. Or, to illustrate how thorough such gatherings could be, take Lord Nelson's death, a few hours after a musket ball entered his shoulder during the Battle of Trafalgar. The ball, with a part of the braid from his epaulette adhering to it, was removed by the surgeon William Beatty, who placed it in a locket. Queen Victoria accepted it as a gift in 1844. Nelson's coat with the hole in the left shoulder, his bloody stockings, his pigtail cut off whole from his corpse, and the pocket watch worn when he died—all entered museums. Souvenir boxes fashioned from the HMS *Victory*, his ship during the fatal battle, held snuff, his hair, and other keepsakes. Nelson's compatriots buried him in a coffin made partially from a piece of the mainmast of *L'Orient*, the French ship he and his crew blew up during the Battle of the Nile. Given Nelson's and Napoleon's outsized roles in shaping Western history, it isn't surprising that their deaths were treated so differently from Charlotte's. But when considered in light of the hagiography surrounding Dickens's last moments (not to mention Shelley's, with those saved bits of bone, ash, and heart) just fifteen years after Charlotte's, which matched Napoleon's closely, except for the penis snipping, the comparison is striking.[7]

Charlotte's death was heroic in an entirely different way, one barely recognized by her contemporaries; illnesses that befell only women were not openly discussed, nor were they viewed as valiant in the way men's often were. It is now generally agreed that Charlotte died of hyperemesis gravidarum, or violent vomiting as a result of pregnancy. She became sick about six months after her marriage, when her "stomach seemed quite suddenly to lose its tone," causing "continual faint sickness," as she explained to Ellen in a letter, hinting also that she might be pregnant. The nausea and vomiting grew worse, until she was so weak and skeletal she couldn't leave her bed. Perhaps suspecting that the end was near, Charlotte wrote her will, leaving her estate to her husband, trusting that he would take care of her elderly father. She died, along with her unborn child, nine months after her wedding.[8]

It is a shame that Charlotte's powerful female friends weren't with her during her final illness. "How I wish I had known!" Elizabeth Gaskell exclaimed when she heard about it. "I do fancy that if I had come, I could have induced her,—even though they had all felt angry with me at first,—to do what was so absolutely necessary, for her very life." Could she have convinced them to terminate the pregnancy, and did Nicholls or Patrick consider it, or Charlotte herself? While abortion was illegal in Britain in 1855, it was widespread, if underground and often dangerous. Much hand-wringing among doctors (all male at this time) against the "elimination of pregnancy" can be found in medical journals of the 1850s and '60s. The journalist Henry Mayhew wrote in 1862 about the "immense number of embryo children who are made away with by drugs and other devices." Most women who wanted to abort took the advice of female friends or midwives and used herbs or mixtures, bought at local herbalists and chemists, such as pennyroyal, oil of savin, and gin and gunpowder. Many of these drugs, described in terms like "menstrual stimulators" and "remedies in obstructed menstruation," produced muscular contractions and vomiting, which sometimes caused abortion, although more often they failed to work. Abortifacients were also advertised in the press under euphemisms such as "female pills" and remedies for "ailments of the female system." One firm that called itself "Madame Frain" sold a "magic Mixture" with this label: "on no account to be taken by persons desirous of becoming mothers." Local women often acted as abortionists, their profession spread by word of mouth, and they went under such names as "granny" and used crochet or knitting needles to induce termination (sometimes resulting in death from infection). Established abortionists advertised offices for "temporary retirement" for ladies.[9]

While Gaskell was deeply religious, she also knew firsthand the problems women faced when they didn't have access to birth control or other methods of preventing childbirth. She worked alongside her husband, a Unitarian clergyman, among the poor in Manchester and wrote with sympathy in her novels of unwed mothers and the difficulties of prostitutes when pregnant. With a wide circle of female friends and associates of all classes, Gaskell must have had some knowledge about abortion, or at the very least, she would have known the right woman to give her advice. Some doctors would perform discreet abortions on their patients, especially if the woman's life was in danger, so perhaps Gaskell would have tried a doctor. Or did she have herbs or mixtures in mind? It is hard not to wish, looking back from a modern perspective, that Gaskell had been given the chance to at least try. What books might Charlotte have written if she had made it past her thirty-ninth birthday?[10]

Patrick had now lost the last member of his large family. He wrote of his astonishment with the situation to his children's nurse, who had emigrated to America when the Brontë children were still small: "When You, and Your sister Nancy, first came to us at Thornton, My Dear Wife, and all my Dear Children were living—six, in number— They are all, now dead—and, I, bordering, on the age of eighty years, am left Alone." No wonder he found himself "laboring under, so great a weight of sorrow," as he wrote to another correspondent. But he had a recently minted son to look after him as his health slowly declined. When Gaskell's wildly popular biography of Charlotte came out two years after her death, Patrick and Nicholls had to field pilgrims and souvenir hunters, who, having trickled in earlier, began to stream in steadily. When Patrick decided to have a new memorial tablet made for the family, he had them in mind when he took down the current one. Hung on an interior wall of the church, near where the family was interred, the old tablet had become so full from the family deaths that the later names had to be crowded in a tiny font at the bottom, leaving no room for his own name. He had the sexton break it up and bury it in the garden, not wanting it to be grabbed by the likes of Charles Hale, who had written about slabs removed from the parsonage walls: "Mr. Nicholls having neglected to bury these stones I might have brought one to America had they not been too heavy."[11]

Patrick finally succumbed to various illnesses on June 12, 1861, at the age of eighty-four. Hundreds of local people attended his funeral, and the shops in the town closed for the day as a mark of respect. The family vault received its last body; the new memorial tablet was completed with its final name. The natural promotion of Arthur Nicholls from curate to incumbent didn't happen, to the surprise of many townsfolk and to Nicholls himself. The trustees voted him out by a narrow margin, for reasons that have remained cloudy. Forced to move out of the parsonage so that Wade, the vicar of Bradford and the choice of the majority of trustees, could move in, Nicholls was given only days to pack. Bewildered about where to go, he returned to live with his aunt in Banagher, taking with him the Brontë manuscripts, including the miniature booklets and Anne's and Emily's diary papers. He also packed up many of the inscribed volumes from the family's library. Some of the girls' samplers went to Ireland with him, as did the desk boxes and workboxes with their contents. He took a dog and maybe dog collars, some of Charlotte's clothing, and locks of family hair. He carried a few mementos of Patrick, who had left him almost everything in his will, a mark of how close the two had finally become. Patrick's notebook of French phrases, which he had made for his trip to Brussels when he escorted his daughters to school, was kept by Nicholls, as was his rifle. In an act of possessiveness and perhaps jealous mourning, Nicholls had Charlotte's bed destroyed to prevent its reuse, or its treasuring as a relic.[12]

Nicholls didn't have room for most of the contents of the parsonage, so a sale by the local auctioneer, Mr. Cragg, dispersed what remained. Not widely advertised, the sale on October 1 and 2, 1861, went unnoticed by Brontë lovers, who then looked back on it with wistfulness, including Hale, who arrived just three weeks after its completion. Neighbors bought household goods for their own use, such as toilet covers, bed hangings, blankets, mattresses, pots, and baskets. Many books were sold, mostly unnamed in the auction catalog, listed only as "small books," "old books," or "sundry books." Some odds and ends went because of their sentimental associations, others probably for a mix of both handiness and sentiment. John Greenwood, the stationer who had sold reams of paper to the Brontë girls, purchased some bric-a-brac, as did relations of the servant Martha Brown, including her brother John, the sexton who had been friends with Branwell. The black horsehair sofa associated with Emily's last hours was bid for by William Hudson, a Haworth man, presumably for seating in his parlor.[13]

Locals found that extra money could be made on the Brontë tourist trade. Greenwood had his Brontë stationery printed, on which Hale wrote his letter to his mother in 1861. Edwin Feather, a postmaster who had handled many of the Brontë manuscripts when sent back and forth to publishers, became a souvenir purveyor. He had a shop close to the church, and he sold postcards with reproductions of Patrick's photo, a drawing of Charlotte by George Richmond, Nicholls's photo, and depictions of the church, both exterior and interior, and the parsonage. One postcard sold by him in the 1860s contains all of these pictures crowded on its front. When the old church was pulled down, Feather and others collected oak from the interior to make souvenirs, such as saltboxes and candleholders. These were the first glimmerings of a tourist trade that would pick up speed in the twentieth century and continues to flourish today.[14]

Brontë "relics" began to bring in cash. Martha Brown had been given some keepsakes by Patrick and Nicholls, including letters, some of the children's miniature books, Charlotte's wedding veil, and the silk dress she wore when she set off for her honeymoon. When Martha died, she willed them to her five sisters, who, being poor, either used them or sold them, or in some cases did one and then the other. Some of Charlotte's dresses that still survive were adjusted to be worn by other bodies. One sister, Ann Binns née Brown, used some gray alpaca material that had belonged to the Brontës to sew a tea apron with a lace border. She wore the apron, then later sold it as a Brontë artifact, a gesture combining thrift with memory of the fabric's previous owners. Relic culture melded with the world of women's domestic handicraft; the memento was worked by hand into something useful for the house, and then later it became a keepsake once again. Or something decorative: scraps of Charlotte's dresses became doll clothing. This apron and these dolls remind us of the wallpaper covers of the Brontë children's stories and of the little snippets of rolled paper stuck to the tea caddy Charlotte made for Ellen. It's hard to imagine this sort of household recycling with relics of Napoleon, say, or those of Dickens or Shelley. Take Dickens's chamber pot, now at the Dickens museum in London: Did someone else fill it, before it became museum worthy and thus retired forever?[15]

Rather astonishingly, the first attempt at a Brontë museum didn't attract enough funds to stay in business. It was a small, slightly tawdry affair, put together by Martha's cousins Francis and Robinson Brown, into whose hands many of the local keepsakes had fallen over the years. "Brown's Temperance Hotel and Museum of Brontë Relics" opened on Main Street in 1889. They eventually moved it to Blackpool and then on to the Chicago World's Fair in 1893, setting up not far from Buffalo Bill's Wild West Show. Finally most of the Brown collection went up for sale at an 1898 auction, including the lock of hair cut from Charlotte's corpse by Martha and numerous pincushions and pen-wipers.[16]

Meanwhile, in Ireland, Nicholls went on to marry his cousin Mary Bell in 1864, but still felt, those who knew him attested, that Charlotte had been his only true love. One wonders how Mary felt about Charlotte's wedding dress, gloves, and shoes preserved in a drawer upstairs, not to mention the Richmond portrait of Charlotte that hung over their sofa. A story, perhaps apocryphal, of this painting falling on Mary as she napped on the sofa, knocking her on the head and stunning her temporarily, has a poetic truth. When her husband died, she sold off the goods in two Sotheby's auctions, in 1907 and 1916, taking in a tidy bundle of cash. Who can blame her?[17]

Well before his death, Nicholls himself had sold off or lent some of the manuscripts. As his first wife's fame swelled, enthusiasts came up to Ireland to see him. Clement Shorter, a journalist and Brontë devotee who went on to write the 1896 *Charlotte Brontë and Her Circle* and other Brontë biographies, was able to carry off letters, Emily's and Anne's diary papers, many of the miniature books, and a handful of Branwell's manuscripts, simply by befriending Nicholls. Nicholls lent some of the papers to Shorter for his research; others Nicholls sold to him with the promise that they would ultimately be donated to the South Kensington Museum (now the Victoria and Albert). Shorter also visited Ellen

Nussey, convincing her to sell him her letters from Charlotte, with the same promise that they would eventually end up in a public institution. Shorter was working with the bibliophile Thomas J. Wise, who fronted much of the money to acquire the manuscripts. Both Nicholls and Nussey began to have suspicions about the shadiness of Shorter and Wise, especially the latter. Nicholls once misplaced a lock of Charlotte's hair, which ended up somehow in Shorter's hands. When it was returned to Nicholls, it was "sadly reduced in size since I had it—a few hairs in stead of a long thick tress."[18]

Wise, born into a working-class family, came to devote his life to manuscripts, rare editions, and literary memorabilia, amassing a collection he called the "Ashley Library"—after his house in north London at 52 Ashley Road, Hornsey Rise—which was eventually sold to the British Museum. Wise combined being a serious bibliographer—he put together, with Alexander Symington, an important early edition of the Brontë letters, even serving as the Brontë Society president for a time—with being a forger and garden-variety fraudster. His main trick involved printing a copy of a rare first edition and then claiming it as genuine, or even a "pre-first" edition privately printed by the author. He forged a series of pamphlets of this sort, of poems by Alfred Lord Tennyson, Elizabeth Barrett Browning, George Eliot, and others. He eventually began stealing from the British Museum, where he had special privileges, ripping out pages of rare works and having them bound into editions he owned. Somehow Wise's love of books bled into faking them, akin to a painter who begins making copies of the old masters out of reverence and then, eventually, for cash. Most of the money he made went into buying authentic manuscripts and rare books for his collection, his dishonesty serving his bibliophilia.[19]

Wise never intended to donate the Brontë manuscripts; some he kept for his collection, others he sold off to make money. He did "increase" the number of items he could sell by unbinding a few of Charlotte's handmade miniature booklets. He split up Emily's 1839 poetry notebook, mounting each page separately. He sold Branwell's manuscripts as Charlotte's or Emily's, since their work fetched much higher prices. When he produced his *Bibliography of the Writings in Prose and Verse of the Members of the Brontë Family*, it was a significant piece of Brontë scholarship except that he included his own fakery, thus institutionalizing it. As far as is known, he didn't make any forgeries of Brontë material, but since a number of fake letters and inscribed books made by anonymous hands exist, we have to wonder. For instance, an inscription on the flyleaf of an edition of *Les Psaumes de David, Mis en Vers Français*, supposedly from Charlotte in Paris to Emily, saying that Emily could use it to "polish up your French," is not in Charlotte's handwriting. Fake letters purporting to be from Charlotte and other family members crop up on occasion, such as one supposedly from Charlotte written in Rome, where she never went. Perhaps some of the Brontë material believed to be genuine might be fakes more clever than these.[20]

Worries about the authenticity of many of the Brontës' possessions plagued museums and scholars from the start. The Brontë Society formed in 1893 and two years later opened a museum at the peak of the hill on Main Street, above the Yorkshire Penny Bank (which moved to the Brontës' old home in 1928). By the 1950s, we find the society's president worrying about the "idolatry" in "Brontëism" and the problem "a generation ago" of zealous hunters of Brontë relics: "The West Riding tinkled with the faint notes of ancient pianos which were alleged, on more or less specious grounds, to have been used by the Brontës at Haworth. So many of these instruments obligingly came to light that, if all were genuine, a piano must have stood in every room at the Parsonage, including the kitchen and the peathouse." He complained about hoards of "Brontë Cradles" and heaps of supposed paintings and photographs of Emily. But he also claimed that the society had weeded out whatever was of "doubtful genuineness." The researcher today who sifts the Brontë archives naturally finds herself wondering about the thoroughness of this culling.[21]

Take, say, the linked jet ovals with Charlotte's and Emily's names scratched on them, pictured at the start of this chapter. What Brontë enthusiast wouldn't want to believe in their authenticity? They thrill as "autographs," like holograph manuscripts, with the vestige of the hand and its character. They seem to embody sisterly collaboration, reminiscent of the joint signatures on the diary paper of 1834, with Emily's and Anne's inked names touching. A household object has a second life, another Brontë hallmark: two panels of a mourning bracelet, which likely consisted of four or five of these ovals, connected by string. Raised flowers and leaves—black foliage carved out of a black backdrop—decorate the reverse side of each link. The Brontë family had other pieces of jet jewelry, including another bracelet fallen into fragments. Jet, made from fossilized driftwood, was mined near the town of Whitby, along the North Yorkshire coast. An inky, coal-like substance, jet was one of the cheaper materials for jewelry making and had a softness ideal for amateur carvers. It would become popular for mourning jewelry during Queen Victoria's reign, but by the start of the nineteenth century it was already associated with sentimentality and sympathy. The bracelet could have belonged to their aunt or mother, since the Branwell family in Penzance could afford such trinkets, unlike Patrick's humble Irish clan. The sisters kept similar raw materials in their workboxes and desk boxes, as we have seen, bits and bobs salvaged from old clothing and jewelry. One small sewing box of painted wood, with a sliding top, has six compartments, holding ribbon, parts of broken jewelry, and metal clothing fasteners. Perhaps a young Charlotte first picked up the pieces of the old bracelet, took a scissors' tip, and scratched this graffiti. Then Emily added her own statement of identity, a kind of "here I am," becoming "here we are." When Lucy, in *Villette*, crafts a watchguard for Paul Emanuel, she puts it in a shell box, and inside its lid she "graved with my scissors' point certain initials." Maybe Charlotte based this incident on her own "graving" in jet. Catherine Earnshaw's scratching of variations on her name into the paint of the window ledge inside her bed also springs to mind.[22]

Are these artifacts the real thing? They could be—the signatures are similar to theirs—but their provenance is so opaque that their authenticity is impossible, as far as I can tell, to confirm. The novelist Stella Gibbons said she found them in a "small, dirty junk shop, with no pretentions, in Kentish Town Road," during World War II. "I asked the man, a dreary creature and plainly poor, if he knew where they came from and I *think* he said 'from a big 'ouse' but I also *remember* his saying he knew nothing about them." She paid five pounds for them, and they knocked about in her jewelry box for years before she sent them to the biographer Winifred Gérin in 1971, whom she had met at the Royal Society of Literature. Gérin was about to bring out her book on Emily Brontë, and she had already made a name for herself with her award-winning biography of Charlotte. Gibbons herself professed her doubt as to their genuineness, wondering if they were "a child's joke," or if the man at the shop scratched them himself, but if so, she wondered why he didn't ask for more money. "Do whatever you like with them," Gibbons ends her letter to Gérin.[23]

They could have been a Gibbons lark. A great wit, in 1932 she wrote *Cold Comfort Farm*, a parody of fiction about earthy connections to nature and people with a "slow, deep, primitive, silent down-dragging link" to beasts. "They lay close to the earth, and something of earth's old fierce simplicities had seeped into their beings." She was making gentle fun of D. H. Lawrence's work and "ruralist" novels of the

1910s and '20s, but her satire also touched the melodrama of *Wuthering Heights*. Her urbane heroine, Flora Poste, takes a trip to her country relations, farmers with names like Starkadder and Lambsbreath living in a house called Howling. Flora's cousin, a tall girl named Elfine, is something of an Emily Brontë stereotype, a poetry lover and "shy dryad" who dances "in the woods with the wind-flowers and birds." Flora civilizes them, teaching the women about birth control, dressing Elfine in current fashions, and marrying her off to the rich local landowner, Dick Hawk-Monitor.[24]

While in the countryside, Flora encounters a young intellectual working on a study about Branwell which argues that he wrote all of the Brontë novels and let his sisters, who were drunkards (especially Anne with a love of gin), take the credit. Gibbons was ridiculing the theory, first made in the 1860s, that Branwell wrote *Wuthering Heights*. "You see, it's obvious that it's his book and not Emily's. No woman could have written that. It's male stuff," says Gibbons's intellectual. Lucasta Miller makes the astute point that Gibbons caricatures Brontë biographers, who had become a "source of mystification" by the 1930s, filling out the gaps in Emily's life story with wild speculations. In fact, according to Gibbons's nephew, who attended many of these Royal Society of Literature lectures with her in the 1970s, she didn't like Gérin and tried to avoid her. Was Gibbons parodying the treatment of any stray stuff that might be connected to the Brontë story as meaningful by sending the jet ovals to Gérin?[25]

Whether or not they are authentic, they represent the deep attention the Brontë story still elicits, a yearning that falls so often on place and matter. To many, the Brontës remain secular saints; the things they may have touched bring their personal magic closer. Without these strong emotions, these objects go the way of all matter, obscurity lapping at their edges. They speak of our need to believe that a life can be recalled through its material remnants, that not everything of that loved body's movement through time has been lost for good. The Brontë story can bring a peculiar immortality to the things it brushes, even when not originally associated with it. The lack of clear provenance can gradually disappear out of historical memory, and the body of Brontë objects can expand instead of contract as time passes. Our desire makes finitude fall away.

Such unruly longings can be found in Haworth still. Since the early twentieth century, the town has crawled with tourists. On a recent fall trip, I stayed at the Brontë Cottage Bed and Breakfast and slept in the Anne Brontë room located in the basement; the Emily and Charlotte rooms were on the second floor. Busloads of tourists arrived to trawl along the main street, filling guided tours to the "Brontë waterfalls" and the "Brontë chair." I passed people in Victorian dress in the churchyard, and a film crew, shooting a segment about Brontëland, crowded one day into the library at the museum where I was studying Brontë artifacts. Dishes, hand towels, and tee-shirts with pictures of the Brontë sisters could be bought in the shops, and tea could be had at the Villette coffeehouse.[26]

Despite all of this, the town, the parsonage, the churchyard, and—especially—the moors have an atmosphere that really does, as Virginia Woolf put it, "express" the Brontës and fit them "like a snail its shell." It's hard to deny the stirring gloominess of the moorland scenery, with its sky usually darkly lowering. The barren Pennines ring with the calls of the grouse, as they suddenly start out of the brush and heather when a walker nears. Boggy spots dot the land, and stands of ferns grow at the edges of streams and rocky cliffs. Many a dog lover lives in Haworth and can be found out on the moors even well after darkness, their canine companions running ahead. The steep, cobbled street that Gaskell described in her biography remains, as do many of the soot-darkened eighteenth-century buildings. The townsfolk still burn coal (and sometimes peat) fires, which permeate the air with a heaviness and an oily smell. Some afternoons and early evenings a thick fog descends, making it impossible to see more than five feet ahead. It rained almost incessantly when I visited, and the penetrating chill increased when darkness fell by 4:30. Bright-green moss grew on the gray slate rooftops. Rooks cawed eerily among the trees in the churchyard.[27]

One afternoon when I was starting up the steep incline of Main Street, I passed a young woman in black leather pants, her long hair dyed black. She stood still. Her face showed such fervor that I found myself looking away. The raw strength of her passion felt too private for a stranger to gaze on. It is easy to ridicule such intense feeling, easy to feel contempt at such naïve sentimentality. But then again, why not admire it? Is there a better place to look to find heroines on which to model one's life?

Notes

ABBREVIATIONS USED IN NOTES

AB   Anne Brontë
BB   Branwell Brontë
CB   Charlotte Brontë
EB   Emily Brontë
EN   Ellen Nussey
PB   Patrick Brontë

Berg   Henry W. and Albert A. Berg Collection of English and
        American Literature, New York Public Library
BPM   Brontë Parsonage Museum
BST   Brontë Society Transactions
LCB   The Letters of Charlotte Brontë, ed. Margaret Smith, vols. 1–3
        (New York: Oxford University Press, 1995).
PML   Pierpont Morgan Library and Museum

PREFACE: THE PRIVATE LIVES OF OBJECTS

1   The apostles cabinet is now at the BPM, F32.
2   Constance Classen, "Touch in the Museum," in Constance Classen, ed., *The Book of Touch* (Oxford, UK: Berg, 2005), 275–77; quoted in ibid., 277; Zacharias Conrad von Uffenbach, *Oxford in 1710*, ed. W. H. Quarrell and W. J. C. Quarrell (Oxford, UK: Blackwell, 1928), 31; quoted in Asa Briggs, *Victorian Things* (Chicago: University of Chicago Press, 1989), 29.
3   See Elaine Freedgood, *The Ideas in Things: Fugitive Meaning in the Victorian Novel* (Chicago: Chicago University Press, 2006), chap. 1. Other important works on material culture include Bill Brown, *A Sense of Things: The Object Matter of American Literature* (Chicago: University of Chicago Press, 2003), and John Plotz, *Portable Property: Victorian Culture on the Move* (Princeton, NJ: Princeton University Press,

2009). Philosophers have thought about materiality, of course: Immanuel Kant separated human consciousness from objects, arguing that we can never know the "thing-in-itself" since as soon as we encounter it, we color it with our own concepts of space and time. Martin Heidegger extended Kant's ideas by seeing the object, such as a jug, as a sort of meeting place of the central elements of earth, sky, mortals (us), and divinities. But this was only when we could encounter the thing authentically, which Heidegger felt was becoming ever more impossible in a world full of trivial noise and hurry. Expanding on Heidegger, Graham Harman and others in the field of object-oriented ontology (and the related one of speculative realism) have removed the human from the center of everything and instead privileged the thing and its relationship to other things. "All human and non-human entities have equal status" in this philosophy, and the "real object lies deeper than any relations with people or other objects," explains Harman in *The Quadruple Object* (Hants, UK: Zero, 2011), 21, 29, 46, 123. See also Martin Heidegger, "The Thing," *Poetry, Language, Thought*, trans. Albert Hofstadter (New York: Harper and Row, 1971).

4 Caroline Walker Bynum, *Christian Materiality: An Essay on Religion in Late Medieval Europe* (New York: Zone, 2011), 233; touchpieces were used by royals who didn't like direct contact with commoners but knew that their subjects would want the benefits of their touch. The Wellcome Collection has a few of these, such as a lodestone, made of slate and silver, A641031 (ca. 1702–1714), thought to have belonged to Queen Anne; Walter Woodburn Hyde, "The Prosecution and Punishments of Animals and Lifeless Things in the Middle Ages and Modern Times," *University of Pennsylvania Law Review* 64 (1915–1916), 726.

CHAPTER ONE: TINY BOOKS

1 For a floor plan of the house (and grounds) before CB had it renovated after the deaths of all her siblings, see F. Mitchell's map in *BST* 9, no. 1 (1936), 27. See also Elizabeth Gaskell's description in *The Life of Charlotte Brontë* (New York: Penguin, 1997), 39. Gaskell was friends with CB, and she visited her at the parsonage. The first edition of Gaskell's biography was published in 1857, two years after CB's death. All references to the weather come from the daily recordings of the local meteorologist Abraham Shackleton, a contemporary of the Brontës who lived in nearby Keighley. His manuscript weather records are in Cliffe Castle Museum, Keighley. See Edward Chitham, *A Life of Emily Brontë* (Oxford, UK: Blackwell, 1987), 17, for his argument that the fires in the house were of peat.

2 Juliet Barker argues that Maria was something of a bluestocking and that the children were there at their mother's death. See *The Brontës* (New York: St. Martin's, 1994), 48, 104; for the nurse's account, see Elizabeth Gaskell to Catherine Winkworth, Aug. 25, 1850, *LCB*, vol. 2, 447.

3 CB's manuscript "The History of the Year," Mar. 1829, BPM, Bonnell 80 (11).

4 I am tempted to imagine that the scissors she used are the rusty steel ones, one handle partly bound in kid, that still exist at the BPM, H128. Her process of making the

book can be seen when one holds the book itself—no record of her making it sur-
vives. It is at the Houghton Library, Harvard University, MS Lowell 1(5). The poet
Amy Lowell was given the manuscript by the bibliophile and forger Thomas James
Wise on September 11, 1905, in London. Wise had purchased it from CB's husband,
Arthur Bell Nicholls, in 1895, using the Brontë biographer Clement Shorter as inter-
mediary (more about this in chap. 9). Amy Lowell donated the book to Harvard in
1925. For helpful transcriptions of CB's juvenilia, see Christine Alexander, ed., *An
Edition of the Early Writings of Charlotte Brontë*, 3 vols. (Oxford, UK: Blackwell,
1987); Gaskell, *Life*, 74.

5 The tiny text reads, "In the year 1829, lived Captain Henry Dunally, a man whose
possessions in this world bring him £200,000 a year. He was the owner of a beautiful country seat, about 10 miles from Glass Town and lived in a style which, though
comfortable and happy, was some thousands below his yearly income. His wife, a
comely lady in the 30th year of her age, was a person of great management and
discretion, and given to use her tongue upon occasion. They had 3 children, the
eldest of whom was 12, the second 10 and the youngest 2 years of age. They went by
the separate names of Augusta Cecilia, Henry Fearnothing (the name of a maternal
uncle of no great character among the more sober part of mankind and to this class
both Dunally and his wife belonged) and Cina Rosalind. These children had, as may
be supposed, each a different character. Augusta was given to . . ."; CB, "History of
the Year"; see Margaret Oliphant, *Annals of a Publishing House, William Blackwood
and His Sons, Their Magazine and Friends* (Edinburgh: Blackwood, 1897); BB's first
"Blackwood's" is at the Houghton Library, Harvard University, MS Lowell 1(8).
For excellent photos of BB's first issue of the miniature magazines, owned by Harvard, go to http://nrs.harvard.edu/urn-3:FHCL.HOUGH:1077557. Indeed, all
nine of the Brontë miniature books at Harvard can be viewed through the library
catalog; CB's first issue of "Blackwood's" is also at the Houghton, MS Lowell 1(6);
Elizabeth Gaskell to George Smith, July 1856, in J. A. V. Chapple and John Geoffrey
Sharps, eds., *Elizabeth Gaskell: A Portrait in Letters* (Manchester, UK: Manchester
University Press, 1980), 149.

6 CB, "Characters of the Celebrated Men of the Present Time," original manuscript
lost. Alexander, *Early Writings*, vol. 1, 127.

7 For much more about the Brontë juvenilia, see Fannie Ratchford, *The Brontës' Web
of Childhood* (New York: Russell and Russell, 1964); see Barker, *Brontës*, chap. 6, for
a list of the children's toys. Some of these toys still exist in the BPM, such as a carved
wooden lion, H163.3; a child's tea set picturing three women around a table and
the bit of verse "Ladies all I pray make free / And tell me how you like your tea,"
H167.1-4; and a brass toy clothes iron, H165; CB, "History of the Year."

8 BB, "History of the Young Men," British Library, Ashley 2468. For transcriptions
of BB's miniature books, see Victor Neufeldt, ed., *The Works of Patrick Branwell
Brontë*, 3 vols. (New York: Garland, 1999).

9 BB, "History of the Young Men."

10 Ratchford, *Brontës' Web*, 19, describes the made-up language; the miniature books
that make up the volumes of the "Tales of the Islanders" have been, sadly, disas-

sembled and mounted in a large, leather-bound volume made for the purpose. All, dated March 12, 1829–July 30, 1830, are at the Berg.

11 CB, "History of the Year."

12 Ibid.

13 At least two versions of the story of the cherry tree, which happened sometime between 1828 and 1830, exist, told by locals about the family. This version comes from J. A. Erskine Stuart, *The Brontë Country* (London: Longmans, 1888), 189–90. Another version has their servant, Sarah Garrs, as the one stepping out onto the tree, playing an escaping prince. For this second version, see Marion Harland, *Charlotte Brontë at Home* (London: Putnam's, 1899), 32.

14 Unlike most other writings by the children, the earliest surviving one, BPM, Bonnell78, isn't dated, so 1826 is a careful guess based on the dates of the other manuscripts and the evidence of maturity of handwriting and skill. Christine Alexander, in *Early Writings*, vol. 1, 3, calls this CB's first extant manuscript. While they are all small, the size of these books vary, as does the print. Some of the text is impossible to read without magnification, despite it also being neat and clearly written out. Probably the smallest book, with the tiniest print, is CB's "The Poetaster," vol. 2, June 8–July 12, 1830, PML, MA 2696.10; for the size of the books as related to the size of the children's bodies, see Kate E. Brown, "Beloved Objects: Mourning, Materiality, and Charlotte Brontë's 'Never-Ending Story,' " *English Literary History* 65, no. 2 (1998), 395–421; CB, "Third Volume of the Tales of the Islanders," Berg.

15 Gaskell, *Life*, 81; Christine Alexander and Juliet McMaster, eds., *The Child Writer from Austen to Woolf* (Cambridge, UK: Cambridge University Press, 2005). For Ruskin's juvenilia, see his autobiography *Praeterita* (New York: Oxford University Press, 1949), 43–45.

16 Richard Altick, *The English Common Reader: A Social History of the Mass Reading Public, 1800–1900*, 2nd ed. (Columbus: Ohio State University Press, 1998), 262–78; CB, "Last Will and Testament of Florence Marian Wellesley . . . ," Jan. 5, 1834, PML, Bonnell Collection.

17 There has been much debate among Brontë biographers about where the family got their books—borrowed from the nearby landowners, the Heatons of Ponden Hall, or from the Keighley Mechanics' Institute. Barker makes a convincing case that they subscribed to a Keighley (the closest town to Haworth) circulating library. See Barker, *Brontës*, 147–49; CB to Hartley Coleridge, Dec. 10, 1840, in *LCB*, vol. 1, 240; Maria Branwell to Patrick Brontë, Nov. 18, 1812, in Thomas James Wise and John Alexander Symington, eds., *The Brontës: Their Lives, Friendship and Correspondence* (Oxford, UK: Blackwell, 1932), vol. 1, 21.

18 The Brontës' edition of *Poems of Ossian* is now at the BPM, bb203; BB, "Blackwood's," June 1829, Houghton Library, Lowell 1(7); CB to W. S. Williams, July 21, 1851, in *LCB*, vol. 2, 667.

19 *Russell's General Atlas of Modern Geography*, PML, 129886; BB, "The Liar Detected," BPM, Bon 139; CB, "Leaf from an Unopened Volume," Jan. 1834, BPM, 13.2.

20 Gaskell, *Life*, 93, describes the Brontës' books; BB, "Liar Detected."

21 For rebinding as a handicraft, usually practiced by women, see Talia Schaffer, *Novel*

Craft: Victorian Domestic Handicraft and Nineteenth-Century Fiction (New York: Oxford University Press, 2011), 16; Harvard's Houghton Library has some of these dress-bound volumes, in the Lowell Collection; *Sermons or homilies appointed to be read in churches in the time of Queen Elizabeth*, BPM, bb57. Inscription transcribed by Barker, *Brontës*, 30.

22 CB, "History of the Year." Like other personal effects of Maria and Elizabeth, this book is, inexplicably, lost.

23 New Testament, PML, Printed Books 17787.

24 Prayer book, PML, MA 2696.

25 John Frost, *Bingley's Practical Introduction to Botany*, 2nd ed. (London: Baldwin, Cradock and Joy, 1827), BPM, 2004/47.9; Susanna Harrison, *Songs in the Night* (London: Baynes, 1807), BPM, bb30. In addition to many pressed ferns and other plants, there is also a tipped-in calling card, from a Mrs. T. Lord, from the nearby Lower Laith, Todmorden. There is also, unsurprisingly, an inscription, as Patrick gave this book to one Hannah, with his "kind regards."

26 *Iliad*, BPM, Bonnell 35; Bible, PML, 17769; CB, piece of paper, BPM, Bonnell 108.

27 BB, "History of the Young Men."

28 John Greenwood, the local Haworth stationer, reported this to Gaskell, *Life*, 216.

29 For the history of paper, see Altick, *English Common Reader*, 262; and Schaffer, *Novel Craft*, 69; CB, "Third Volume of the Tales of the Islanders"; CB, untitled fragment, BPM, Bonnell 88; CB, "The Poetaster," vol. 1, July 6, 1830, Houghton Library, Lowell I(2).

30 Written on the inside of the cover of BB's November 1833 "The Politics of Verdopolis, A Tale by Captain John Flower" are directions for delivering a package: "Carriage Paid 110, by Red Rover, Lynn Coach, Thursday Night, March 6, 1834," which seems to show that BB sewed his book together some months after he wrote it. BPM, Bonnell 141; BB, "Blackwood's," Jan. 1829, Houghton Library, MS Lowell 1(6); BB, "History of the Rebellion," BPM, BS112; CB, "Albion and Marina," Wellesley College Library, Wellesley, MA. It wasn't just the children who handmade booklets. Their father, PB, also created a small notebook, BPM, BS 178, out of recycled paper, stitched together. He filled it with French phrases to be used on his trip to France and Belgium to escort CB and EB to their school.

31 Leah Price, "Getting the Reading out of It: Paper Recycling in Mayhew's London," in *Bookish Histories; Books, Literature and Commercial Modernity, 1700–1900* (New York: Palgrave, 2009), 154; CB to George Smith, Feb. 5, 1851, in *LCB*, vol. 2, 573.

32 Leah Price, *How to Do Things with Books in Victorian Britain* (Princeton, NJ: Princeton University Press, 2012), 27–29; *Geography for Youth*, 14th ed., trans. Abbé Lenglet du Fresnoy (Dublin: P. Wogan, 1795), BPM, SB 256. This volume, obviously very cheaply made with rag paper unevenly printed—a testament to the poverty of the Brontë clan—has doodles and jottings covering most of the blank pages, including "Hugh Bronte His book in the year 1803" and Walsh Bronte's signature.

33 The Shelley diary is at the Pforzheimer Collection, New York Public Library; Edward Trelawny, *Records of Shelley, Byron, and the Author* (New York: New York Review of Books, 2000), 145; Bodleian Library, Shelley adds. d.6.

34 The skull fragments are unlikely to be authentic. The helpful curators of the collection are themselves doubtful of their authenticity. When I looked at these fragments, I wondered what sort of material they might really be if they aren't bone. What is the story behind that fraud? What are said to be parts of Shelley's jaw are on display at the Keats-Shelley Memorial House in Rome. The beautiful (if grisly) volume that supposedly contains his hair and ashes, British Library, Ashley MS 5022, was created in the 1890s by the bibliophile Thomas James Wise, who was also a known forger and thief (more about him in chap. 9). The manuscripts it contains are definitely authentic, but the Shelley remains probably aren't. Someone's hair *is* set in the front cover, however, but what is in the back cover is anyone's guess. The fragments looked to me like small black and gray rocks. Wise also owned many Brontë manuscripts, and he had CB's manuscript of *The Professor* bound by Joseph Zaehnsdorf, a London binder who occasionally used tanned human skin rather than leather. See "Books Bound in Human Skins," *New York Times*, Jan. 25, 1886.

35 For an engrossing and impeccably researched account of body snatching, the Anatomy Act, and corpse recycling, see Ruth Richardson, *Death, Dissection, and the Destitute* (Chicago: University of Chicago Press, 2000); the pocket book is now at the Museum of the Royal College of Surgeons, Edinburgh.

36 BB, "Young Soults Poems with Notes," BPM, BS114; CB, "An Interesting Passage in the Lives of Some Eminent Men," Houghton Library, Lowell 1(1).

37 Gaskell, *Life*, 14; for graveyard overcrowding, see Barker, *Brontës*, 98; C. Mabel Edgerley, "The Structure of Haworth Parsonage," *BST*, 9, no. 1 (1936), 29; EN's reminiscences, in *LCB*, vol. 1, 600; for the "arvills," see Gaskell, *Life*, 26–27; BB to the editor of *Blackwood's*, Dec. 7, 1835, in Wise and Symington, eds., *Brontës*, vol. 1, 133.

38 Many Brontë scholars argue that the handmade booklets are reactions to grief after the death of the two Brontë sisters. See especially Brown, "Beloved Objects," Robert Keefe, *Charlotte Brontë's World of Death* (Austin: University of Texas Press, 1979), and Winifred Gérin, *Charlotte Brontë: The Evolution of Genius* (London: Oxford University Press, 1967); CB, "An Interesting Passage in the Lives of Some Eminent Men of the Present Time," June 17, 1830, Houghton Library, Lowell I(1).

39 EN's reminiscences, in *LCB*, vol. 1, 597.

40 Gaskell felt the window seats gave the house an old-fashioned feel when she first visited CB there. Gaskell, *Life*, 39, 105. A visitor to the parsonage house today will not be able to see the moors out of most of the windows, but during the Brontës' time, the trees that now block the view either did not exist or were very small. Also, some of the windows that had the best views of the moors no longer exist, such as one in the kitchen and another in an upstairs bedroom; CB's friend Mary Taylor wrote about CB's odd reading in a letter to Gaskell, in ibid., 78.

41 Barbara Whitehead, *Charlotte Brontë and Her 'Dearest Nell': The Story of a Friendship* (Otley, UK: Smith Settle, 1993), 51.

42 CB, "Biographical Notice of Ellis and Acton Bell," first printed in her edition of *Wuthering Heights, Agnes Grey*, and a selection of her sisters' poems, published by Smith, Elder and Co., 1850. Republished as appendix II, in *LCB*, vol. 2, 742.

CHAPTER TWO: PILLOPATATE

1 Abraham Shackleton calls it "a fine day." Manuscript weather records, Cliffe Castle Museum, Keighley.

2 AB and EB, diary paper, Nov. 24, 1834, BPM, Bonnell 131.

3 This box has gone missing, but Clement Shorter described it when Arthur Nicholls lent it to him in 1895. It isn't the one now at the BPM that is said to have belonged to EB, H109, since that one is more than twice as large as the diary papers tin, which was "about two inches long." Shorter, *Charlotte Brontë and Her Circle* (Westport, CT: Greenwood, 1970), 146, originally published in 1896; for discussions of EB's and AB's reading of Moore's *Life of Byron*, see Edward Chitham, *A Life of Emily Brontë* (Oxford, UK: Blackwell, 1987), 83, and Winifred Gérin, *Emily Brontë* (London: Oxford University Press, 1971), 44–45.

4 CB, "A Day at Parry's Palace, by Lord Charles Wellesley," BPM, B85.

5 EN's account of her visit to the parsonage in 1833, reprinted in appendix II, in *LCB*, vol. 1, 596; for EB leading CB close to strange animals, see EN's recollections, quoted in Shorter, *Charlotte Brontë*, 179; CB, "Biographical Notice of Ellis and Acton Bell," in *LCB*, vol. 2, 745, 746.

6 Harriet Martineau, *Autobiography*, ed. Linda Peterson (Peterborough, Ontario: Broadview, 2007), 99, 112, 51.

7 From an interview with Martha Brown, first printed in *Yorkshireman*, and reprinted in *BST* 14, no. 3 (1963), 28–29; "Turning" could also mean putting damp clothes through a mangle, according to Jocelyn Kellett, *Haworth Parsonage: The Home of the Brontës* (Bradford, UK: Brontë Society, 1977), 65.

8 AB's sampler, BPM, S12, was given by CB's husband, Arthur Bell Nicholls, to Clement Shorter, an early Brontë collector and biographer, who then donated it to the BPM.

9 AB's first sampler, BPM, S11; Maria Brontë's sampler, BPM, S5, with a verse from Proverbs, was finished May 18, 1822. Elizabeth's, BPM, S6, was completed on July 22, 1822; Maria Branwell's sampler, April 15, 1791, BPM, S1, and Elizabeth Branwell's, October 11, 1790, BPM, S2. Both were made in Penzance; EB's first sampler, BPM, S9, was finished April 22, 1828, and her second, BPM, S10, on March 1, 1829. CB's first, BPM, S7, was July 25, 1822, her second, BPM, S15, April 1, 1828.

10 Carol Humphrey, *Samplers* (Cambridge, UK: Cambridge University Press, 1997), 5; a framed sampler hanging at the Brontë parsonage was made by one Nellie Cattral when she was thirteen years old, in 1781. It was sold at a Sotheby's auction on July 2, 1898 (lot 41), by Robinson Brown, who inherited it from his father, William Brown, the Haworth church sexton. William probably obtained it from his niece Martha Brown, a servant at the parsonage. See the Sotheby's Sales Catalog, BPM, Bon335; for samplers stitched with hair, see Jane Toller, *The Regency and Victorian Crafts* (London: Ward Lock, 1969), 68–69; one of these Great Exhibition samplers is pictured in Nerylla Taunton, *Antique Needlework Tools and Embroideries* (Suffolk, UK: Antique Collector's Club, 1997), 187; Elizabeth Parker's sampler, Victoria and Albert Museum, T.6-1956.

11 Mary C. Beaudry, *Findings: The Material Culture of Needlework and Sewing* (New Haven, CT: Yale University Press, 2006), 45; CB, "Julia," in Winifred Gérin, ed., *Five Novelettes* (London: Folio Press, 1971), 92.

12 Martineau, *Autobiography*, 323–24.

13 Beaudry, *Findings*, 45. Especially poignant examples of needlework tools that speak of an absent woman are the wooden knitting-sheaths, BPM, H201.1 and H201.2, that belonged to Maria, the Brontës' mother. They have "MB" scratched on them and were used by the daughters after their mother's death; Mary Andere, *Old Needlework Boxes and Tools* (New York: Drake, 1971), 26.

14 Sally Hesketh, "Needlework in the Lives of the Brontë Sisters," *BST* 22, no. 1 (1997), 73.

15 All of the workboxes discussed in this paragraph are featured in Taunton, *Antique Needlework Tools*, 57, 108–9, 113.

16 Hesketh, in "Needlework," 74, describes Aunt Branwell's boxes; CB's leather workcase, BPM, H108; CB's workbox, BPM, H180, was kept by her husband, Arthur Bell Nicholls, and sold at auction in 1907 by his second wife after his death. The BPM bought it at this auction.

17 Andere, in *Old Needlework Boxes*, 24–25, discusses secret compartments.

18 For the contents of CB's workbox, see Juliet Barker, *Sixty Treasures: The Brontë Parsonage Museum* (Haworth, UK: Brontë Society, 1988), n. 50; AB's workbox was sold at a Sotheby's auction in 1916, lot 664, by the Brontë enthusiast J. H. Dixon, who had bought it from Tabitha Radcliffe, the sister of Martha Brown, a servant of the Brontës. The lot also contained an unfinished green purse and a handmade silk purse.

19 Lewis Carroll, *Through the Looking Glass: And What Alice Found There* (Philadelphia: Henry Altemus, 1897), 106; while cloth and clothing began to be made in factories in the early nineteenth century, mass-produced and machine-made clothing didn't begin to widely replace hand sewing until the 1850s and later. The sewing machine was invented in the 1850s, but it would take a few decades before it would be found in many homes. For "it-narratives" and their meaning, see Elaine Freedgood, "What Objects Know: Circulation, Omniscience and the Comedy of Dispossession in Victorian It-Narratives," *Journal of Victorian Culture* 15, no. 1 (2010), 33–100.

20 Umbrella needle-case, Victoria and Albert Museum, T.238-1969; Maria's gift, BPM, H129; CB's needle booklet for Eliza, BPM, H175; for premade cards to turn into needle-cases, see Andere, *Old Needlework Boxes*, 76. Embroidering on paper was a common craft, as was creating "pin-pricked" designs and pictures on paper. See Toller, *Regency and Victorian Crafts*, 46–48; numerous drawings CB made were probably meant for needle-cases, as Christine Alexander and Jane Sellars explain, in *The Art of the Brontës* (London: Cambridge University Press, 1995), 188–89; CB to EN, April 22, 1848, in *LCB*, vol. 2, 53; CB's "housewife," BPM, H149.

21 Basket, BPM, H108.5; book pincushion, part of the contents of CB's portable desk, Berg; CB's pincushion with the inscription was sold at the Sotheby's auction of July 2, 1898, lot 88, BPM, Bon335; the Wordsworth one is pictured in Taunton, *Antique Needlework Tools*, 140–41.

22 CB to EN, Dec. 1839, and Apr. 30, 1840, in *LCB*, vol. 1, 207, 216; CB to EN, Jan. 1847, Apr. 1847, and Sept. 1847, in *LCB*, vol. 1, 515, 523, 543; CB to EN, Apr. 30, 1840, in *LCB*, vol. 1, 216; CB to EN, Dec. 1845, in *LCB*, vol. 1, 441; CB to EN, Apr. 1847, in *LCB*, vol. 1, 523.

23 CB's recitation while sewing comes from EN's reminiscences, in *LCB*, vol. 1, 609; the unfinished patchwork quilt, BPM, D145, might not have been made by the Brontës, though it was sold as such at a Sotheby's auction, on July 2, 1898, lot 47, by Robinson Brown.

24 See Talia Schaffer, *Novel Craft: Victorian Domestic Handicraft and Nineteenth-Century Fiction* (New York: Oxford University Press, 2011), for her theories about the relationship between crafts and novel writing for Victorian women. She explores all of the crafts mentioned in this paragraph. For crafts and class status, see 29; "Catalogue of the Contents of Moor Lane House, Gomersal, to be Sold by Auction on Wednesday and Thursday, May 18 and 19, 1898," BPM, P Sales Cat. 2; CB's quilled tea caddy, BPM, H34, which, according to Barker, *Sixty Treasures*, was a gift for Ellen.

25 Quoted in Asa Briggs, *Victorian Things* (Chicago: Chicago University Press, 1988), 207. See also Rozsika Parker, *The Subversive Stitch: Embroidery and the Making of the Feminine* (London: Women's Press, 1984), 175–79 and Schaffer, *Novel Craft*, 34–35.

26 CB to EN, Dec. 1839, in *LCB*, vol. 1, 207; CB to EN, Jan. 20, 1842, in *LCB*, vol. 1, 278; CB's stockings, BPM, D23; AB, diary paper, July 31, 1845, in private hands; CB to EB, June 8, 1893, in *LCB*, vol. 1, 191.

27 See Sally Hesketh's excellent article, "Needlework," on needlework and the Brontës for more on this. On p. 78 she writes, "Morally strong characters embrace domestic duty (represented by plain sewing), whilst those who are morally weak shirk their obligations in preference of frivolous ornamental work."

28 Ellen Weeton's diaries, partially published as Edward Hall, ed., *Miss Weeton: Journal of a Governess* (London: Oxford University Press, 1939), vol. 2, 396; quoted in Pam Hirsch, *Barbara Leigh Smith Bodichon, Feminist, Artist, and Rebel* (London: Chatto and Windus, 1998), 54.

29 Geoffrey Warren, *A Stitch in Time: Victorian and Edwardian Needlecraft* (London: David and Charles, 1976), 123.

30 See Edward Chitham, *A Life of Anne Brontë* (Oxford, UK: Blackwell, 1991), especially chap. 9, for an extensive analysis of AB's more rational character.

CHAPTER THREE: OUT WALKING

1 "High waving heather 'neath stormy blasts bending," Dec. 13, 1836. All of the quotations from EB's poems come from Janet Gezari, ed., *Emily Jane Brontë: The Complete Poems* (London: Penguin, 1992). If EB didn't title a poem, then I give its first line as a title. The dates provided come from Gezari's scholarly footwork. When they are conjectural, I include a question mark.

2 EN's reminiscences, in *LCB*, vol. 1, 601, 598; EB, "Song," 1844.

3 See Edward Chitham, *A Life of Emily Brontë* (Oxford, UK: Blackwell, 1987), for his discussion of the actual weather in EB's poems. EB, "Often rebuked, yet always back returning," undated. This poem may have been written by CB and attributed to EB, or if EB wrote it, it is probable that CB revised it, as she did with many of EB's poems. Chitham, in *Emily Brontë*, 219, argues the latter. Gezari argues that the poem was wholly written by CB but cast in EB's voice and deliberately attributed to EB by CB. See her *Last Things: Emily Brontë's Poems* (Oxford, UK: Oxford University Press, 2007), especially 141–50.

4 BB's fragment, in Victor Neufeldt, ed., *The Works of Patrick Branwell Brontë* (New York: Garland, 1999), vol. 2, 587.

5 The stick, BPM, SB: 337, was donated in 1917 to the museum by Mr. George Day. He was an annual subscriber to the Brontë Society starting in 1897 and then a lifetime member from 1906 to 1926. Along with the walking stick, he donated funeral cards for CB, BB, PB, and John Brown, as well as other items. Day bought the stick at a Sotheby's auction as lot 668 in December 13–15, 1916, as part of the collection of a well-known Brontë enthusiast and collector of Brontë artifacts, J. H. Dixon of Harrogate. It was accompanied by a silhouette portrait of BB and a framed authentication letter, stating that it was sold by J. Briggs to H. Edmundson, who sold it in turn to C. Stansfield, from whom it was purchased by Mr. Dixon. See "Catalogue of Valuable Illuminated and Other Manuscripts," Sotheby's, Dec. 13–15, 1916, BPM. For Dixon as a collector, see Ann Dinsdale, Sarah Laycock, and Julie Akhurst, *Brontë Relics: A Collection History* (Yorkshire, UK: Brontë Society, 2012), 43; the history and craft of blackthorn sticks comes from A. E. Boothroyd, *Fascinating Walking Sticks* (London: White Lion, 1973), 54–56; in addition to PB's blackthorn stick, there is also a heavy oak one, perhaps used when he was an old man, at the BPM. John Lock and Canon W. T. Dixon, *A Man of Sorrow: The Life, Letters and Times of the Rev. Patrick Brontë, 1777–1861* (London: Ian Hodgkins, 1979), 52.

6 Gerard J. Van Den Broek, *The Return of the Cane: A Natural History of the Walking Stick* (Utrecht: International Books, 2007); Anthony Reál, *The Story of the Stick in All Ages and Lands* (New York: J. W. Bouton, 1876), 234; CB to Mary Taylor, Sept. 4, 1848, in *LCB*, vol. 2, 113; Elizabeth Gaskell, *The Life of Charlotte Brontë* (New York: Penguin, 1997), 166; John Greenwood, the local stationer, told the story about EB's shooting lessons. See Chitham, *Emily Brontë*, 159, for more information.

7 EN quoted in Wemyss Reid, *Charlotte Brontë* (London: Macmillan, 1877), 30; for BB's walks to Bradford, see Juliet Barker, *The Brontës* (New York: St. Martin's, 1994), 305; for BB's walk to Roe Head, see Barbara Whitehead, *Charlotte Brontë and Her 'Dearest Nell': The Story of a Friendship* (Otley, UK: Smith Settle, 1993), 9; CB to EN, June 1840, in *LCB*, vol. 1, 221.

8 Thomas quoted in Lucy Newlyn, "Hazlitt and Edward Thomas on Walking," *Essays in Criticism* 56, no. 2 (2006), 164, a very fine meditation on the walking stick and on foot travel more generally; it would be rather hard to touch Saint Catherine's stick now, however. A portion is displayed in her former house and shrine in Siena, Italy, but it is encased in a reliquary; the Saint John of God statue is now at the Wellcome Collection, London, A 61810.

9 Richard Holmes, *Coleridge: Early Visions* (London: Hodder and Stoughton, 1989), 60; Morris Marples, *Shanks's Pony: A Study of Walking* (London: Dent, 1959), 45; Hucks quoted in Holmes, *Coleridge*, 61.

10 For Dickens and walking, see Anne D. Wallace, *Walking, Literature, and English Culture: The Origins and Uses of Peripatetic in the Nineteenth Century* (Oxford, UK: Oxford University Press, 1993), 230–31; Dickens's compass is at the Berg, his stick at the Library of Congress; Darwin's stick is at the Wellcome Collection, A 4962.

11 For pilgrims' staffs, see Joseph Amato, *On Foot: A History of Walking* (New York: New York University Press, 2004), 53; for sticks containing relics, see Max Von Boehn, *Modes and Manners: Lace, Fans, Gloves, Walking-Sticks, Parasols, Jewelry, and Trinkets* (London: Dent, 1929), 98; for souvenir sticks, see Van Den Broek, *Return of the Cane*, 104–11; a late-nineteenth-century staff, for instance, has Welsh place-names cut all over it, attesting to the walker's indefatigability. In a private collection, but pictured and discussed in Boothroyd, *Fascinating Walking Sticks*, 169.

12 An odd souvenir walking stick of 1832 that fits this composite function had a shaft made of the floating batteries of Gibraltar and a handle mounted with brass from one of its guns. A similar stick, a souvenir of the Bristol Reform Act Riots of 1831, seems almost too fanciful to have existed. It was made out of wood from the prayer desk in the Bishop of Bristol's palace, which was burned down during the riots. The handle came from the pistol that Lieutenant Colonel Thomas Brereton, court-martialed because he withdrew his troops during the riots to save them from being injured, used to kill himself during his trial. The stick also had a "tricolor tassel" made from pieces of the ropes used to hang some of the rioters. This stick and the Gibraltar one are mentioned in "Curiosities Sent to the Naval and Military Museum," *Age*, Feb. 12 (1832), 54; the Nelson stick is in a private collection, but see Boothroyd, *Fascinating Walking Sticks*, 167.

13 As Rebecca Solnit explains, in her eloquent *Wanderlust: A History of Walking* (New York: Penguin, 2001), 72, "Roads are a record of those who have gone before, and to follow them is to follow people who are no longer there"; EB, "Every leaf speaks bliss to me," 1838; AB and EB, diary paper, June 26, 1837, BPM, BS105; EB, "The Prisoner," Oct. 9, 1845; EB drew a picture of herself writing on this stool in her bedroom, on her diary paper of July 1845. The Brontës' servant Martha Brown was given the stool by PB, and she in turn gave it to her sister Tabitha Ratcliffe, who sold it to J. Roy Coventry of Liverpool. Eventually it made its way to the BPM, F11. Tabitha reported seeing EB regularly carry the stool outside to write. Christine Alexander and Jane Sellars, *The Art of the Brontës* (London: Cambridge University Press, 1995), 104.

14 Robert Southey to CB, March 12, 1837, in *LCB*, vol. 1, 166.

15 The quotations about crossing the Alps are from Book 6 of *The Prelude*, lines 629, 635, 640–41, from the passage about crossing Simplon Pass. Initially disappointed because he didn't notice they had gone over the pass, Wordsworth was able to experience this sense of eternity in his imagination, after the fact. Wordsworth, *The Prelude or Growth of a Poet's Mind*, 2nd ed., ed. Ernest de Selincourt (Oxford, UK:

Clarendon Press, 1959), 209–10; Wordsworth, "Tintern Abbey," lines 49, 97–98, in *Lyrical Ballads*, 2nd ed. (Oxford, UK: Oxford University Press, 1980), 113–15; see Wallace, *Walking*, and Solnit, *Wanderlust*, for more on Wordsworth and walking; Coryate is quoted in Marples, *Shank's Pony*, 4.

16 Stephen is quoted in Marples, *Shank's Pony*, 147; for "streetwalkers," see Wallace, *Walking*, 221–22. See also Deborah Epstein Nord, *Walking the Victorian Streets: Women, Representation, and the City* (Ithaca, NY: Cornell University Press, 1995).

17 When EB was teaching at Law Hill in 1838–1839, she may have crossed paths with Anne Lister, whose house, Shibden Hall, was nearby. EB probably heard Lister's story, as Lister was already thought a remarkable character by those who lived nearby. See Jill Liddingon, "Anne Lister and Emily Brontë, 1838–39: Landscape with Figures," *BST* 26, no. 1 (2001); Anne Lister, *I Know My Own Heart: The Diaries of Anne Lister 1791–1840* (New York: New York University Press, 1988), 278; see Marples, *Shank's Pony*, chap. 9, for a general biography of Weeton; Edward Hall, ed., *Miss Weeton: Journal of a Governess* (London: Oxford University Press, 1939), vol. 2, 24, 34, 45; Lister, *I Know My Own Heart*, 113–14.

18 CB to EN, Aug. 14, 1839, in *LCB*, vol. 1, 200; CB to Margaret Wooler, Sept. 27, 1850, in *LCB*, vol. 2, 477.

19 See Solnit, *Wanderlust*, chap. 14, for more on women walking as a form of protest; Frances Wilson, *The Ballad of Dorothy Wordsworth* (London: Faber and Faber, 2008), 54; Dorothy Wordsworth to Mrs. Christopher Crackenthorpe, Apr. 21, 1794, in Ernest de Selincourt, ed., *The Letters of William and Dorothy Wordsworth* (Oxford, UK: Oxford University Press, 1967), vol. 1, 116–17.

20 *Wuthering Heights* has become a key text for feminist literary theory, and the ideas I put forth here are commonplace. The most important essay on EB's contribution to feminism is, arguably, the chapter on *Wuthering Heights* in Sandra M. Gilbert and Susan Gubar, *The Madwoman in the Attic: The Woman Writer and the Nineteenth-Century Literary Imagination* (New Haven, CT: Yale University Press, 1979). Their chapter on *Jane Eyre* in the same volume makes a convincing case for its importance for feminism as well.

21 There has been a good deal of writing about the maternal role of nature in EB's work. For some of the best, see Margaret Homans, "Repression and Sublimation of Nature in *Wuthering Heights*," *PMLA* 93, no. 1 (1978), and Stevie Davies, *Emily Brontë: Heretic* (London: Women's Press, 1994).

22 For facts about EB's walking, I draw on accounts by contemporaries, the most important being walks on the moors that EN took with the sisters during visits, the first in 1833. Only three letters written by EB survive, all of them brief and formal. As we have seen, her childhood writings have gone missing, along with the manuscript of *Wuthering Heights* and part of a new novel that she probably began just before her death. Besides her poetry and her one novel, only a few essays written at school, the diary papers, her drawings, a fragment of an account book, and a couple of text fragments survive. Almost all of what we know about EB—and this holds true for BB and AB as well—comes from CB's comments in letters, general remarks to friends, a couple of short essays written after EB's death, and *Shirley*, with the title

character based in part on EB. As Lucasta Miller has shown, CB had her motives for depicting EB and her other siblings in specific, likely skewed, ways. See *The Brontë Myth* (New York: Knopf, 2001). Many Brontë scholars have debated to what extent EB's poems are autobiographical, especially given that many of them were written about Gondal events and characters, or from these imaginary people's points of view. I read them as personal in this chapter, following the lead of Janet Gezari, in *Last Things*.

23 Quoted in E. M. Delafield, ed., *The Brontës: Their Lives Recorded by Their Contemporaries* (London: Hogarth Press, 1935), 267; these descriptions of EB come from EN as given in her reminiscences in *LCB*, vol. 1, and in conversations with the early biographer of EB, Agnes Mary Francis Robinson, *Emily Brontë* (Boston: Robert Brothers, 1889); CB, "Editor's Preface to the New Edition of *Wuthering Heights*," in *LCB*, vol. 2, 748.

24 CB, "Editor's Preface," in *LCB*, vol. 2, 749; EN quoted in Clement Shorter, *Charlotte Brontë and Her Circle* (Westport, CT: Greenwood, 1970), 179; Gaskell, *Life*, 166.

25 EB, "It was night and on the mountains," 1839?; EB, "The Philosopher," Feb. 3, 1845, and "Julian M. and A.G. Rochelle," Oct. 9, 1845; Wilson, *Ballad*, 54; EB, "I'm happiest when most away," 1838?; Wordsworth, "Tintern Abbey," lines 46–47, in *Lyrical Ballads*; scholarship on the importance of nature in EB's writing is vast. One particularly fine work is Margaret Homans, *Women Writers and Poetic Ideology: Dorothy Wordsworth, Emily Brontë, and Emily Dickinson* (Princeton, NJ: Princeton University Press, 1980).

26 Gaskell to John Forster, 1853, in *LCB*, vol. 3, 198; quotes are from the *Oxford English Dictionary*. See Steven Vine, *Emily Brontë* (London: Twayne, 1998), chap. 4, for an eloquent exploration of the term "wuther."

27 CB, "Editor's Preface," in *LCB*, vol. 2, 749.

28 EB, "Loud without the wind was roaring," Nov. 11, 1838.

29 Gezari, *Last Things*, 17.

30 EB could read German, and it's possible that she was familiar with the term *Sehnsucht*. Brontë scholars have argued that EB should be considered a philosopher in her own right. Janet Gezari, for instance, sees EB as a "self-taught philosopher whose audacity is related to her refusal to create or subscribe to a system" (*Last Things*, 4).

31 CB, "Prefatory Note to 'Selections from Poems by Ellis Bell,' " in *LCB*, vol. 2, 748, 752; EB, "Why ask to know the date—the clime?" Sept. 14, 1846; EB, "All day I've toiled but not with pain," undated; EB, "Honour's Martyr," Nov. 21, 1844; EB, "Loud without the wind was roaring" and "F. De Samara to A.G.A.," Nov. 1, 1838; EB, "Tell me tell me smiling child," 1836?; EB, "The inspiring music's thrilling sound," 1836?

32 EB, "Faith and Despondency," Nov. 6, 1844.

33 Frances Wilson suggests, in *Ballad*, 54, in her exploration of Dorothy Wordsworth's pedestrianism, that walking was "a physical expression of longing"; CB to W. S. Williams, May 22, 1850, in *LCB*, vol. 2, 403.

34 For more about such studies, see Nicola Watson, *The Literary Tourist: Readers and*

Places in Romantic and Victorian Britain (New York: Palgrave, 2006), especially 9; T. P. Grinsted, *The Last Homes of Departed Genius* (London: Routledge, 1867), vi.

35 John Keats to Benjamin Bailey, July 18–22, 1818, in Hyder Edward Rollins, ed., *The Letters of John Keats, 1814–1821* (Cambridge, MA: Harvard University Press, 1958), vol. 1, 342; lines 1–2, in H. W. Garrod, ed., *Keats: Poetical Works* (London: Oxford University Press, 1967), 385; see Simon Goldhill, *Freud's Couch, Scott's Buttocks, Brontë's Grave* (Chicago: University of Chicago Press, 2011), and Watson, *Literary Tourist*, for more about pilgrimages to Abbotsford; the walking stick made from a tree growing out of Scott's grave was given to Andrew Carnegie by Thomas Fox on May 9, 1901, and a photograph of it is at the Carnegie Library, Pittsburgh, CA-522.

36 Miller, *Brontë Myth*, 98; Virginia Woolf, "Haworth, November 1904," *Guardian*, Dec. 21, 1904; Matthew Arnold, "Haworth Churchyard," lines 154–55, in Humphrey Milford, ed., *The Poems of Matthew Arnold, 1804–1867* (Oxford, UK: Oxford University Press, 1909), 280; Emily Dickinson, *The Poems of Emily Dickinson*, ed. R. W. Franklin (Cambridge, MA: Harvard University Press, 2005), 73; see Watson, *Literary Tourist*, 111–18, for more on the confusion about graves and Brontë pilgrimage more generally.

37 It is hard to reconstruct when Parkes went to Haworth. A letter that Gaskell reproduces, without saying who wrote it, in her biography of CB, *Life*, describes a visit to Haworth, and Charles Lemon, who reprints the letter in *Early Visitors to Haworth: From Ellen Nussey to Virginia Woolf* (Haworth, UK: Brontë Society, 1996), attributes it to Parkes and dates it October 3, 1850. Margaret Smith, however, attributes the letter to Jane Forster, and speculates that its date is late January 1851. For her arguments, see *LCB*, vol. 2, 569–70. Emma Lowndes, in *Turning Victorian Women into Ladies: The Life of Bessie Raynor Parkes, 1829–1925* (Palo Alto, CA: Academica, 2012), reports that Parkes's daughter thought she went with Gaskell to Haworth in July 1855. See also the biography of Parkes written by her daughter: Marie Belloc Lowndes, *I, Too, Have Lived in Arcadia: A Record of Love and of Childhood* (London: Macmillan, 1941); Gaskell to an unknown correspondent, quoted in Lemon, *Early Visitors*, 21–23.

38 W. H. Cooke, "A Winter's Day at Haworth," *St. James Magazine* 21 (Dec. 1867–Mar. 1868), 166. Others who walked from Keighley include Charles Hale, in 1861. See Lemon, *Early Visitors*, 73; walking from Bradford on footpaths and roads, then on to Bingley was one route; another went by way of Heaton, Wilsden, Old Allan, and Brae Moor. The anonymous walker who wrote for *The Bradford Observer*, April 30, 1857, took the Bradford route. William Scruton took this latter way, in 1858. See Lemon, *Early Visitors*, 33, 46; Walter White's walking tour, for example, detailed in his 1858 *Month in Yorkshire*, had a stop in Haworth. See Lemon, *Early Visitors*, 42; E. P. Evans, "Two Days at the Home of the Brontës," *Treasury of Literature and the Ladies' Treasury*, Dec. 2 (1872), 302–4; Helen H. Arnold, "Reminiscences of Emma Huidekoper Cortazzo, 1866–1882," *BST* 13 (1958), 221.

39 Sylvia Plath, *The Unabridged Journals of Sylvia Plath*, ed. Karen V. Kukil (New York: Anchor Books, 2000), 588–89.

40 Algernon Charles Swinburne, *A Note on Charlotte Brontë* (London: Chatto and Win-

dus, 1877), 74; EB, "Gleneden's Dream," May 21, 1838; Anne Carson, "The Glass Essay," lines 97–101, in *Glass, Irony, and God* (New York: New Directions, 1995), 4.

41 Many of these objects are held at the BPM. They include the pew fronts, urns, candlesticks, and the walking stick, Ch30, which has an ivory handle and a silver plate with the following inscription: "R.A. Hey, Sawwood OXENHOPE Oak from Haworth Church / erected in the year 670." It was donated to the museum by Mrs. Foster Bannister, Mill Hey, Haworth, in 1947, according to *BST* 11, no. 2 (1947), 115. The escritoire might be the desk at the BPM, TA 230, which was purchased in 1970 and was used in the library, according to *BST* 15, no. 5 (1970), 333.

CHAPTER FOUR: KEEPER, GRASPER, AND OTHER FAMILY ANIMALS

1 EB, diary paper, July 30, 1841, manuscript missing, but a facsimile can be found in Clement Shorter, *Charlotte Brontë and Her Circle* (Westport, CT: Greenwood, 1970); CB gave this account to Elizabeth Gaskell. See Gaskell's *Life of Charlotte Brontë* (New York: Penguin, 1997), 200–201. Some Brontë scholars doubt its truth, or at the very least think it was embellished by Gaskell. This is perhaps true; we can never know, of course. However, there are many other accounts of EB's relations with animals and evidence in her own writing that seem to support Gaskell's tale, at least in its bare bones.

2 According to Gaskell, *Life*, 200, Keeper was a gift to EB. She doesn't specify from whom—perhaps PB —nor do we know where Keeper came from nor how old he was when he arrived, although he wasn't a puppy if he already had such a reputation; the quote is from John Stores Smith, who described Keeper's breed after he visited Haworth and met PB and Keeper. He later published an account of his visit in *Free Lance*, Mar. 14, 1868; Gaskell, however, calls Keeper a "bull-dog" and in other sources he is called a "bull mastiff." Jane Sellars, in *The Art of the Brontës* (London: Cambridge University Press, 1995), 122, speculates that he is a Labrador mix, which is unlikely given that the breed wasn't introduced to England until the late eighteenth century and remained rare until many decades later, according to Carson I. A. Ritchie, *The British Dog: Its History from Earliest Times* (London: Robert Hale, 1981), 151–52. I am speculating on Keeper's breed by studying the watercolor EB made of him in 1838 and comparing it to the many paintings of bull terriers around the time in William Secord's wonderful and comprehensive *Dog Painting 1840–1940* (Suffolk, UK: Antique Collector's Club, 1992); on the history of dog breeding, see Harriet Ritvo, *The Animal Estate: The English and Other Creatures in the Victorian Age* (Cambridge, MA: Harvard University Press, 1987), 91–98; for bull-baiting in Haworth, see Barbara Whitehead, *Charlotte Brontë and Her 'Dearest Nell': The Story of a Friendship* (Otley, UK: Smith Settle, 1993), 113; for working dogs and the history of animal cruelty legislation, see Ritchie, *British Dog*, 180, 141–44, 183–84.

3 Ritchie, *British Dog*, 25.

4 See Walter Woodburn Hyde, "The Prosecution and Punishment of Animals and Lifeless Things in the Middle Ages and Modern Times," *University of Pennsylvania*

Law Review 64 (1915–1916), 730; William Ewald, "Comparative Jurisprudence (I): What Was It Like to Try a Rat?" *University of Pennsylvania Law Review* 143 (1994-1995), 1889; and Keith Thomas, *Man and the Natural World: A History of the Modern Sensibility* (New York: Pantheon, 1983), 97–98; William Shakespeare, *The Merchant of Venice*, 4.1; see Ewald, "Comparative Jurisprudence (I)," 1915, for the basic rights of animals in the past.

5 These ancient beliefs all come from Thomas, *Man and the Natural World*, 27, 75, 78, 98, 137; CB, "Like wolf—black bull or goblin hound," from Victor Neufeldt, ed., *The Poems of Charlotte Brontë: A New Text and Commentary* (New York: Garland, 1985), 425.

6 For instance, see the 1803 engraving of a lurcher by Philip Reinagle, in *The Sportsman's Cabinet* (London: Cundee, 1804), 102; see Lisa Surridge, "Animals and Violence in *Wuthering Heights*," *BST* 24, no. 2 (1999), 161–73, for a discussion about working animals in the novel, as opposed to pets.

7 From Queen Victoria's diary, quoted in Katharine MacDonogh, *Reigning Cats and Dogs* (New York: St. Martin's, 1999), 133.

8 Henry Mayhew, *London Labour and the London Poor* (New York: Dover, 1968), vol. 2, 48–50; Margaret Forster, *Elizabeth Barrett Browning: A Biography* (London: Chatto and Windus, 1988), 117–18.

9 Ritvo, *Animal Estate*, 86; The titles of illustrations come from Thomas, *Man and the Natural World*, 108; Secord, *Dog Painting*, 252, and Ritchie, *British Dog*, 20, discuss dogs put in human roles and stuffed pets; the poodle-shawl story comes from MacDonogh, *Reigning Cats and Dogs*, 135. Even PB fell into some of this sentimentalism, writing two letters from the point of view of dogs, one as Flossy; the Dickens letter opener is now at the Berg.

10 See Stevie Davies, *Emily Brontë: Heretic* (London: Women's Press, 1994), for this view of EB's feelings about dogs and human nature, especially 104–5. See also Ivan Kreilkamp, "Petted Things: *Wuthering Heights* and the Animal," *Yale Journal of Criticism* 18, no. 1 (2005), 87–110, and Surridge, "Animals and Violence in *Wuthering Heights*"; EB, "Le Chat," in Sue Lonoff, ed. and trans., *The Belgian Essays* (New Haven, CT: Yale University Press, 1996), 56–58.

11 EN's observation comes from Shorter, *Charlotte Brontë*, 179–80; the quote from the acquaintance is from Gaskell, *Life*, 199.

12 EN's account of Keeper on EB's lap, a common occurrence, quoted in Shorter, *Charlotte Brontë*, 179–80; see Davies, *Emily Brontë*, chap. 3, for her remark that EB found animals to be "blood relatives."

13 CB, "Eamala is a gurt bellaring bull," June 1833, in Neufeldt, ed. *Poems of Charlotte Brontë*, 109; John Greenwood, the Haworth stationer, from his diary of village events, quoted in Winifred Gérin, *Emily Brontë* (London: Oxford University Press, 1971), 147.

14 CB told the rabies story to Gaskell. See *Life*, 200; the surgeon Gordon Stables, for instance, wrote in the 1870s that the best remedy involved immediate cauterization of the bite. See *Dogs in Their Relation to the Public* (London: Cassell, 1877), 28.

15 CB, "Editor's Preface to the New Edition of *Wuthering Heights*," in *LCB*, vol. 2, 749; *Cornhill Magazine*, July 28, 1873, 66.

16 Kreilkamp, "Petted Things," 87–110; CB, "Editor's Preface," in appendix II, in *LCB*, vol. 2, 751.

17 Davies, *Emily Brontë*, 118.

18 EB, "Le Papillon," in Lunoff, ed. and trans., *Belgian Essays*, 176; see Davies, *Emily Brontë*, chap. 3, for an eloquent meditation on animals, especially the lapwing; EB, "Redbreast early in the morning," 1837, and "And like myself lone wholly lone," Feb. 27, 1841, from Janet Gezari, ed., *Emily Jane Brontë: The Complete Poems* (London: Penguin, 1992).

19 Our society today also abuses dogs and animals of all sorts, and it's not always possible to argue that we are more humane than people of earlier eras. Much like the work dogs of the eighteenth and nineteenth centuries, huskies are used to pull sleds and are then abandoned, and the use of greyhounds for racing can cause painful damage to their legs. We have our puppy mills, our drugged race horses, our industrial farms where chickens and livestock are kept in horrific conditions, and much more. Keeper's collar, BPM, H110, belonged to a Miss Lucy Lund, from Ilkley, who lent it to the museum in 1898 and then donated it in 1902. It is possible that she bought it at the 1861 sale of the contents of the parsonage, after PB died, or from relatives of the Brontë servants, who were given such personal items by PB; quoted in MacDonogh, *Reigning Cats and Dogs*, 132; for the history of the dog tax, see P. B. Munsche, *Gentlemen and Poachers: The English Game Laws, 1671–1831* (London: Cambridge University Press, 1981), 82–83; George Clark murdered a tax collector, on May 18, 1862. "Accidents and Offences," *Trewman's Exeter Flying Post or Plymouth and Cornish Advertiser*, Mar. 5, 1862, 3; for the dog tax as a means to exert class control, see Ritvo, *Animal Estate*, 188.

20 Prince Albert's walking stick is now in the Royal Collection, 31205.

21 For where collars were sold, see Elizabeth Wilson, "Foreword," in *Four Centuries of Dog Collars at Leeds Castle* (London: Leeds Castle Foundation, 1979), 2; for a collar with an inside lining, see the gilt copper one, lined with red morocco leather and blue velvet, inscribed with "This dog belongs to his Royal Highness George Augustus, Prince of Wales, 1715," now at the Armoury at Windsor Castle. See MacDonogh, *Reigning Cats and Dogs*, 131; "Advertisements and Notices," *Belfast News-Letter*, June 28, 1866; for pictures of early metal collars, see Secord, *Dog Painting*, especially 37; for working dogs on ships, see Ritchie, *British Dog*, 149–50; *Ipswich Journal*, Oct. 16, 1841; Nicolás C. Ciarlo, Horacio De Rosa, Dolores Elkin, and Phil Dunning, "Evidence of Use and Reuse of a Dog Collar from the Sloop of War HMS *Swift* (1770), Puerto Deseado (Argentina)," *Technical Briefs in Historical Archeology* 6 (2011), 20–27.

22 The Dog Collar Museum in Leeds Castle has lots of these engraved collars, such as one inscribed with "Tabinet / The Property of Earl Talbot. The winner of the Great Champion all aged stakes for all England. 32 dogs at 20 guin's each at Ashdown Park, Dec. 14th 1838"; the Wellesley collar and the Wimbledon Jack charity collar

are at the Dog Collar Museum. See also *Four Centuries of Dog Collars*, no. 38 and no. 48.

23 The Bicknell collar is British, from the eighteenth century, and in the Dog Collar Museum; two collars have these inscriptions: "I'm the Marquis of Granby's Dog Putton, Whose Dog are you?" and "I am Mr. Pratt's Dog, King St. Nr. Wakingham, Berks. Whose Dog are You?" Both are pictured in *Four Centuries of Dog Collars*, no. 52 and no. 22; the Nelson collar is at the National Maritime Museum, London, PLT0138; the Dickens collar is in private hands; For the Burns collar, see George R. Jesse, *Researches into the History of the British Dog* (London: Hardwicke, 1866), vol. 1, 67; CB, "The Poetaster," vol. 1, July 6, 1830, Houghton Library, Harvard University, Lowell I(2).

24 For EB's account book, see Edward Chitham, *A Life of Emily Brontë* (Oxford, UK: Blackwell, 1987), 195; Flossy's collar, BPM, H111, is also missing its padlock and has a "JW" hallmark; the error about Flossy's breed seems to have originated with EN, who wrote in pencil on one of CB's letters that "Mr. B" had given her "a King Charles Dog," Flossy's offspring. This note was written many years after the dog, and CB herself, had died, so it may have been a failure on the part of EN's memory (see *LCB*, vol. 1, notes, 362). Flossy's breed is never described by any of the Brontës in letters or diaries, nor does Gaskell describe it. A contemporary engraving of one of these springing spaniels chasing after birds, in the anonymous *Sportsman's Cabinet*, 181, looks remarkably like EB's drawing of Flossy running, chasing a butterfly; for spaniel breeds, see Ritchie, *British Dog*, 163–64.

25 CB to EN, July 1, 1841, in *LCB*, vol. 1, 258–59. In her diary paper of July 1845 (in private hands), AB points out that CB is "now sitting sewing in the Dining-Room Emily is ironing upstairs . . . Keeper and Flossy are I do not know where." A few lines later, she announces that CB has "let Flossy in by the bye and he is now lying on the sopha."

26 See Alexander and Sellers, *Art of the Brontës*, 22, for more about the importance of Bewick's *History of British Birds* to the Brontës' art; BB, "Thomas Bewick," first published in the *Halifax Guardian*, Oct. 1, 1842, reprinted in Viktor Neufeldt, ed., *Works of Patrick Branwell Brontë* (New York: Garland, 1999), vol. 3, 397–400.

27 BB's oil painting, now known as the "Gun Group," went missing after it was photographed around 1860, except for a cut-out segment that pictures EB, now in the National Portrait Gallery, London. For the history of this painting and reproductions of it, see Alexander and Sellers, *Art of the Brontës*, 307–10; Juliet Barker discusses the theories as to why BB was dismissed at length. See *The Brontës* (New York: St. Martin's, 1994), 334–35; BB, "The Shepherd's Chief Mourner," in Neufeldt, ed., *Works*, vol. 3, 337. He revised this poem numerous times, and it was published in the *Yorkshire Gazette* on May 10, 1845.

28 AB, diary paper, July 30, 1841, manuscript missing; Mrs. Ellis H. Chadwick, *In the Footsteps of the Brontës* (London: Pitman, 1914), 124.

29 EB, diary paper, July 30, 1845, in private hands.

30 CB to EB, Sept. 2, 1843, in *LCB*, vol. 1, 329; CB to EB, Dec. 1, 1843, in *LCB*, vol. 1, 331.

31 EN's account, quoted in Whitehead, *Charlotte Brontë and Her 'Dearest Nell,'* 150; CB to PB, June 2, 1852, in *LCB*, vol. 3, 50.

32 EN to Mary Gorham, July 22, 1845, in *LCB*, vol. 1, 405; CB to EN, Aug. 1844 and Nov. 14, 1844, in *LCB*, vol. 1, 363, 374; AB to EN, Jan. 26, 1848, in *LCB*, vol. 2, 19.

33 CB to W. S. Williams, June 25, 1849, in *LCB*, vol. 2, 224; CB to EN, June 23, 1849, in *LCB*, vol. 2, 222.

34 Elizabeth Gaskell to an unidentified person, 1853, in *LCB*, vol. 3, 198; CB to EN, Dec. 8, 1851, in *LCB*, vol. 2, 726; CB to EN, Dec. 7, 1854, in *LCB*, vol. 3, 306.

35 The information about Plato and Cato comes from PB's notebook, BPM, BS 173. See also John Lock and Canon W. T. Dixon, *A Man of Sorrow: The Life, Letters, and Times of the Rev. Patrick Brontë, 1777–1861* (London: Ian Hodgkins, 1979), 482–83; the third brass collar, BPM, 2000.2, is shinier and in much better shape than Keeper's (although its padlock is missing). It is also engraved in a more skilled manner, with decorative flourishes, and would have been more expensive than Keeper's. For these reasons, I speculate that this collar did belong to one of the later dogs, since PB would have been more comfortably off at this point because of royalties from CB's books (even though CB left most of her estate to her husband in her will, PB benefited from it since the two men lived together and shared in it). It is possible that the collar is not authentic. Although the provenance of the collars cannot be traced back to Arthur Nicholls, it seems likely that he took them with him when he moved back to Ireland. He was also a dog lover and took Flossy for walks after AB died. After PB's death, Arthur took Plato with him, who died in 1866, and maybe Cato, although he is never mentioned in any letters by Nicholls. Nicholls wrote to Martha Brown, one of the former parsonage servants, "Poor Plato died about a fortnight ago; he had become very helpless, wasted away like Keeper." This third collar was on loan to the BPM until May 2013, when it was donated. See *BST* 26, no. 1 (2001), 108.

CHAPTER FIVE: FUGITIVE LETTERS

1 CB to EN, Mar. 1855, in *LCB*, vol. 3, 328; CB to EN, May 11, 1831, and July 21, 1832, in *LCB*, vol. 1, 109, 114.

2 CB to EN, Oct. 18, 1832, and Nov. 10, 1834, in *LCB*, vol. 1, 119, 133; CB to EN, Dec. 5 and 6, 1836, in *LCB*, vol. 1, 156.

3 CB to EN, Sept. 5 and July 21, 1832, and May 1836, in *LCB*, vol. 1, 117, 115, 145; CB to EN, July 2, 1835, in *LCB*, vol. 1, 140; CB to EN, Aug. 20, 1840, in *LCB*, vol. 1, 226; CB to EN, Mar. 6, 1843, in *LCB*, vol. 1, 312.

4 CB to EN, Dec. 5 and 6, 1836, in *LCB*, vol. 1, 156; CB to EN, Sept. 1840, in *LCB*, vol. 1, 227–28.

5 See Kathryn Crowther, "Charlotte Brontë's Textual Relics: Memorializing the Material in *Villette*," *Brontë Studies* 35, no. 2 (2010), 131–32.

6 Paulina in *Villette* plaits together the "spoils" from her fiancé's head, a "grey lock" from her father's, and a thread of her own, and "prisoned it in a locket, and laid it on her heart." When Catherine Earnshaw dies in *Wuthering Heights*, the locket around her neck contains a wisp of blond hair from her husband.

7 The details of Branwell's affair come from Juliet Barker, *The Brontës* (New York: St. Martin's, 1994), 456–70; this letter from BB to John Brown is now missing, but Richard Monckton Milnes copied extracts of it into his commonplace book. Quoted in ibid., 459–61.

8 CB to EN, July 21, 1832, in *LCB*, vol. 1, 115.

9 Harriet Martineau, *Autobiography*, ed. Linda Peterson (Peterborough, Ontario: Broadview, 2007), 370–71, 136.

10 CB to EN, Feb. 11, 1834, in *LCB*, vol. 1, 125; CB to EN, July 4, 1834, in *LCB*, vol. 1, 129.

11 AB cross-wrote a letter to EN on October 4, 1847. She probably did it not to save on postage but rather because she had only small sheets of paper, since the national penny post had already been instituted. *LCB*, vol. 1, 544–45; John Pearce, *A Descant on the Penny Postage* (London: J. Born, 1841), 6.

12 James Wilson Hyde, *The Royal Mail: Its Curiosities and Romance* (London: Blackwell, 1885), 259, 181.

13 CB to EN, Aug. 24, 1838, in *LCB*, vol. 1, 180; CB to EN, early 1837, in *LCB*, vol. 1, 163.

14 CB to EN, May 8, 1835, in *LCB*, vol. 1, 137.

15 William Lewins, *Her Majesty's Mails: An Historical and Descriptive Account of the British Post Office* (London: Sampson Low, 1864), 100.

16 CB to EN, Jan. 12, 1840, in *LCB*, vol. 1, 208.

17 For the history of valentines, Christmas cards, and so on, see Asa Briggs, *Victorian Things* (Chicago: University of Chicago Press, 1988), 364.

18 Catherine J. Golden, *Posting It: The Victorian Revolution in Letter Writing* (Gainesville: Florida University Press, 2009), 27, 122; CB to EN, Dec. 1852, in *LCB*, vol. 3, 91; CB to George Smith, Feb. 17, 1852, in *LCB*, vol. 3, 21.

19 The letter with the wallpaper snippet is now at the Berg, with Gaskell's handwritten note on the back of the wallpaper: "Slip of the paper with which Charlotte Brontë papered her future husband's study, before they were married. —ECG"; CB to Amelia Ringrose, Mar. 31, 1850, in *LCB*, vol. 2, 373; CB to Elizabeth Smith, May 25, 1850, in *LCB*, vol. 2, 407. The socks and the letter are at the BPM; CB to EN, Apr. 1847, in *LCB*, vol. 1, 523. The piece of lace was reputedly given by EN to a Mrs. Cameron and was passed down as a family heirloom. See Barbara Whitehead, *Charlotte Brontë and Her 'Dearest Nell': The Story of a Friendship* (Otley, UK: Smith Settle, 1993), 137, n. 1; CB to EN, Jan. 1847, in *LCB*, vol. 1, 515.

20 Michael Finlay, *Western Writing Implements in the Age of the Quill Pen* (Cumbria, UK: Plain Books, 1990), 59; CB to EN, June 19, 1834, in *LCB*, vol. 1, 128.

21 Michael Champness and David Trapnell, *Adhesive Wafer Seals: A Transient Victorian Phenomenon* (Kent, UK: Chancery House, 1996), 4–5, 13. For envelopes and their gumming, see Finlay, *Western Writing Implements*, 59.

22 These examples of wafers are all discussed and pictured in Champness and Trapnell, *Adhesive Wafer Seals*, 13–146.

23 Many of the envelopes for CB's letters no longer exist, and it's also likely that CB sent letters that disappeared without a trace, so we can't know if she used wafers with other correspondents; CB to EN, Aug. 9, 1846, in *LCB*, vol. 1, 491–92.

24 CB to EN, Sept. 1847, PML, MA 7315.

25 Some Brontë biographers have argued that EB had a lover. See, for instance, Sara Fermi, "Emily Brontë: A Theory," *Brontë Studies* 30, no. 1 (2005), 71–74. Also, after EB died, CB had possession of EB's desk, so it is possible the seals were actually CB's.

26 Champness and Trapnell, *Adhesive Wafer Seals*, 4.

27 For issues of privacy in the Victorian post, see Kate Thomas, *Postal Pleasures: Sex, Scandal, and Victorian Letters* (London: Oxford University Press, 2012); Champness and Trapnell, *Adhesive Wafer Seals*, 99, 107–111.

28 CB to BB, May 1, 1843, and CB to EN, May 1842, in *LCB*, vol. 1, 317, 184; CB to Constantin Heger, July 24, 1844, British Library, add. MS 38, 732A. See also *LCB*, vol. 1, 357–59; the account of the fate of the letters comes from Louise Heger, the daughter of the Hegers, who heard it from her mother. She then told it to M. H. Spielmann. See Spielmann's "The Inner History of the Brontë-Heger Letters," *Fortnightly Review*, Apr. (1919), 345–50.

29 CB to Constantin Heger, Oct. 24, 1844, British Library, add. MS 38, 732B. See also *LCB*, vol. 1, 370; Spielmann, "Inner History," 346.

30 CB to Constantin Heger, Jan. 8, 1845, British Library, add. MS 38, 732D. See also *LCB*, vol. 1, 379–80; Spielmann, "Inner History," 346.

31 Spielmann, "Inner History," 346. See also Margaret Smith, "The History of the Letters," in *LCB*, vol. 1, 64; CB to Constantin Heger, Nov. 18, 1845, British Library, add. MS 38, 732C. See also *LCB*, vol. 1, 435–37.

32 Spielmann, "Inner History," 346.

33 Ibid., 348.

34 CB to Constantin Heger, July 24, 1844, in *LCB*, vol. 1, 357; CB to Constantin Heger, Oct. 24, 1844, in *LCB*, vol. 1, 370; CB to Constantin Heger, Jan. 8, 1845, in *LCB*, vol. 1, 379.

35 The detail about Madame Heger reading *Villette* comes from Barker, *Brontës*, 787.

36 A special packet of letters given to CB by her father must have been profoundly moving to her. One day, he handed her a small collection of love letters written to himself by her mother before they were married. "Yellow with time," the letters she read now for the first time held "a rectitude, a refinement, a constancy." CB found it strange to peruse what she called "the record of a mind whence my own sprang." The experience was at once sad and sweet for her, especially the "gentleness about them indescribable." They made her wish that "she had lived and that I had known her." CB to EN, Feb. 1850, in *LCB*, vol. 2, 347; CB to EN, early 1837 and Dec. 5 and 6, 1836, in *LCB*, vol. 1, 162, 156; CB to EN, Sept. 26, 1836, in *LCB*, vol. 1, 152; CB to EN, Oct./Nov. 1836, in *LCB*, vol. 1, 154–55; Victoria Glendinning, *Vita: The Life of V. Sackville-West* (New York: Knopf, 1983), 168.

37 CB to EN, Oct. 1852, in *LCB*, vol. 3, 73; CB to EN, Oct. 13, 1843, in *LCB*, vol. 1, 334; CB to Margaret Wooler, July 14, 1851, in *LCB*, vol. 2, 666; EN's account, given in a letter to Lady Morrison, quoted in Whitehead, *Charlotte Brontë and Her 'Dearest Nell,'* 156.

38 Elaine Miller makes a convincing argument about the importance of CB and EN's passionate love, and that it has been mostly ignored by biographers who look at

it with a heterosexist bias. See "Through All Changes and through all Chances: The Relationship of Ellen Nussey and Charlotte Brontë," in *Not a Passing Phase: Reclaiming Lesbians in History 1840–1985* (London: Women's Press, 1989).

39 See Sharon Marcus, *Between Women: Friendship, Desire, and Marriage in Victorian England* (Princeton, NJ: Princeton University Press, 2007). CB's ardent language in her letters to EN was also not unusual for the time. Marcus discusses many letters between women with similar language.

40 Anne Longmuir argues that the character Shirley was possibly based, in part, on the lesbian Anne Lister, in her "Anne Lister and Lesbian Desire in Charlotte Brontë's *Shirley*," *Brontë Studies* 31 (2006), 145–55; CB explained to Gaskell that Shirley was based on EB. See Gaskell, *Life*, 299.

41 CB to EN, Mar. 12, 1839, in *LCB*, vol. 1, 187; See Marcus, *Between Women*, for an exploration of the way Victorian heterosexual relationships were often secondary to female friendships and love.

42 CB's favoring the name Charles for herself comes from Whitehead, *Charlotte Brontë and Her 'Dearest Nell,'* 45.

43 Sandra M. Gilbert and Susan Gubar, *The Madwoman in the Attic: The Woman Writer and the Nineteenth-Century Literary Imagination* (New Haven, CT: Yale University Press, 1979).

44 CB to EN, Oct. 31, 1854, in *LCB*, vol. 3, 296; EN to Arthur Nicholls, Nov. 1854, in *LCB*, vol. 3, 297.

45 CB to PB, June 9, 1849, in *LCB*, vol. 2, 218.

46 Abraham Shackleton, manuscript weather records, Cliffe Castle Museum, Keighley.

CHAPTER SIX: THE ALCHEMY OF DESKS

1 AB diary paper, July 1845, in private hands.

2 An example of EB's paper recycling can be seen on a version of the "chained bird" poem at the Berg, dated February 27, 1841, written on the back of a handwritten text in Latin; the sheet with eight poems is at the Berg, beginning "When days of Beauty deck the vale," with poems dated from September to November 1836; Derek Roper discusses these manuscripts in great detail, in his introduction to *The Poems of Emily Brontë* (Oxford, UK: Clarendon, 1995), especially 13–21.

3 In this first notebook, British Library, Ashley MS 175: 1839, EB recorded the dates of composition and transcription. It was made in 1839 and contained the best of her poems going back to 1837. She wrote in a cursive hand, which was very unusual for her. The Gondal notebook is also at the British Library, add. MS. 43483. It retains its original binding, but the 1839 one was disassembled and the leaves remounted by the collector Thomas Wise. The non-Gondal one, now known as the Honresfeld MS, went missing in the twentieth century, but a facsimile copy was made in 1934, in volume 17 of the Shakespeare Head edition of the Brontës' writing: Thomas Wise and John Alexander Symington, eds., *The Poems of Emily Jane Brontë and Anne Brontë* (Oxford, UK: Shakespeare Head, 1934). EB started both notebooks in February 1844.

4 Both EB's and CB's desks, along with their contents, were kept by CB's husband, Arthur Nicholls, after CB's death. After *his* death, they were sold by his second wife at a Sotheby's auction in 1907. See "Catalogue of Valuable Books and Manuscripts," July 26–27, BPM, P.S. Cat. 3. CB's desk was bought by Alexander Murray Smith, the son of her publisher George Smith, who later donated it to the BPM. EB's desk was bought by Henry Houston Bonnell, the bibliophile and Brontëana collector from Philadelphia, who later donated it to the BPM; a non-portable standing desk at the BPM is also believed to have belonged to CB, probably bought by her in the 1850s, when her writing was bringing in fairly steady royalties; AB, diary paper, July 1841, manuscript missing.

5 The drawing of EB's that makes it clear that she is representing the page she is currently writing is the diary paper of June 26, 1837, BPM, BS105, which pictures AB and EB sitting at a table, the diaries they are working on in front of them and labeled "the papers."

6 The velvet's border on CB's desk repeats the star pattern, in brass set into the wood, on the outside of the box. The slope of AB's desk has an especially feminine appearance, with a cerise-pink-velvet lining. AB's desk has the most obscure provenance and was donated to the BPM empty. The Haworth stationer John Greenwood owned it, and his great-granddaughter Mary Preston donated it to the museum in 1961; the hair, BPM, BS 171, is accompanied by a note in PB's hand that says, "Anne Brontë / May 22 1833 / Aged 13 / years," and was in CB's desk at the Sotheby's sale in 1907. It is unclear when the hair was put there and by whom: CB, or her father or husband after her death; see Christine Alexander and Jane Sellars, *The Art of the Brontës* (London: Cambridge University Press, 1995), for more information about the sewing patterns, especially 265; coin purse pattern, BPM, C36.

7 Nicholls's pulling of the tin box out of a desk comes from Clement Shorter, *Charlotte Brontë and Her Circle* (Westport, CT: Greenwood, 1970), 146; it's possible that CB sent some sections of *The Professor* in the mail for friends or others to read, before she began sending it around to publishers—thus, these sections may have been folded to fit into envelopes. See, for instance, the introduction by Margaret Smith and Herbert Rosengarten to *The Professor* (Oxford, UK: Clarendon, 1987), where they explore this possibility; the information about the second tin comes from EB's account book. Edward Chitham, *A Life of Emily Brontë* (Oxford, UK: Blackwell, 1987), 195.

8 EB and CB each had paint boxes, and EB had a leather box that was specially made to hold her geometry set (which included a folding bone ruler and a retractable pen with a steel nib); George Eliot's lace box is at Nuneaton Museum and Art Gallery, X/R0723.

9 CB, "Last Will and Testament of Florence Marian Wellesley," PML, Bonnell Collection; George Eliot's desk was stolen in 2012 from a museum in Nuneaton, Warwickshire; Nightingale's desk is at the Florence Nightingale Museum, London, FNM: 0371.

10 For the Lund warehouse, see Michael Finlay, *Western Writing Implements in the Age of the Quill Pen* (Cumbria, UK: Plain Books, 1990), 127; for Michi, see David Harris, *Portable Writing Desks* (Buckinghamshire, UK: Shire, 2001), 20; the Byam quote is from Catherine J. Golden, *Posting It: The Victorian Revolution in Letter Writing*

(Gainesville, FL: Florida University Press, 2009), 132; the features of the elaborate desks come from Mark Bridge, *An Encyclopedia of Desks* (London: Apple Press, 1988), 84; Gaskell desk, BPM, LI.2005.7.1; Lewis Carroll, *Alice's Adventures in Wonderland* (Boston: Lee and Shepard, 1896), 7.

11 William Makepeace Thackeray, *Vanity Fair* (New York: Penguin, 2003), 565, 168.

12 CB to EB, June 8, 1839, in *LCB*, vol. 1, 191; CB's Roe Head Journal, BPM, Bonnell 98; CB to EN, June 30, 1839, and May 1842, in *LCB*, vol. 1, 191, 193, 253.

13 Jane Austen to Cassandra Austen, Oct. 24, 1798, Deirdre Le Faye, ed., *Jane Austen's Letters*, 3rd ed. (Oxford, UK: Oxford University Press, 1995), 15; J. F. Haywood, *English Desks and Bureaux* (London: Victoria and Albert Museum, 1968), 2, and John R. Bernasconi, *The English Desk and Bookcase* (Reading, UK: College of Estate Management, 1981), 28; CB, "The Secret," Nov. 7, 1833, Elmer Ellis Library, University of Missouri-Columbia.

14 I have not been able to trace the provenance of the second desk box of CB's, although it belonged to Dr. Albert A. Berg, who probably bought it from William Thomas Hildrup Howe, a major collector and president of the American Book Co. His collection, which included Dickens and Brontë artifacts, went on sale when he died in 1939. I have been unable to find a list of Howe's collection. Berg donated CB's desk to the New York Public Library with the following items stored inside: what is said to be a lock of CB's hair (collected by Martha Brown from the corpse); another, anonymous lock of hair; the visiting cards of CB and her husband, in an envelope addressed to EN; a hand-painted cardboard box; a velvet bracelet that belonged to CB, according to an accompanying letter from EN; funeral cards for EB, CB, BB, and PB; and a few other odds and ends.

15 Anthony Trollope, *North America* (New York: Harper, 1862), 263–64; Anthony Trollope, *Autobiography* (New York: Dodd, Mead, 1912), 89, 299; Anthony Trollope to Rose Trollope, Mar. 17, 1875, in N. John Hall, ed., *The Letters of Anthony Trollope* (Stanford, CA: Stanford University Press, 1983), vol. 2, 654.

16 CB to EN, July 31, 1845, in *LCB*, vol. 1, 412; BB to J. B. Leyland, Sept. 10, 1845, in *LCB*, vol. 1, 424; Juliet Barker, *The Brontës* (New York: St. Martin's, 1994), 476.

17 CB to EN, Nov. 14, 1844, in *LCB*, vol. 1, 374.

18 EB, "The Prisoner," Oct. 9, 1845, in Janet Gezari, ed., *Emily Jane Brontë: The Complete Poems* (London: Penguin, 1992); some, such as Gezari, believe that the notebook CB found was the Gondal one, but others, such as Barker, in *Brontës*, 481, think it was the non-Gondal notebook; CB described finding EB's poetry a few years later to her publisher and eventual friend W. S. Williams, in a letter of September 1848, in *LCB*, vol. 2, 119; she gives another version of the finding in CB, "Biographical Notice of Ellis and Acton Bell," in *LCB*, vol. 2, 742.

19 For a sustained analysis of the distance that sprang up between CB and EB during this time, see Chitham, *Emily Brontë*, chap. 6.

20 CB to W. S. Williams, Sept. 1848, in *LCB*, vol. 2, 119; see Winifred Gérin, *Charlotte Brontë: The Evolution of Genius* (London: Oxford University Press, 1967), 309, for her argument that the pseudonyms were upon EB's insistence; CB to W. S. Williams, July 31, 1848, in *LCB*, vol. 2, 94.

21 The large, gate-legged table they paced around, which EB pictured on her 1837 diary paper, is in a private collection; the fact about pacing at Roe Head comes from Barbara Whitehead, *Charlotte Brontë and Her 'Dearest Nell': The Story of a Friendship* (Otley, UK: Smith Settle, 1993), 3; we don't know exactly when they each began their novels, but estimates by most Brontë scholars put their completion within a year. See especially the introductions to the Clarendon editions of *Wuthering Heights*, ed. Hilda Marsden and Ian Jack (Oxford: Clarendon, 1976), of *Agnes Grey*, Hilda Marsden and Robert Inglesfield (Oxford, UK: Clarendon, 1988), and of *The Professor*, ed. Margaret Smith and Herbert Rosengarten.

22 CB, "Editor's Preface to the New Edition of *Wuthering Heights*," in *LCB*, vol. 2, 749.

23 CB to W. S. Williams, Sept. 17, 1849, in *LCB*, vol. 2, 255; CB to George Smith, Oct. 30, 1852, in *LCB*, vol. 3, 74. CB had been writing passionate, gothic stories like *Jane Eyre* since she was a girl, but she needed the influence of *Wuthering Heights* to show her how this type of writing could be incorporated into a novel.

24 CB to EN, Oct. 7, 1847, in *LCB*, 547.

25 From a letter Mary Taylor wrote to Elizabeth Gaskell, see Gaskell, *The Life of Charlotte Brontë* (New York: Penguin, 1997), 81.

26 For EB's struggles with pens, see Edward Chitham, *The Birth of Wuthering Heights: Emily Brontë at Work* (New York: St. Martin's, 1998), 10; CB's pen-wiper, BPM, H223. It is also listed in "Museum of Brontë Relics: A Descriptive Catalogue of Brontë Relics Now in the possession of R. and F. Brown, 123, Main St., Haworth, 1898," BPM, P. Bib. 1; CB to EN, Feb. 16, 1849, in *LCB*, vol. 2, 183.

27 This history of pens draws on Leonée Ormond, *Writing: The Arts and Living* (London: Victoria and Albert Museum, 1981), 57.

28 J. Hunt, *The Miscellany* (Buckingham, UK: J. Seeley, 1795), 47.

29 Gaskell, *Life*, 234.

30 CB, "Biographical Notice," in *LCB*, vol. 2, 743.

31 CB wrote the quoted words in 1836 on a snippet of diary that shares the page with her poem "Diving," about plunging into the mind, into "depths so black and profound." This snippet, Bonnell 98(7), BPM, makes up part of the journal notes called "The Roe Head Journal"; Harriet Martineau, "Obituary," *Daily News*, Apr. 6, 1855; Gaskell, *Life*, 233.

32 CB was eventually able to pry some money out of Newby, four years after the novels were published. See Barker, *Brontës*, 747.

33 Ileana Martin speculates that CB used heron-shaped scissors (the legs comprising the blades), part of the collection at the BPM, for her cutting and pasting of *Shirley*. See "Charlotte Brontë's Heron Scissors: Cancellations and Excisions in the Manuscript of *Shirley*," *Brontë Studies* 38, no. 1 (2013), 19–29.

34 It is not known when AB began her second novel. Barker, in *Brontës*, 530, believes she probably started it in April 1847, while others give the start date as early as September 1846 (Chitham, *Emily Brontë*, 197), and still others estimate she began it six months later.

35 Barker, for instance, makes a strong case that EB had started a second novel. See *Brontës*, 532–33.

36 The information about the siblings possibly playing the game High Water comes from Whitehead, *Charlotte Brontë and Her 'Dearest Nell,'* 110.

37 For CB's things in EB's desk, see Juliet Barker, *Sixty Treasures: The Brontë Parsonage Museum* (Haworth, UK: Brontë Society, 1988), 43; CB to EN, Feb. 1852, in *LCB*, vol. 3, 17.

38 CB to W. S. Williams, Apr. 16, 1849, in *LCB*, vol. 2, 203.

CHAPTER SEVEN: DEATH MADE MATERIAL

1 The amethyst bracelet, BPM, J14, belonged to CB and was kept by her husband, Arthur Nicholls, after her death. After his death, it was sold with another bracelet (probably BPM, J43) made of AB's and EB's hair, by Nicholls's second wife, at the 1907 Sotheby's auction. Both were part of lot 34 and came in CB's small satinwood box with a blue bead necklace and eyeglasses. The lot was purchased by the BPM. See "Catalogue of Valuable Books and Manuscripts," July 26 and 27, 1907, 4, BPM, P.S. Cat. 3.

2 BB to J. B. Leyland, June 1846, in *LCB*, vol. 1, 475; BB to John Brown, Aug. 1848, in *LCB*, vol. 2, 110.

3 CB to W. S. Williams, Oct. 6, 1848, in *LCB*, vol. 2, 124; CB to W. S. Williams, Oct. 2, 1848, in *LCB*, vol. 2, 122.

4 Charles Dickens, *Dombey and Son* (New York: Penguin, 2002), 297, *The Old Curiosity Shop* (New York: Penguin, 2001), 522, and *Oliver Twist* (London: Penguin, 2002), 192; information about the "good death" comes from Pat Jalland, *Death in the Victorian Family* (Oxford, UK: Oxford University Press, 1996), especially 19–38; quote from ibid., 22.

5 A page from Branwell's sketchbook that has the drawing of his aunt is reproduced in Brian Wilks, *The Brontës* (London: Hamlyn, 1975), 79; Dickens's daughter is quoted in Peter Ackroyd, *Dickens* (New York: Harper Perennial, 1990), xii; the Millais pencil sketch and a plaster cast of the marble bust by Woolner can be viewed today at the Dickens Museum, London, along with many other relics, such as his "commode," the china monkey that sat on his desk, and a clock from Gad's Hill. There is also a table with a brass plaque nailed to it that reads, "Table (from the Chalet) upon which Charles Dickens penned his last words"; for the display of death masks around the house, see Jalland, *Death in the Victorian Family*, 290, and Philippe Ariès, *Images of Man and Death* (Cambridge, MA: Harvard University Press, 1985), 128; Elizabeth Gaskell, *My Lady Ludlow* (New York: Harper, 1858), 17.

6 CB to W. S. Williams, Oct. 1848, in *LCB*, vol. 2, 138; CB to EN, Oct. 29, 1848, in *LCB*, vol. 2, 130; CB to EN, Dec. 10, 1848, in *LCB*, vol. 2, 152; Elizabeth Gaskell, *The Life of Charlotte Brontë* (New York: Penguin, 1997), 277; CB to W. S. Williams, Nov. 22, 1848, in *LCB*, vol. 2, 142; CB to W. S. Williams, Dec. 7, 1848, and CB to Dr. Epps, Dec. 9, 1848, in *LCB*, vol. 2, 148, 151.

7 CB, "Biographical Notice," in *LCB*, vol. 2, 746; the detail about EB feeding the dogs comes from A. Mary F. Robinson, *Emily Brontë* (London: W. H. Allen, 1883), 228.

8 The details about EB in her room come from the servant Martha Brown's account, given in an interview to Gaskell, who then wrote about it in a letter to John Forster, in September 1853, in J. A. V. Chapple and Arthur Pollard, eds., *The Letters of Mrs. Gaskell* (Manchester, UK: Manchester University Press, 1997), 246; Martha Brown passed the bone comb (BPM, H121)—probably given to her by Patrick—on to her sister, who gave it to her own daughter. The daughter's husband, a Mr. Alderson of Shipley, sold it to J. H. Dixon, who put it up for sale at the Sotheby's 1916 auction. See "Catalogue of Valuable Illuminated and Other Manuscripts," Dec. 13–15, 1916, BPM. Lucasta Miller casts doubt on the authenticity of this comb, citing Godfrey Fox Bradby, *The Brontës and Other Essays* (Oxford, UK: Oxford University Press, 1932), 37, who remarks that "rumour has it that five other combs with charred teeth were aspirants for the honor of admission to the glass case." Yet he gives no source for this "rumor," so it's hard to credit Miller's conviction that "five combs with charred teeth would eventually battle it out for the honour of a place under glass in the Brontë Parsonage Museum," based wholly on an unsourced rumor. See Miller, *The Brontë Myth* (New York: Knopf, 2001), 213; CB to EN, Dec. 19, 1848, in *LCB*, vol. 2, 154; EB's words quoted in Gaskell, *Life*, 68. The black sofa now sits where it did when Emily died, in the parlor at the BPM. There has been much debate among Brontë biographers about whether she died in the parlor or in her bed upstairs; CB to EN, Apr. 12, 1849, in *LCB*, vol. 2, 200.

9 The coffin size comes from extracts from William Wood's account book, BPM; one set of mourning gloves is at the BPM, D60. It is of white knitted silk and was given to a Mrs. Uttley; CB to EN, Dec. 23, 1848, in *LCB*, vol. 2, 157; the mourning cards are at the Berg. It's not clear who had these made.

10 This letter, CB to EN, Dec. 23, 1848, is at the Berg. Also in *LCB*, vol. 2, 157; CB to W. S. Williams, Dec. 25, 1848, in *LCB*, vol. 2, 159; CB to W. S. Williams, Jan. 2, 1849, in *LCB*, vol. 2, 165.

11 The notion of a suburb in the sky comes from Michael Wheeler, *Death and the Future Life in Victorian Literature and Theology* (New York: Cambridge University Press, 1990), 121; John Wolffe, in his survey of nineteenth-century British sermons preached on the deaths of the famous and his study of thousands of consolation letters, found a heavy emphasis on the dead as active in heaven. See *Great Deaths: Grieving, Religion, and Nationhood in Victorian and Edwardian Britain* (Oxford, UK: Oxford University Press, 2000), 63, 179; CB to EN, Aug. 6, 1843, in *LCB*, vol. 1, 328; W. S. Williams to CB, Dec. 21, 1848, in *LCB*, vol. 2, 156; PB to Eliza Brown, June 10, 1859, in Dudley Green, ed., *The Letters of the Reverend Patrick Brontë* (Stroud, UK: Nonsuch, 2005), 279; PB to the Reverend John Buckworth, Nov. 27, 1821. in ibid., 43.

12 CB to W. S. Williams, June 4, 1849, in *LCB*, vol. 2, 216; CB to W. S. Williams, June 13, 1849, in *LCB*, vol. 2, 220; from EN's diary, quoted in *LCB*, vol. 2, 215n.

13 Mary Taylor told Gaskell about this incident in a letter. See Gaskell, *Life*, 104.

14 Jalland, in *Death in the Victorian Family*, recounts the Horsley story and discusses the practice generally. See especially 214. According to Bertram Puckle, *Funeral Customs: Their Origins and Development* (London: T. Werner Laurie, 1926), the

ancient Greeks would cut the hair of a child whose parent had died, as a token of grief. A lock of the child's hair would then be buried with the parent. See especially 269.

15 For Horsley, see Jalland, *Death in the Victorian Family*, 214; for Keats, see Andrew Motion, *Keats* (London: Faber and Faber, 1975), 564; Ruth Richardson tells the anecdote of the postman. See *Death, Dissection, and the Destitute* (Chicago: University of Chicago Press, 2000), 4.

16 Numerous such artifacts were found among the archaeologist Margaret Cox's excavations of eighteenth- to nineteenth-century burial vaults underneath Christ Church, Spitalfields, London, including a small wooden barrel containing two molars. See Cox, *Life and Death in Spitalfields 1700–1850* (London: Council for British Archaeology, 1996). She also discusses the popular belief in resurrection, which "demanded complete mortal remains" (101). She explains that the lead coffins, found among her excavations, were a means to keep remains together, free from rot; as Richardson puts it, in *Death, Dissection, and the Destitute*, 29: "Dissection represented . . . the deliberate mutilation or destruction of identity, perhaps for eternity." See also Puckle, *Funeral Customs*, 206.

17 "The Relic," lines 6, 11. In Donne's "The Funeral," the speaker hopes that when he dies, the one who shrouds him will not harm or "question much" that "subtle wreath of hair which crowns my arm" (lines 1–2). Donne, *The Poems of John Donne*, ed. Herbert J. C. Grierson (London: Oxford University Press, 1966), vol. 1, 58, 62–63; "Locksley Hall," lines 56–58, in Tennyson, *The Poems of Tennyson*, 2nd ed., ed. Christopher Ricks (Harlow, Essex, UK: Longman, 1987), vol. 2, 123; "Triumph of Time," lines 114–115, 120, in Algernon Charles Swinburne, *Poems and Ballads and Atalanta in Calydon* (London: Penguin, 2000), 32.

18 Many of these superstitions were practiced without a clear sense as to why, their origins having been forgotten. Ruth Richardson, in *Death, Dissection, and the Destitute*, 7, 27, describes what she calls a popular "folk theology" during this time, a mixture of "orthodox, obsolete, and ersatz Christianity and what can only be called quasi-pagan beliefs." Mirrors were covered for other reasons as well, such as in Jewish tradition where covering mirrors and not bathing during a wake are means to honor the dead by putting aside all considerations of personal appearance.

19 For Antoni Forrer, see Irene Guggenheim Navarro, "Hairwork of the 19th Century," *Magazine Antiques* 159 (2001), 484–93. Shirley Bury also discusses Forrer in *Jewellery, 1789–1910: The International Era* (Woodbridge, UK: Antique Collector's Club, 1991); the details from the Great Exhibition come from *Official Descriptive and Illustrated Catalogue of the Great Exhibition of 1851* (London: Spicer Brothers, 1851), 1137, 683, and 1149. For a French example of a hair portrait, see Flaubert's *Madame Bovary* (New York: Penguin, 2002), 36. Emma has a memorial card for her mother made out of the dead woman's hair; the growth of the Victorian hair jewelry industry is explored in Christian Holm, "Sentimental Cuts: 18th-Century Mourning Jewelry with Hair," *Eighteenth-Century Studies* 38 (2004), 139–43; Pamela Miller, "Hair Jewelry as Fetish," in Ray B. Browne, ed., *Objects of Special Devotion: Fetishes and Fetishism in Popular Culture* (Bowling Green, OH: Bowling Green University Press,

n.d.); Diana Cooper and Norman Battershill, *Victorian Sentimental Jewellery* (London: Newton Abbot, 1972); and Bury, *Jewellery*; the journals that discussed hairwork include *New belle assemblee* and *The Cornhill Magazine*. For more on Victorian hair jewelry, see Marcia Pointon, *Brilliant Effects: A Cultural History of Gem Stones and Jewellery* (New York: Yale University Press, 2010). For the Rembrandt in cross-stitch, see Nerylla Taunton, *Antique Needlework Tools and Embroideries* (Suffolk, UK: Antique Collector's Club, 1997), 63; CB, "Passing Events," PML, Brontë 02, 1836, and "Captain Henry Hastings," 1839, Houghton Library, Harvard University.

20 Helen Sheumaker's history of hairwork in America describes different types of hairwork and how these pieces were made (and by whom). See *Love Entwined: The Curious History of Hairwork in America* (Philadelphia: University of Pennsylvania Press, 2007). Although American hairwork was quite different from British hairwork in terms of use and history, its patterns and manufacture were similar; The bracelet made from AB's hair, BPM, J8, was sold at the 1898 auction of EN's things after she died (as lot 212, "plaited chain of hair in two strips, fastened with gold barrel-shaped fasteners") and was acquired by the BPM from Mrs. Worthing Needham in 1932 (see *BST* 8, no. 1 [1932], 43–46). It almost matches a hair necklace, made from EB's and AB's hair, that was bought by the BPM in 1927 at an auction (lot 27), now J12. A very thin, long tress of tightly woven hair made into a necklace, BPM, J51, looks like it was also made with a table. It is said to be EB's hair, passed down through the servant Martha Brown; "Catalogue of the Contents of Moor Lane House, Gomersal, to Be Sold by Auction on Wednesday and Thursday, May 18 and 19, 1898," BPM, P Sales Cat. 2.

21 CB, "Passing Events"; EB, "Why ask to know the date—the clime?" Sept. 14, 1846, in Janet Gezari, ed., *Emily Jane Brontë: The Complete Poems* (London: Penguin, 1992). Locket, BPM, J42, SB: 636; the brooch, BPM, J15, was also bought at the Nussey auction, by a Mr. James Miles, and there seems to be some uncertainty about whose hair it contains, either AB's or CB's.

22 Gold brooch, Victoria and Albert Museum, M.21-1972, 1855; Elizabeth Gaskell, *Cranford* (New York: Longmans, 1905), 104.

23 Snippets of hair on velvet backdrop, BPM, J81. Juliet Barker, *The Brontës* (New York: St. Martin's, 1994), 134, identifies Sarah Garrs as the one who cut and took the hair. Garrs later married and emigrated to the United States. She wrote to PB from Iowa when she heard that CB had died. Aunt Branwell's hair is not represented in the grouping, but Garrs would not have known her very well, since Aunt Branwell didn't move into the parsonage permanently until after Garrs had left. The whole collection was donated to the BPM in 1989 by Dr. John D. Stull, *BST* 21 (1994), 3.

24 According to Joan Evans, the sapphire amulet was buried with Charlemagne at Aix-la-Chapelle in 814 and rediscovered when the tomb was opened by Otto III in 1000. Preserved in the treasury of the cathedral, it was given by the canons to Empress Josephine in 1804, who wore it at her coronation, set into her crown. It is now in the treasury of the Palace of Tau, in Reims, France. See Evans, *A History of Jewellery, 1100–1870* (Boston, MA: Boston Book and Art, 1970), 42; for Charles I relics, see Diana Scarisbrick, *Ancestral Jewels* (London: Deutsch, 1989), 67–68. Some of the Charles I hair jewels are at the Victoria and Albert Museum, including a brooch,

M. 103-1962, ca. 1650, with his cypher in gold wire mounted over his hair, and this inscription on the back: "CR REX MARTYR."

25 Numerous examples of talismanic jewelry can be seen at the Victoria and Albert Museum, including at least four toadstone rings. The museum also has a number of amulets containing the teeth or horns of various animals—such as wolf or deer teeth—also thought to be protective or nurturing; jewel with caul, British Museum, Cat. 229-30, 577.

26 CB, "The Search after Happiness," Aug. 17, 1829, British Library, Ashley 156; CB, "The Foundling," 1833, British Library, Ashley 159.

27 CB, "Caroline Vernon," in Winifred Gérin, ed., *Five Novelettes* (London: Folio Press, 1971), 301; Jane Austen, *Sense and Sensibility* (London: Richard Bentley, 1833), 84.

28 Dickens, *Oliver Twist*, 313; CB, "The Secret," Nov. 7, 1833, Elmer Ellis Library, University of Missouri-Columbia.

29 Bury, in *Jewellery*, 681, discusses the scandal of replacing the beloved's hair with anonymous hair. For a similar occurrence in the hairwork industry in America, see Sheumaker, *Love Entwined*. Both Bury and Sheumaker discuss the busy traffic in human hair during the nineteenth century. The most popular hairwork instructional manual of the day, Alexanna Speight's *Lock of Hair* (London: Goubaud, 1872), has an extensive discussion on the shearing of women's hair for sale; *The Family Friend* 5 (1853), 55. *The Englishwoman's Domestic Magazine* makes a similar point: "When we think of the imperishable nature of human hair, we can easily understand the anxiety with which a tress or lock cut from the forehead of a friend who is perhaps long among the dead . . . is preserved." *Cassell's Home Journal* also played on these fears, as do all of the hairwork instructional manuals.

30 Mary Taylor is quoted in Gaskell, *Life*, 103; inkstand, Royal Collection, 15955. See also Jonathan Marsden, ed., *Victoria and Albert: Art and Love* (London: Royal Collection, 2010), 206; Examples of teeth jewelry are held in the archives at Frogmore House, Windsor Castle. They are matching earrings and a pendant made of gold-mounted enamel, RCIN, nos. 52540, 52541.1, and 52541.2, in the shape of fuchsia flowers, which symbolized humble love, and their stamens are represented by the baby teeth of Princess Beatrice. The pendant has written on it, in gold, "Our baby's first tooth." It also has a case built for a plait of hair, but no hair is in it. Another example is a gold and enamel brooch representing a thistle that holds, as its flower, a milk tooth of Princess Victoria. An inscription on the back states that it was pulled by her father, Prince Albert, on September 13, 1847. Balmoral Castle, RNIN 13517; charm bracelet: Royal Collection, 65293. See also Marsden, *Victoria and Albert*, 337.

31 Christopher Hibbert, *Queen Victoria: A Personal History* (London: HarperCollins, 2000), 286–87; quoted in Bury, *Jewellery*, 666. Navarro, "Hairwork of the 19th Century," discusses the many hair jewels given by Queen Victoria as well as those she received.

32 Quoted in Hibbert, *Queen Victoria*, 293; quoted in Wolffe, *Great Deaths*, 204–5; for discussions of the materiality of spiritualism and its general history, see Janet Oppenheim, *The Other World: Spiritualism and Psychical Research in England, 1850–1914* (New York: Cambridge University Press, 1985), Alex Owen, *The Darkened*

Room: Women, Power, and Spiritualism (Philadelphia: University of Pennsylvania Press, 1990), and Marlene Tromp, *Altered States: Sex, Nation, Drugs, and Self-Transformation in Victorian Spiritualism* (Albany, NY: SUNY Press, 2006); for Katie King, see Owen, *Darkened Room*, 55; the detail about CB's ghost comes from Miller, *Brontë Myth*, 89.

33 Clément Chéroux, Andreas Fischer, Pierre Apraxine, et al., eds., *The Perfect Medium: Photography and the Occult* (New Haven, CT: Yale University Press, 2005); Thomas Wilmot included the picture of CB in his *Twenty Photographs of the Risen Dead* (Birmingham, UK: Midland Educational Company, 1894). See also Miller, *Brontë Myth*, 89.

34 According to Susan R. Foister, in "The Brontë Portraits," *BST* 18 (1984), 352, the negative was one of thousands at the National Portrait Gallery that came from the studio of the photographer Sir Emery Walker. The studio card index states that it is "from a carte-de-visite of Charlotte Brontë, taken within a year of her death." As Foister points out, the carte de visite wasn't introduced into Britain until 1857 at the earliest, so she theorizes that the *carte* was taken of the 1854 photograph (by re-photographing). See also Juliet Barker, "Charlotte Brontë's Photograph," *BST* 19, nos. 1–2 (1986), 27–28, who makes an even stronger case for the photo being authentic, based on the discovery of a print of the negative in a different collection. Barker later cast some doubt on her own conclusion, however, suspecting along with others that the photograph might actually be of EN. Audrey Hall speculates about other photos, in "Two Possible Photographs of Charlotte Brontë," *BST* 21, no. 7 (1996), 293–302.

35 Jalland, *Death in the Victorian Family*, 6, 373, 374. See also Audrey Linkman, *Photography and Death* (London: Reaktion, 2011), 69; Jay Winter remarks that "those who tried to reunite the living and the dead, to retrieve their bodies and to give them a secure and identifiable resting place, faced staggering problems." See *Sites of Memory, Sites of Mourning: The Place of the Great War in European Cultural History* (New York: Cambridge University Press, 1995), 28.

36 Ian and Catherine Emberson, "A Necktie and a Lock of Hair: The Memories of George Feather the Younger," *Brontë Studies* 31 (2006), 161.

37 EN to George Smith, Mar. 28, 1860, quoted in Barker, *Brontës*, 773; PB to Elizabeth Gaskell, Apr. 5, 1855, in Green, *Letters of Reverend Patrick Brontë*, 227.

38 British Library, Egerton MS 3268B. Other locks EN gave away, BPM, J26 and E.2007.9, both curls in envelopes; Nicholls's ring, BPM, J29.

CHAPTER 8: MEMORY ALBUMS

1 CB to PB, June 7, 1851, in *LCB*, vol. 2, 630–31; CB to Amelia Taylor, June 7, 1851, in *LCB*, vol. 2, 633; "Thingville" comes from Kathryn Crowther, "Charlotte Brontë's Textual Relics: Memorializing the Material in *Vilette*," *Brontë Studies* 35, no. 2 (2010), 129.

2 The detail of the small box inside a big one comes from Yoshiaki Shirai, "Ferndean:

Charlotte Brontë in the Age of Pteridomania," *Brontë Studies* 28 (2003), 124; the information about Paxton and fern houses comes from Sarah Whittingham, *Fern Fever: The History of Pteridomania* (London: Frances Lincoln, 2012), 108, 113; for the cases shaped like the Crystal Palace, see Nicolette Scourse, *The Victorians and Their Ferns* (London: Croom Helm, 1983), 89.

3   Kingsley promoted the "mania," feeling that it brought women outdoors and in contact with nature. As a fervent evangelical, Kingsley saw nature as expressing the glory of God, and he hoped "botanizing" would replace women's desire for "novels and gossip, crochet and Berlin-wool" work, a popular type of embroidery. Charles Kingsley, *Glaucus; Or, the Wonders of the Shore* (Cambridge, UK: Macmillan, 1855), 4; for ferns as a design motif, see David Elliston Allen, *Naturalists and Society: The Culture of Natural History in Britain, 1700–1900* (Aldershot, UK: Ashgate, 2001), 16; water jug, BPM, H28; for fern ware, see Nerylla Taunton, *Antique Needlework, Tools, and Embroideries* (Suffolk, UK: Antique Collector's Club, 1997), 160.

4   For fern laws, see Allen, *Naturalists and Society*, 17; Whittingham, *Fern Fever*, 173.

5   For the Wordsworths as fern lovers, see Whittingham, *Fern Fever*, 13; Ward's Tintern Abbey case is pictured in Allen, *Naturalists and Society*, 401; the popular association of ferns with graveyards and ruins comes from Charlotte Yonge's 1853 *Herb of the Field* (London: Macmillan, 1887), 69–70; Whittingham, *Fern Fever*, 225, includes a picture of a "phantom bouquet"; For ruins inside Wardian cases, see Allen, *Naturalists and Society*, 404; the Glenny anecdote comes from Whittingham, *Fern Fever*, 119.

6   John Ruskin, "Remarks Addressed to the Mansfield Art Night Class, 14 October 1873," in *A Joy for Ever* (London: George Allen, 1904), 238.

7   EB, "There shines the moon, at noon of night," Mar. 6, 1837, "Weaned from life and torn away," Feb. 1838, and "Often rebuked, yet always back returning," date unknown, in Janet Gezari, ed., *Emily Jane Brontë: The Complete Poems* (London: Penguin, 1992); Yonge, *Herb of the Field*, 74; and Scourse, *Victorians and Their Ferns*, 169.

8   David Elliston Allen, *The Victorian Fern Craze: A History of Pteridomania* (London: Hutchinson, 1969), 11–12; quoted in Whittingham, *Fern Fever*, 26–27.

9   Quoted in Whittingham, *Fern Fever*, 216.

10 An example of fairies dancing in ferny settings can be found in Charles Kingsley, *The Water Babies: A Fairy Tale for a Land Baby*, ed. Brian Alderson and Robert Douglas-Fairhurst (Oxford, UK: Oxford University Press, 2013). See Whittingham, *Fern Fever*, 40–41, for more about the linkage between fairies and ferns and for some Victorian-era illustrations of them; for ferns and invisibility, see Yonge's chapter on ferns, in *Herbs of the Field*, 69, and "How to Become Invisible," *Punch*, Aug. 11 (1866), 65. For lunacy and ferns, see Whittingham, *Fern Fever*, 223.

11 CB to Mrs. Rand, May 26, 1845, in *LCB*, vol. 1, 393; CB to EN, July 10, 1846, in *LCB*, vol. 1, 483; CB to EN, Jan. 1850, in *LCB*, vol. 2, 337.

12 CB to EN, July 1851, in *LCB*, vol. 2, 671.

13 CB to EN, Dec. 15, 1852, in *LCB*, vol. 3, 93.

14 CB to EN, Jan. 2, 1853, in *LCB*, vol. 3, 101; CB to EN, Apr. 6, 1853, in *LCB*, vol. 3, 149; CB to EN, May 16, 1853, in *LCB*, vol. 3, 165–66.

15 CB to EN, May 27, 1853, in *LCB*, vol. 3, 168.

16 Elizabeth Gaskell to John Forster, Apr. 23, 1854, in *LCB*, vol. 3, 248.

17 CB to EN, May 21, 1854, in *LCB*, vol. 3, 263; the wedding dress was bequeathed by Nicholls to his niece, named, strangely, Charlotte Brontë Nicholls, with the promise that she burn it before she died so that it couldn't be sold. In 1954 she did burn it, although a copy was made using the memory of it retained by her niece, according to Juliet Barker, *Sixty Treasures: The Brontë Parsonage Museum* (Haworth: Brontë Society, 1988), item 53. The bonnet and veil do still exist, however: BPM, D97; CB to an unknown recipient, June 1854, in *LCB*, vol. 3, 266; CB to EN, June 11, 1854, in *LCB*, vol. 3, 268–69.

18 This travel dress is at the BPM, D74.

19 Some rare ferns had been found in Yorkshire, such as this "filmy fern" with transparent leaves, called the dwarf creeping fern when first found near Bingley in 1724, later renamed the Killarney fern when it was rediscovered in Ireland; Mary Taylor to CB, Apr. 1850, in *LCB*, vol. 2, 393; the vasculum often hung with a leather strap across the body. A collecting press was a wooden case, which could be strapped and buckled in order to flatten the ferns, such as the "Botanist's Portable Collecting Press," available at such shops as Mr. Bogue of 3 St. Martin's Place, London, in three sizes. Whittingham, *Fern Fever*, 67.

20 "A Devonian Period," *Punch*, Sept. 14, 1889; The Miss Myers story comes from Whittingham, *Fern Fever*, 66; CB to Catherine Winkworth, July 27, 1854, in *LCB*, vol. 3, 280; the "Phantom" tale comes from Eanne Oram, "Charlotte Brontë's Honeymoon," *BST* 25 (1975), 343–44, and *LCB*, vol. 3, 280–81.

21 CB's fern album, BPM, bb238, has this inscription on the flyleaf: "F.E. Bell / Jan. 25th 1914 / From Mrs. Nicholls Hill House Banagher / Ferns collected and pressed by Charlotte Brontë at Killarney / On her honeymoon." Since some of the pages of the album have a watermark of 1869, they were not all made by CB. It's possible CB arranged the ferns on some of the pages, and members of the Bell family arranged others, and then the leaves were bound into an album later, a common practice at the time. It's also possible that CB only collected and pressed the ferns, and the Bell family later made them into an album. The album came from Frances Bell, whose aunt was Arthur Nicholls's second wife, the Mrs. Nicholls referred to here. She gave it to Frances, who then handed it down to her niece, Mrs. Marjorie Gallop. It was donated to the BPM by her descendants, Christopher and Nigel Gallop. See *BST* 21 (1994), 4; lithographs of fern fronds, sometimes called "mixed fern" sheets, were cut up and pasted into albums, often alongside real pressed ferns. See Whittingham, *Fern Fever*, 184; Allen, *Victorian Fern Craze*, 52–53. These "albums" are reminiscent of the purpose-built photo albums that were soon to be made, with slots for plants rather than photographs. The same sorts of printed books containing dried specimens of seaweed or moss, with decorative frames and information, could also be bought. One was Mary Wyatt's *Algae Damnonienses, or Dried Specimens of Marine Plants*, which came out in several volumes from 1834 to 1840. Another was Mary Howard's *Ocean*

Flowers and Their Teachings (Bath, UK: Binns and Goodwin, 1847). See Carol Armstrong, ed., *Ocean Flowers: Impressions from Nature* (Princeton, NJ: Princeton University Press, 2004), for reproductions of some of the pages of these gorgeous books.

22 Nicholls's commonplace book, BPM, BS 244; the Victoria and Albert Museum has a marvelous pattern book, by a Sarah Bland, made c. 1836–1854, E.372:343-1967. Also, the Fales Collection, at New York University's Bobst Library, has numerous British and American albums with handwritten recipes, some from the 1800s and others that are older. Felicia Hemans's son gave the commonplace book to Browning; the term "commonplace book" is flexible and is often used for many sorts of albums, including what I call friendship or souvenir albums. David Allen, *Commonplace Books and Reading in Georgian England* (Cambridge, UK: Cambridge University Press, 2010), 29–34; even though it is about America, Ellen Gruber Garvey's wonderful *Writing with Scissors: American Scrapbooks from the Civil War to the Harlem Renaissance* (New York: Oxford University Press, 2013) has much to say about album culture in nineteenth-century Europe. She posits that scrapbooks didn't become common in America until around the 1850s.

23 The autograph album had a long history before the Victorian period, however, and dates back at least to the seventeenth century. See Martha Langford, *Suspended Conversations: The Afterlife of Memory in Photographic Albums* (Montreal: McGill-Queens University Press, 2001), 23; the snippet of Docwra's, BPM, E.2006.2. At least seven letters from PB still exist that say something very similar to this one: "Dear Madam, The annexed scrap, is all I can spare, of the autograph, of my dear daughter Charlotte Brontë, I have had so many applications, that my store is nearly exhausted. Yours very respectfully, P. Brontë." PB to Miss Jenkins, July 9, 1857, in Dudley Green, ed., *Letters of the Reverend Patrick Brontë* (Stroud, UK: Nonsuch, 2005), 256. A page removed from an anonymous, nineteenth-century album, to give another example, has a letter from PB pledging support for a parliamentary candidate mounted on it, and pasted above it is a piece cut from a letter that says, "Believe me / Yours sincerely / C Brontë," MSS 001, box 21, folder 16b, Fales Collection, New York University Bobst Library; Harriet Martineau, *Autobiography*, ed. Linda Peterson (Peterborough, Ontario: Broadview, 2007), 219; The Enoch signatures are reproduced in Thomas Wise and John Alexander Symington, *The Shakespeare Head Brontë* (Oxford, UK: Shakespeare Head, 1938), vol. 2, 104.

24 See CB to EN, July 31, 1845, in *LCB*, vol. 1, 413 and n. 14, 414. See also EN's reminiscences, in *LCB*, vol. 1, 609; Mary Pearson's commonplace book is at the Harry Ransom Center, University of Texas, Austin. See Christine Alexander and Jane Sellars, *The Art of the Brontës* (London: Cambridge University Press, 1995), 355, and Barker, *Brontës*, 512.

25 Roe Head Album, BPM, C109; Christine Alexander discusses this album and speculates that some or all of the pages may have been sold loose, then drawn or written on by the girls, and then finally bound together later. See "Charlotte Brontë, Her School Friends, and the Roe Head Album," *Brontë Studies* 29 (2004), 1–16.

26 Wagner album, Pforz BND-MSS (Wagner, A.), Pforzheimer Collection, New York Public Library; for the Stovin albums for Walker, see S. P. Rowlands, "An Old Fern

Collection," *British Fern Gazette* 6, no. 10 (1934), 260–62; the Stovin album given to Nightingale, Florence Nightingale Museum, FNM: 1072.

27 The album with birds comes from Jane Toller, *The Regency and Victorian Crafts* (London: Ward Lock, 1969), 58; for albums with cards and stamps, see Asa Briggs, *Victorian Things* (Chicago: Chicago University Press, 1988), 267, 350–52; the war album, Florence Nightingale Museum, FNM: 0600. There is another Crimean War album with pressed plants from battlefields, made by Arthur Walber, here: FM 0601.1-2; Wilkie Collins, *The Law and the Lady* (New York: Penguin, 1999), 82.

28 For the queen's seaweed album, see Thad Logan, *The Victorian Parlour* (New York: Cambridge University Press, 2001), 124; for more of her albums, see Jonathan Marsden, ed., *Victoria and Albert: Art and Love* (London: Royal Collection, 2010), 185, 355.

29 It is possible that CB didn't bring this album back with her to Haworth. She may have left it with the Bells in Ireland, or left the pressed ferns there, and one of the Bells put them into the album; CB to EN, Aug. 9, 1854, in *LCB*, vol. 3, 283–84.

30 CB to EN, July 1850, and CB to Margaret Wooler, Nov. 15, 1854, in *LCB*, vol. 3, 282, 301; CB to EN, Dec. 26, 1854, in *LCB*, vol. 3, 312; CB to Amelia Taylor, Feb. 1855, in *LCB*, vol. 3, 327.

31 Souvenir album of Haworth, BPM, E 2013.2; collection of photographs titled "Views taken during 1903," Berg, box PB7. This box contains an assortment of random Brontë-related items, like two locks of hair, loose photos of the Haworth environs, and disassembled album pages that contain other area pictures, some snipped from print sources.

32 Here are a few scrap albums, of many more, devoted strictly to the Brontës: BPM, TA.125, two albums, one brown, the other blue, of newspaper clippings, postcards, and a few letters, made by Mabel Edgerley. BPM, TA.138, newspaper cuttings in a brown album with blue spine, possibly compiled by Miles Hartley. BPM, SB:1258A, album with postcards, clippings, and photos, donated by Mrs. Chadwick. BPM, SB:764, scrap album with a blue spine, dated 1855; Brown album, BPM, SB:2352; Scruton album, BPM, TA.198. A red hardback edition of *The Temple Dictionary of the Bible*, ed. Rev. W. Ewing (London: Dent, 1909); Turner album, BPM, SB:2288.

CHAPTER NINE: MIGRANT RELICS

1 Charles Hale to Sarah Hale, Nov. 8, 1861, reprinted in Charles Lemon, ed., *Early Visitors to Haworth: From Ellen Nussey to Virginia Woolf* (Haworth, UK: Brontë Society, 1996), 73–85.

2 Martine Bagnoli, Holger A. Klein, C. Griffith Mann, and James Robinson, eds., *Treasures of Heaven: Saints, Relics, and Devotion in Medieval Europe* (New Haven, CT: Yale University Press, 2010), 10–11. The British Museum has some of these Holy Land tokens made from earth from various sites. Stones, earth, and other materials from places like Cavalry and the Holy Sepulchre were set into reliquaries, such as one held at the Katholisches Münsterpfarramt, Zwiefalten, Germany, with stones from these sites behind gems, along with fragments of the True Cross.

3 For Hardy and Keats, see Claire Tomalin, *Thomas Hardy* (New York: Penguin, 2006), 235. For more information about the taking of souvenirs from Keats's burial place, see Samantha Matthews, *Poetical Remains: Poets' Graves, Bodies, and Books in the Nineteenth Century* (New York: Oxford University Press, 2004), 12 and chap. 4. For Shakespeare's tree and Burns souvenirs, see Nicola Watson, *The Literary Tourist: Readers and Places in Romantic and Victorian Britain* (New York: Palgrave, 2006), 69; the writer didn't even have to be dead to be transportable, in the minds of some fans, to be possessable through the matter she had touched. Harriet Martineau told of slight acquaintances visiting her, with strangers who would filch her pen "from the inkstand, still wet" in order to "be framed or laid up in lavender." Martineau, *Autobiography*, ed. Linda Peterson (Peterborough, Ontario: Broadview, 2007), 309.

4 Mrs. M. H. Spilmann, of Kent, was sent heather from the moors near the parsonage in 1935, from Mrs. de l'Hopital, BPM, BSC 2.6.4. Sydney Biddell brought his copy of Gaskell's biography (now at the BPM) when he traveled to Haworth in 1879 and made annotations about what he saw. He pressed between its pages a leaf from a black currant bush and a sprig of heather; burial in Burns land started in the 1840s. See Watson, *Literary Tourist*, 74.

5 Virginia Woolf, "Haworth, November 1904," *Guardian*, Dec. 21, 1904; Sylvia Plath, *The Unabridged Journals of Sylvia Plath*, ed. Karen V. Kukil (New York: Anchor Books, 2000), 589.

6 CB, "The Death of Napoleon," in Sue Lonoff, ed. and trans., *The Belgian Essays* (New Haven, CT: Yale University Press, 1996), 272; it appears that Napoleon's coffin that was broken up had been buried for around twenty years, making it an even eerier relic. A contemporary described the original set of coffins thus: "composed first of tin, lined with white satin, which having been soldered down, was enclosed in another of mahogany, a third of lead, and the whole in a fourth of mahogany, secured with iron screws." Quoted in Mark R. D. Seaward, "Charlotte Brontë's Napoleonic Relic," *BST* 17, no. 3 (1978), 186–87; fragment of coffin, BPM, BS20a. See also Juliet Barker, *Sixty Treasures: The Brontë Parsonage Museum* (Haworth, UK: Brontë Society, 1988), item 16.

7 The ball in a locket is discussed in the *London Times*, June 17, 1844, p. 6, col. G. It is now part of the Royal Collection, Windsor Castle; Nelson's coat (UN 10024), the other items mentioned, and much more of the same are now at the National Maritime Museum, London. Much jewelry was made with Lord Nelson's hair, such as a brooch belonging to a Lady Neville, inscribed with such details as "Lost to his country Oct. 21, 1805"; For example, the British Library holds a wooden box, add. MSS 56226, made from a fragment of the HMS *Victory* shot off during the Battle of Trafalgar. It contains a sample of Nelson's hair, taken at the same battle. The box has a small brass plate on the lid, inscribed with "Victory Trafalgar. Octr 21 1805." A snuffbox at the Victoria and Albert Museum, partly made of the oak from one of Nelson's ships, the HMS *Bellerophon*, reproduces his death mask in miniature.

8 Even though the attending physician wrote, "Phthisis," or general wasting disease, on CB's death certificate, Brontë biographers have made a solid argument for

extreme morning sickness. See Juliet Barker, *The Brontës* (New York: St. Martin's, 1994), 772; H. W. Gallagher, "Charlotte Brontë: A Surgeon's Assessment," *BST* 18 (1995), 363–69; and *LCB*, vol. 3, 320–21, n. 3; CB to EN, Jan. 19, 1855, in *LCB*, vol. 3, 319.

9 Elizabeth Gaskell to John Greenwood, Apr. 12, 1855, in J. A. V. Chapple and Arthur Pollard, eds., *The Letters of Mrs. Gaskell* (Manchester, UK: Manchester University Press, 1997), 337; for more about Gaskell's reference to abortion, see Barker, *Brontës*, 774–75; for references to abortions in medical journals, see J. A. and Olive Banks, *Feminism and Family Planning in Victorian England* (Liverpool: University of Liverpool, 1964), 86; Mayhew quoted in Patricia Knight, "Women and Abortion in Victorian and Edwardian England," *History Workshop* 4 (1977), 57. The history of herbs, mixtures, and advertisements comes from ibid., 60–62, and John M. Riddle, *Eve's Herbs: A History of Contraception and Abortion in the West* (Cambridge, MA: Harvard University Press, 1997), 202–3. Knight explains that the men behind the "Madame Frain" mixture spent time in prison for "conspiring to incite women to abortion" (62). See also R. Sauer, "Infanticide and Abortion in Nineteenth-Century Britain," *Population Studies* 32 (1978), 88.

10 James Whitehead, a physician at the Manchester Lying-in Hospital, wrote a report in 1847 about his clinical experience. Out of 2,000 women he questioned, 747 said they had aborted at least once. Whitehead performed a few abortions himself, he admitted, when the woman's life was in danger, by administering ergot of rye. Riddle, *Eve's Herbs*, 238.

11 PB to Mrs. Sarah Newsome (formerly Garrs), June 12, 1855, in Dudley Green, ed., *The Letters of the Reverend Patrick Brontë* (Stroud, UK: Nonsuch, 2005), 231; PB to Elizabeth Gaskell, June 20, 1855, in ibid., 235; the sexton William Brown told the story of the buried memorial tablet to Charles Hale. Charles Hale to Sarah Hale, Nov. 8, 1861, in Lemon, *Early Visitors to Haworth*, 79–80.

12 See Barker, *Brontës*, 822–25, who covers the different theories and possibilities as to why Nicholls wasn't able to take PB's place; PB's notebook, BPM, BS 178. See Barker, *Sixty Treasures*, item 15; the detail about the destruction of the bed comes from Alan H. Adamson, *Mr. Charlotte Brontë: The Life of Arthur Bell Nicholls* (Montreal: McGill-Queen's University Press, 2008), 125.

13 The manuscript auction catalog for this sale, BPM, SB:349, is extremely vague as to what was sold. Most of the books, for instance, were just listed as "books," without any other information, except for in rare cases such as listings for "Brontë poems," "3 vols. Jane Eyre," and "History of Rome"; the "Greenwood" listed as a buyer at the auction may have been a local landowner rather than the stationer, who was unrelated to these other Greenwoods. The "Smith" who walked away with a few artifacts may have been George Smith, Charlotte's publisher. The Brontë piano was also sold at this auction, to John Booth of Oxenhope, now BPM, F13. Barker, *Sixty Treasures*, items 8 and 23.

14 The Berg has one of these postcards, part of box PB7; the information about the salt-boxes and candleholders comes from the catalog of the 1916 Sotheby's sale: "Catalogue of Valuable Illuminated and Other Manuscripts," Dec. 13–15, 1916, 97.

15 The veil and dress are now at the BPM, D97 and D74. EB's wooden stool and CB's corset also passed from Martha to the sisters, then eventually to the BPM; Barker, *Sixty Treasures*, item 51, discusses the altering and reusing of CB's dresses; the apron was eventually donated to the BPM, by Miss Omerod, Beach House, Hawarden Road, Colwyn Bay. See *BST* 11, no. 2 (1947), 115; a "pot" doll, BPM, H153, wears bits of what CB wore, once owned by Mrs. Grayson, Keighley. See also *BST* 11, no. 1 (1946), 49.

16 Ann Dinsdale, Sarah Laycock, and Julie Akhurst, *Brontë Relics: A Collection History* (Yorkshire, UK: Brontë Society, 2012), 25; "Catalogue of Brown Collection of Brontë Relics," Sotheby's sale, July 1898, BPM, P.S. Cat. 1, and "Museum of Brontë Relics, a Descriptive Catalogue of Brontë Relics Now in the Possession of R. and F. Brown," BPM, P. Bib. 1.

17 Adamson, *Mr. Charlotte Brontë*, 136.

18 Ibid., 147–155; quoted in ibid., 156.

19 See John Collins, *The Two Forgers: A Biography of Harry Buxton Forman and Thomas James Wise* (Aldershot, UK: Scolar, 1992), and Wilfred Partington, *Forging Ahead: The True Story of the Upward Progress of Thomas James Wise* (New York: Putnam, 1939).

20 For Wise, the Brontë manuscripts, and his bibliography, see Dinsdale et al., *Brontë Relics*, 41; "Forgeries and Uncertain Attribution," in *LCB*, vol. 3, 375–78; there are also a couple of letters to Thackeray to whom CB did write, but her letters to him didn't survive.

21 Donald Hopewell, "The President on 'Follies of Brontë Obsession,' " *BST* 12, no. 4 (1954), 308, and "New Treasures at Haworth," *BST* 12, no. 1 (1951), 21.

22 The Brontë Parsonage Museum bought the ovals, BPM, J82, at a Sotheby's auction held on February 24, 2000. They were listed in the sales catalog for £600 to £800 and probably had been inherited by a relative of Gérin, who died in 1989. See *BST* 26, no. 1 (2001), 106; fragments of jet bracelet: BPM J75.2; sewing box: BPM, H171.

23 Stella Gibbons to Winifred Gérin, Nov. 5, 1971, BPM, BS IX Gib.1971-11-05. In the letter, Gibbons mentions that she had offered the ovals to someone at the Brontë Society in the 1950s, but he wasn't enthusiastic. She also writes, "The reason why I haven't sent on the clasps before is Procrastination, the Thief of Time."

24 Stella Gibbons, *Cold Comfort Farm* (New York: Penguin, 1994), 36, 123, 126.

25 Lucasta Miller, *The Brontë Myth* (New York: Knopf, 2001), 206–7, 216, tells the history of the theories of BB's authorship of EB's novel; Gibbons, *Cold Comfort Farm*, 102; Miller, *Brontë Myth*, 339; Gibbons's nephew, Reggie Oliver, went on to write a biography of Gibbons. See *Out of the Woodshed: A Portrait of Stella Gibbons* (London: Bloomsbury, 1998), 238; Gibbons would have been close to seventy when she sent the ovals to Gérin, so she may have aged out of her satirical period, although maybe she became ever more witty as she grew older.

26 See Miller, *Brontë Myth*, 106–8, for more about what she calls the "Brontë brand."

27 Virginia Woolf, "Haworth, November 1904," *Guardian*, Dec. 21, 1904; the tall trees in the churchyard were not there during the Brontës' time; they were planted in the 1860s in order to break up the overcrowded corpses in the graveyard. Barker, *Brontës*, 98.

Further Reading

Armstrong, Tim. *Modernism, Technology, and the Body: A Cultural Study.* Cambridge, UK: Cambridge University Press, 1998.

Bachelard, Gaston. *The Poetics of Space.* Boston: Beacon Press, 1964.

Barthes, Roland. *Camera Lucida.* New York: Hill and Wang, 1981.

Bataille, Georges. *Literature and Evil: Essays.* London: Boyars, 1997.

Batchen, Geoffrey. *Forget Me Not: Photography and Remembrance.* New York: Princeton Architectural Press, 2004.

Bebbington, D. W. *Evangelicalism in Modern Britain: A History from the 1730s to the 1980s.* London: Unwin Hyman, 1989.

Bourke, Joanna. *Dismembering the Male: Men's Bodies, Britain and the Great War.* London: Reaktion, 1996.

Bradley, Ian. *The Call to Seriousness: The Evangelical Impact on the Victorians.* New York: Macmillan, 1976.

Bronfen, Elisabeth. *Over Her Dead Body: Death, Femininity and the Aesthetic.* Manchester, UK: Manchester University Press, 1992.

Brown, Bill, ed. *Things.* Chicago: University of Chicago Press, 2004.

Brown, Peter. *The Cult of Saints.* Chicago: University of Chicago Press, 1981.

Cohen, Deborah. *Household Gods: The British and Their Possessions.* New Haven, CT: Yale University Press, 2006.

Cottom, Daniel. *Unhuman Culture.* Philadelphia: University of Pennsylvania Press, 2006.

Curl, James. *The Victorian Celebration of Death.* Stroud, Gloucestershire, UK: Sutton, 2000.

Davey, Richard. *A History of Mourning.* London: Jay's, 1889.

Dávidházi, Péter. *The Romantic Cult of Shakespeare.* New York: Palgrave, 1998.

Davies, Stevie. *Emily Brontë: The Artist as a Free Woman.* Manchester, UK: Carcanet, 1983.

Di Bello, Patrizia. *Women's Albums and Photography in Victorian England.* Aldershot, UK: Ashgate, 2007.

Douglas-Fairhurst, Robert. *Victorian Afterlives: The Shaping of Influence in Nineteenth-Century Literature.* London: Oxford University Press, 2004.

Du Maurier, Daphne. *The Infernal World of Branwell Brontë.* New York: Doubleday, 1961.

Eagleton, Terry. *Myths of Power: A Marxist Study of the Brontës*. Basingstoke, UK: Macmillan, 1975.

Elfenbein, Andrew. *Byron and the Victorians*. Cambridge, UK: Cambridge University Press, 1996.

Fraser, Rebecca. *Charlotte Brontë: A Writer's Life*. New York: Pegasus, 2008.

Fumerton, Patricia. *Cultural Aesthetics: Renaissance Literature and the Practice of Social Ornament*. Chicago: University of Chicago Press, 1991.

Fussell, Paul. *The Great War and Modern Memory*. New York: Oxford University Press, 1975.

Gallagher, Catherine, *The Body Economic: Life, Death and Sensation in Political Economy and the Victorian Novel*. Princeton, NJ: Princeton University Press, 2006.

Gallagher, Catherine, and Stephen Greenblatt. *Practicing New Historicism*. Chicago: University of Chicago Press, 2000.

Gere, Charlotte, and Judy Rudoe. *Jewellery in the Age of Queen Victoria: A Mirror to the World*. London: British Museum Press, 2010.

Gérin, Winifred. *Branwell Brontë*. London: Hutchinson, 1972.

Glen, Heather. *Charlotte Brontë: The Imagination in History*. Oxford, UK: Oxford University Press, 2002.

Gordon, Lyndall. *Charlotte Brontë: A Passionate Life*. New York: W. W. Norton, 1996.

Hallam, Elizabeth, and Jenny Hockey. *Death, Memory, and Material Culture*. Oxford, UK: Berg, 2001.

Harris, Jose. *Private Lives, Public Spirit: A Social History of Britain 1870–1914*. New York: Oxford University Press, 1993.

Harvey, Anthony, and Richard Mortimer. *The Funeral Effigies of Westminster Abbey*. Woodbridge, UK: Boydell, 1994.

Heidegger, Martin. *Being and Time*. Trans. Joan Stambaugh. New York: State University of New York Press, 1996.

Herrmann, Frank. *The English as Collectors: A Documentary Chrestomathy*. New York: W. W. Norton, 1972.

Hotz, Mary Elizabeth. *Literary Remains: Representations of Death and Burial in Victorian England*. New York: State University of New York Press, 2009.

Jupp, Peter, and C. Gittings. *Death in England: An Illustrated History*. New Brunswick, NJ: Rutgers University Press, 2000.

Kucich, John. *Repression in Victorian Fiction: Charlotte Brontë, George Eliot, and Charles Dickens*. Berkeley: University of California Press, 1987.

Lee, Hermione. *Virginia Woolf's Nose: Essays on Biography*. Princeton, NJ: Princeton University Press, 2007.

Llewellyn, Nigel. *The Art of Death: Visual Culture in the English Death Ritual c. 1500–c. 1800*. London: Reaktion, 1991.

Logan, Peter. *Victorian Fetishism: Intellectuals and Primitives*. Albany: State University of New York Press, 2009.

Lutz, Deborah. *Relics of Death in Victorian Literature and Culture*. Cambridge, UK: Cambridge University Press, 2015.

Maynard, John. *Charlotte Brontë and Sexuality*. New York: Cambridge University Press, 1984.

Miller, J. Hillis. *The Disappearance of God; Five Nineteenth-Century Writers*. Cambridge, MA: Harvard University Press, 1963.

Mitchell, Sally. *The Fallen Angel: Chastity, Class and Women's Reading*. Bowling Green, OH: Bowling Green Popular Press, 1981.

Ousby, Ian. *The Englishman's England: Taste, Travel, and the Rise of Tourism*. New York: Cambridge University Press, 1990.

Pascoe, Judith. *The Hummingbird Cabinet: A Rare and Curious History of Romantic Collectors*. Ithaca, NY: Cornell University Press, 2006.

Pearce, Susan. *On Collecting: An Investigation into Collecting in the European Tradition*. London: Routledge, 1995.

Plotz, John. *Portable Property: Victorian Culture on the Move*. Princeton, NJ: Princeton University Press, 2009.

Polhemus, Robert. *Erotic Faith: Being in Love from Jane Austen to D. H. Lawrence*. Chicago: University of Chicago Press, 1990.

Richter, David. *The Progress of Romance: Literary Historiography and the Gothic Novel*. Columbus: Ohio State University Press, 1996.

Rosenman, Ellen Bayuk. *Unauthorized Pleasures: Accounts of Victorian Erotic Experience*. Ithaca, NY: Cornell University Press, 2003.

Schaaf, Larry J. *Sun Gardens: Victorian Photograms by Anna Atkins*. New York: Aperture, 1985.

———. *Sun Pictures: British Paper Negatives 1839–1864*. Catalog 10. New York: Hans P. Kraus Jr., ca. 2001.

Schor, Esther. *Bearing the Dead: The British Culture of Mourning from the Enlightenment to Victoria*. Princeton, NJ: Princeton University Press, 1994.

Shuttleworth, Sally. *Charlotte Brontë and Victorian Psychology*. Cambridge, UK: Cambridge University Press, 1996.

Siegel, Elizabeth, Patrizia Di Bello, Marta Weiss, et al. *Playing with Pictures: The Art of Victorian Photocollage*. Chicago: Art Institute of Chicago, 2009.

Stewart, Susan. *On Longing: Narratives of the Miniature, the Gigantic, the Souvenir, the Collection*. Durham, NC: Duke University Press, 1993.

Taylor, Lou. *Mourning Dress: A Costume and Social History*. London: Allen and Unwin, 1983.

Thormählen, Marianne. *The Brontës and Education*. Cambridge, UK: Cambridge University Press, 2007.

———. *The Brontës and Religion*. Cambridge, UK: Cambridge University Press, 1999.

Thurschwell, Pamela. *Literature, Technology, and Magical Thinking, 1880–1920*. New York: Cambridge University Press, 2001.

Westover, Paul. *Necromanticism: Traveling to Meet the Dead, 1750–1860*. New York: Palgrave Macmillan, 2012.

Zigarovich, Jolene. *Writing Death and Absence in the Victorian Novel: Engraved Narratives*. New York: Palgrave, 2012.

Index

Page numbers beginning with 257 refer to endnotes.